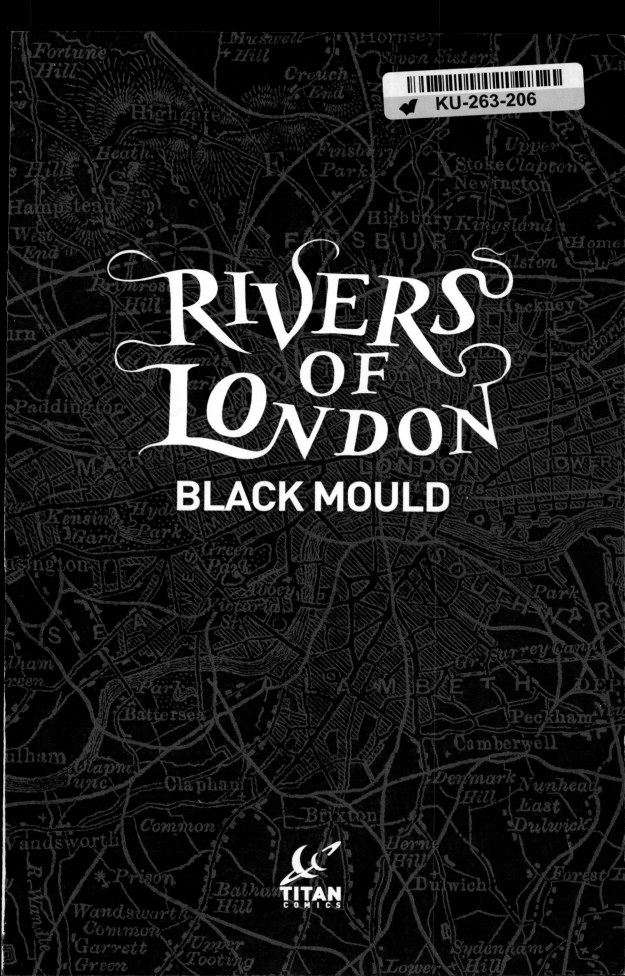

RIVERS OF LONDON

BLACK MOULD

TITAN
COMICS

RIVERS OF LONDON: BLACK MOULD
PB ISBN: 9781785855108
FP HC ISBN: 9781785863851

TITAN COMICS

EDITOR STEVE WHITE
DEPUTY EDITOR JESSICA BURTON
SENIOR DESIGNER ANDREW LEUNG

Senior Comics Editor Andrew James
Titan Comics Editorial Tom Williams, Amoona Saohin,
Lauren McPhee, Jonathan Stevenson, Lauren Bowes
Production Supervisor Maria Pearson
Production Controller Peter James
Senior Production Controller Jackie Flook
Art Director Oz Browne
Senior Sales Manager Steve Tothill
Directt Sales and Marketing Manager Ricky Claydon
Commercial Manager Michelle Fairlamb
Head of Rights Jenny Boyce
Publishing Manager Darryl Tothill
Publishing Director Chris Teather
Operations Director Leigh Baulch
Executive Director Vivian Cheung
Publisher Nick Landau

Published by Titan Comics
A division of Titan Publishing Group Ltd.
144 Southwark St.
London
SE1 0UP

A CIP catalogue record for this title is available from the British Library.

First edition: June 2017
10 9 8 7 6 5 4 3 2

Printed in Spain.
Titan Comics.

For rights information contact jenny.boyce@titanemail.com

WWW.TITAN-COMICS.COM

Become a fan on Facebook.com/comicstitan

Follow us on Twitter @ComicsTitan

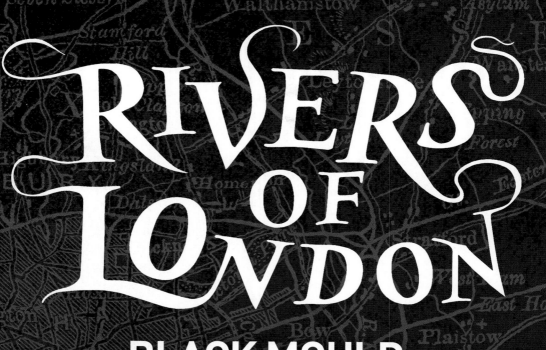

RIVERS OF LONDON

BLACK MOULD

WRITTEN BY
ANDREW CARTMEL & BEN AARONOVITCH

ART BY
LEE SULLIVAN

COLORS BY
LUIS GUERRERO

LETTERING BY
ROB STEEN

TITAN
COMICS

CHARACTER PROFILES

THOMAS NIGHTINGALE

Peter's boss. Runs the Folly, home of the SAU. Age unknown, but older than he looks. Had a rum time of it during World War II. Bit of a technophobe. Likes rugby.

SAHRA GULEED

Regular cop and self-professed Muslim ninja. Found herself roped into all this Falcon nonsense. Outranks Peter; although, in matters of the supernatural, defers to him – but never say that to her face.

PETER GRANT

Only Police constable in the Special Assessment Unit – and trainee wizard. Big on architecture. Geek about town.

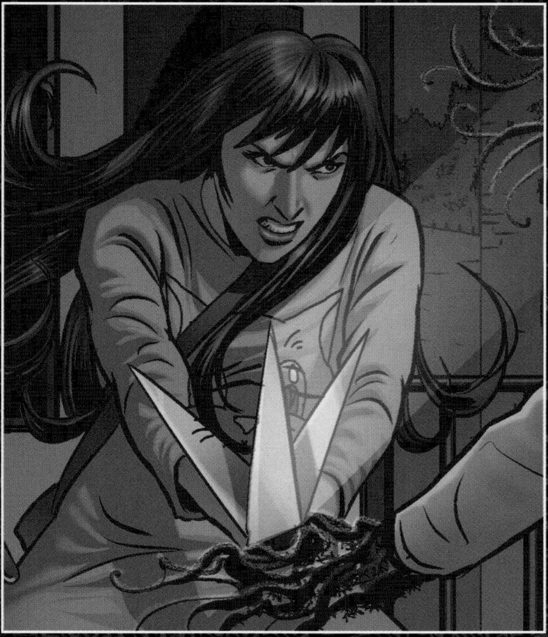

MOLLY
Maid. Makes dreadful sandwiches, but handy with a blade. Considered spooky.

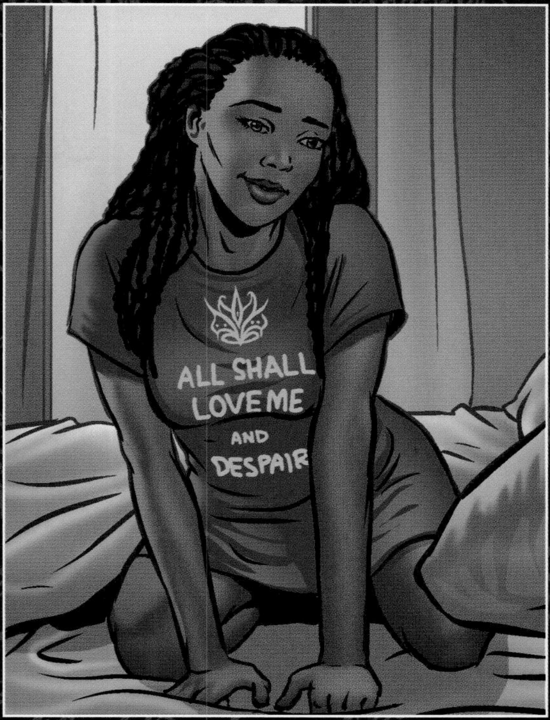
ALL SHALL LOVE ME AND DESPAIR

BEVERLEY BROOK
River goddess and Peter's girlfriend, although she'd probably say Peter was *her* boyfriend. Can make men behave in strange ways.

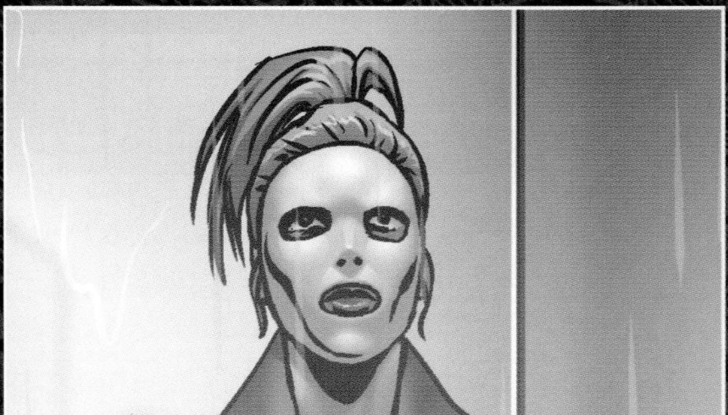

LESLEY MAY
Was Peter's partner, during which time her face was mutilated by magical fall-out during an incident in Covent Garden. Went rogue and betrayed Peter, about which he is still really pissed off. Lesley now seems to be working for the Folly's nemesis, the Faceless Man, in an effort to get her face back.

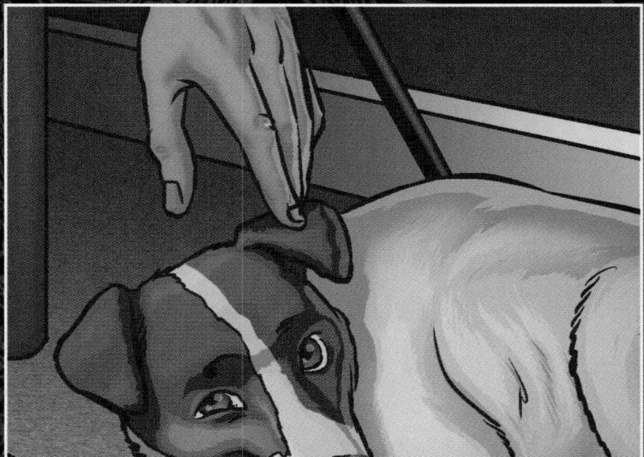

TOBY
Dog. Not in the *Scooby Doo* or 'rescuing-Peter-who's-down-the-well, Lassie' sense. More the 'stealing sausages off your plate' sense.

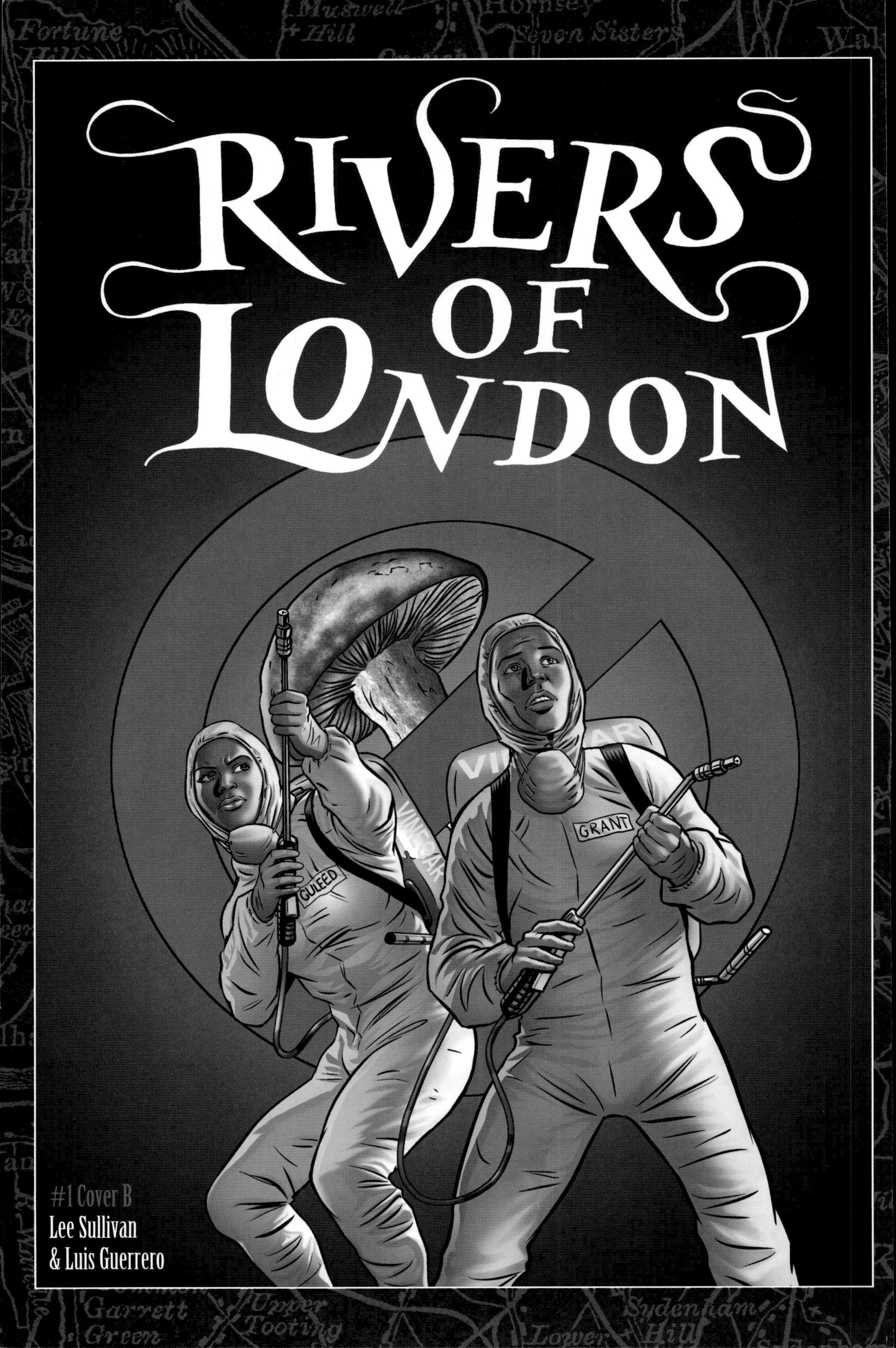
Fortune
Muswell
Hill
Hornsey
Seven Sisters
RIVERS OF LONDON
VINEGAR
GRANT
GULEED
#1 Cover B
Lee Sullivan
& Luis Guerrero
Garrett
Green
Upper
Tooting
Sydenham
Hill
Lower

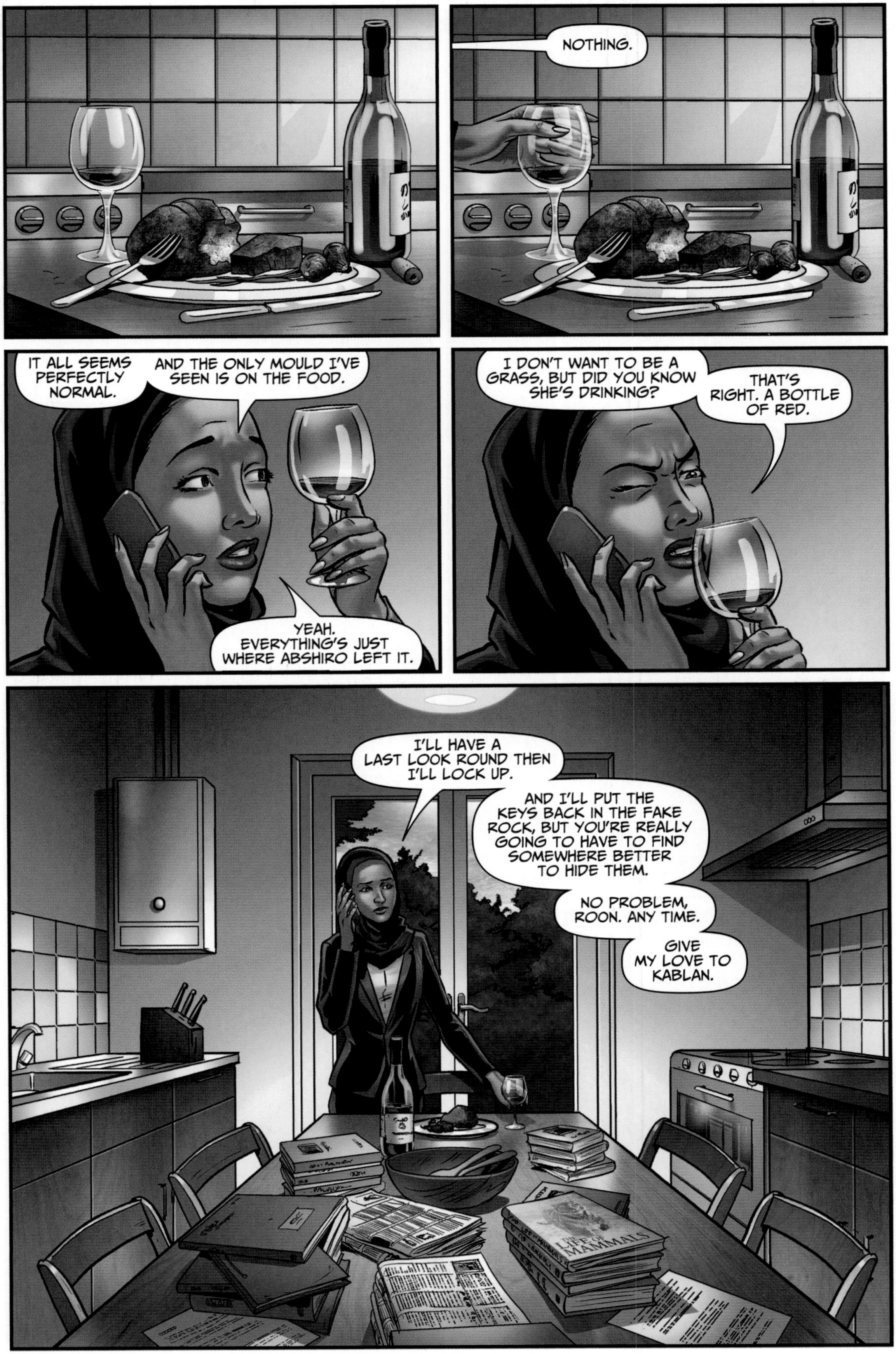
NOTHING.
IT ALL SEEMS PERFECTLY NORMAL.
AND THE ONLY MOULD I'VE SEEN IS ON THE FOOD.
YEAH. EVERYTHING'S JUST WHERE ABSHIRO LEFT IT.
I DON'T WANT TO BE A GRASS, BUT DID YOU KNOW SHE'S DRINKING?
THAT'S RIGHT. A BOTTLE OF RED.
I'LL HAVE A LAST LOOK ROUND THEN I'LL LOCK UP.
AND I'LL PUT THE KEYS BACK IN THE FAKE ROCK, BUT YOU'RE REALLY GOING TO HAVE TO FIND SOMEWHERE BETTER TO HIDE THEM.
NO PROBLEM, ROON. ANY TIME.
GIVE MY LOVE TO KABLAN.
THE LIFE OF MAMMALS

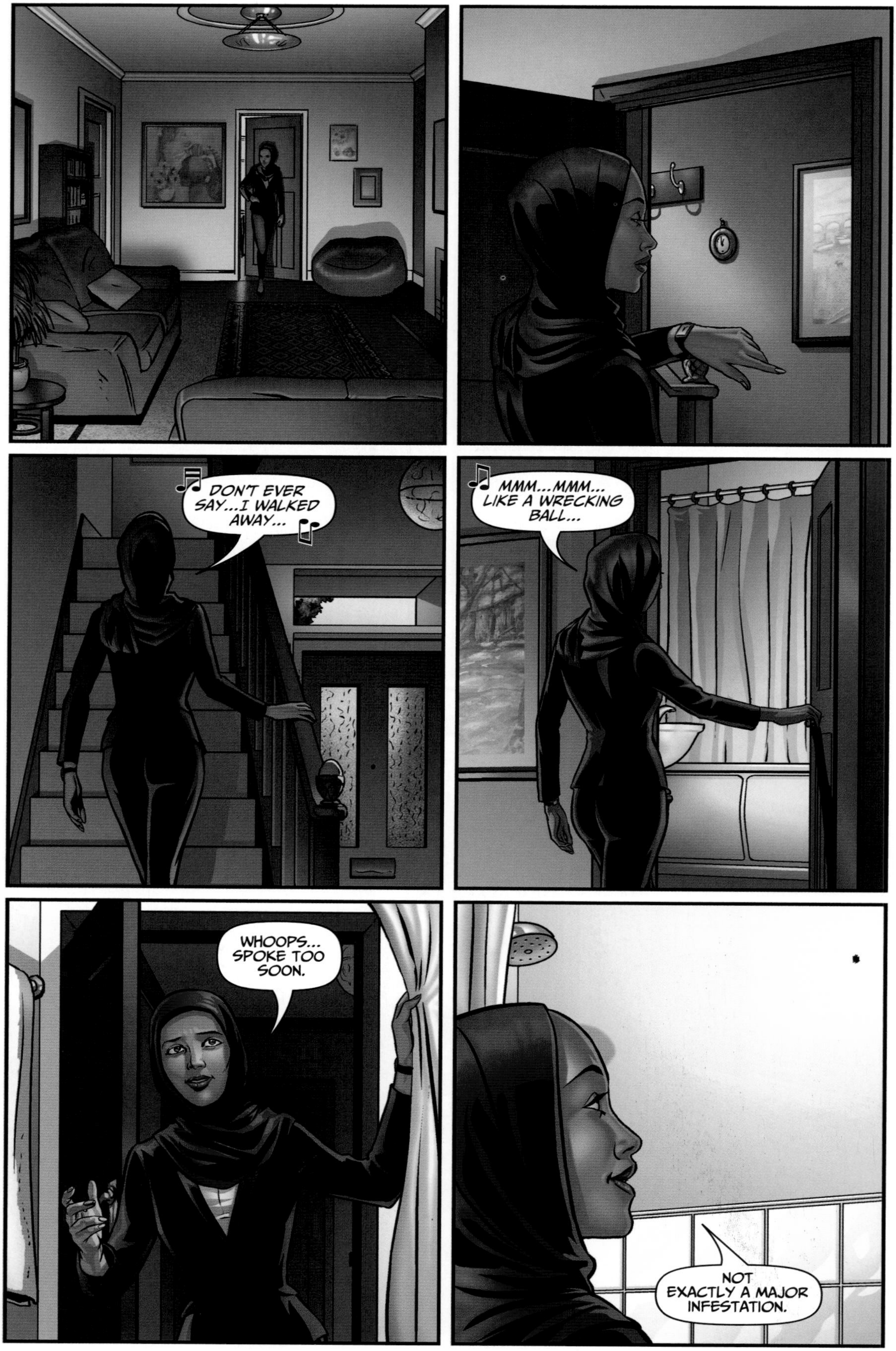
DON'T EVER SAY...I WALKED AWAY...
MMM...MMM... LIKE A WRECKING BALL...
WHOOPS... SPOKE TOO SOON.
NOT EXACTLY A MAJOR INFESTATION.

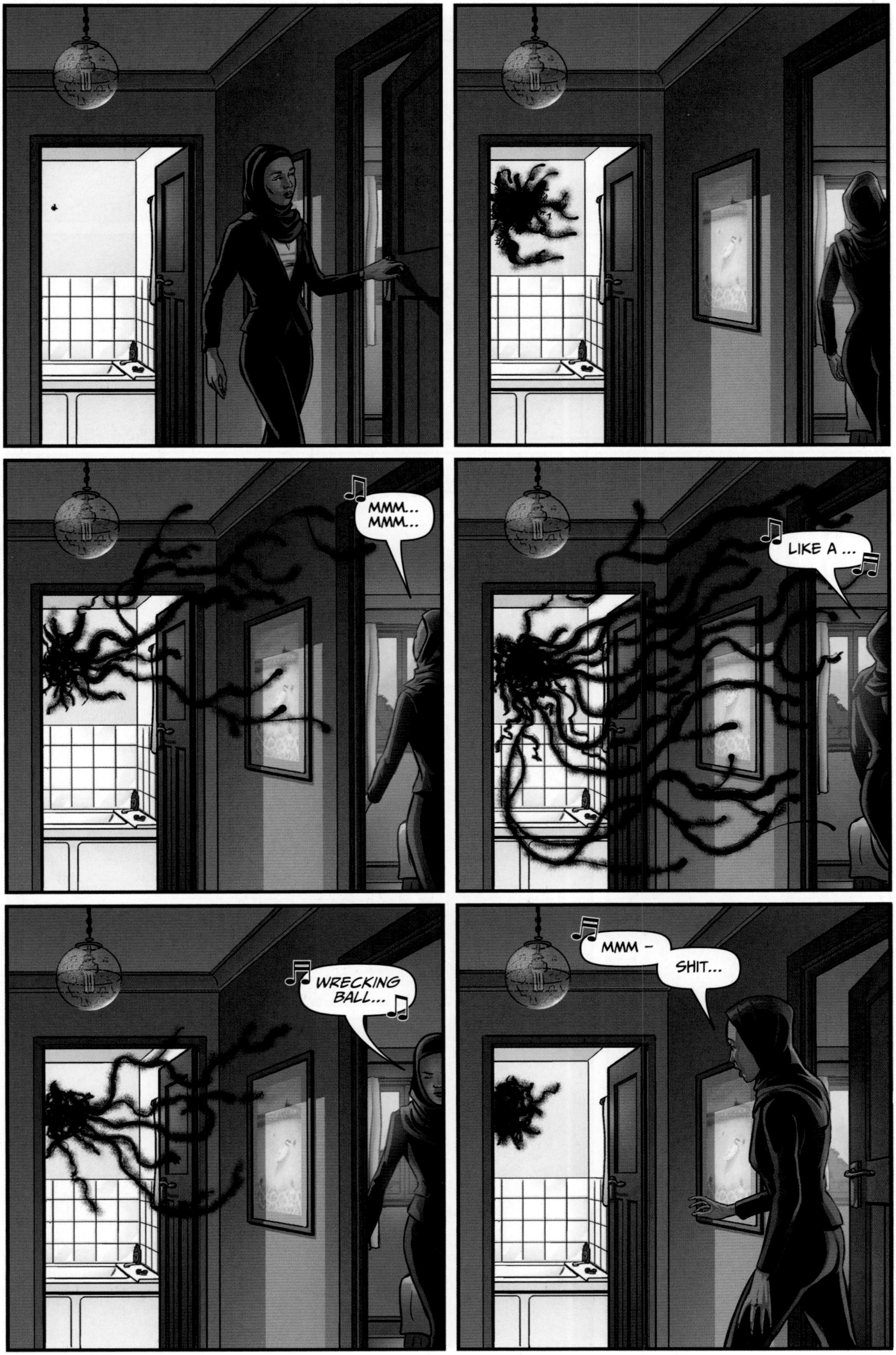
MMM...
MMM...
LIKE A ...
WRECKING
BALL...
MMM –
SHIT...

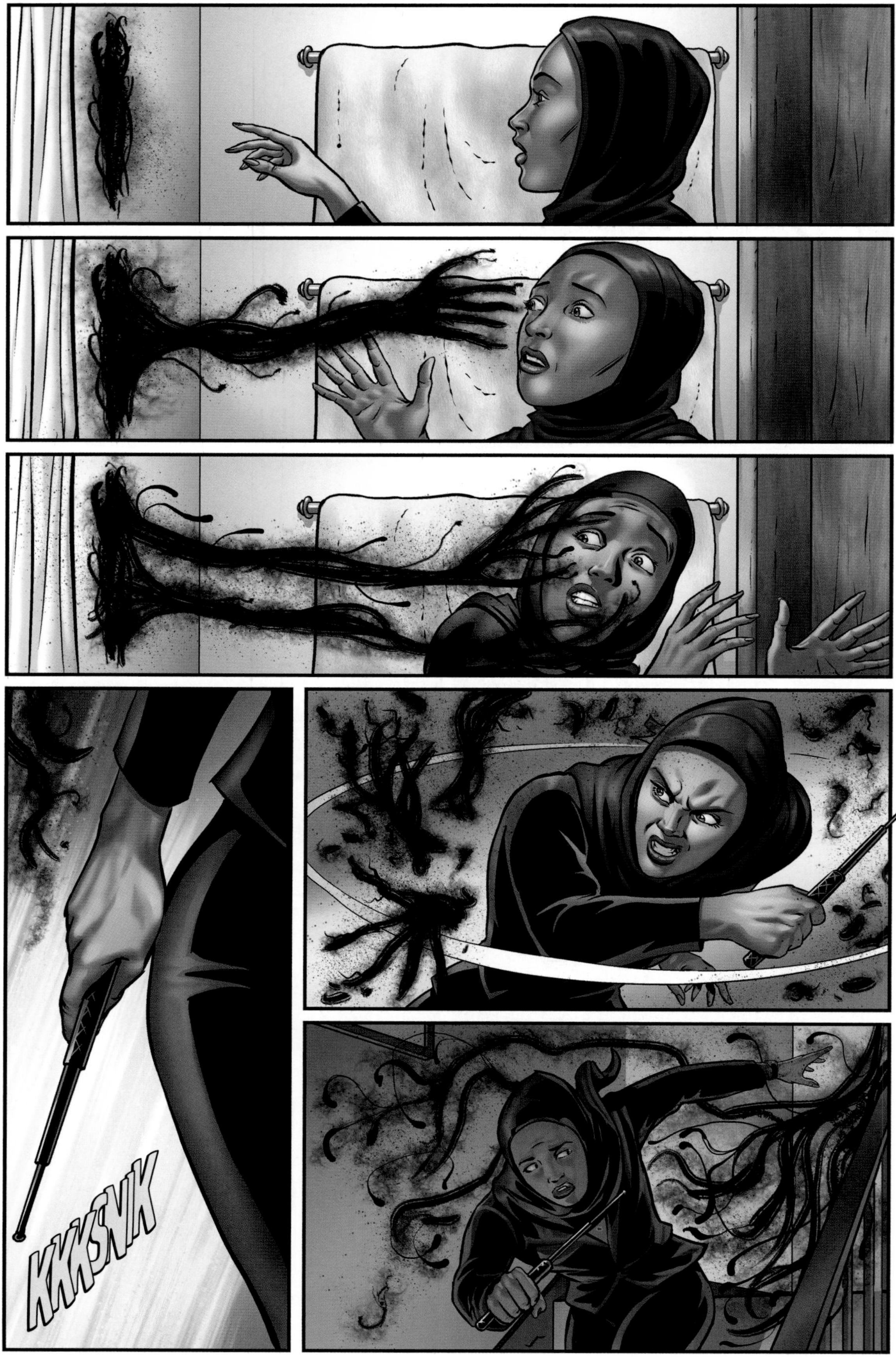
KKKSNIK

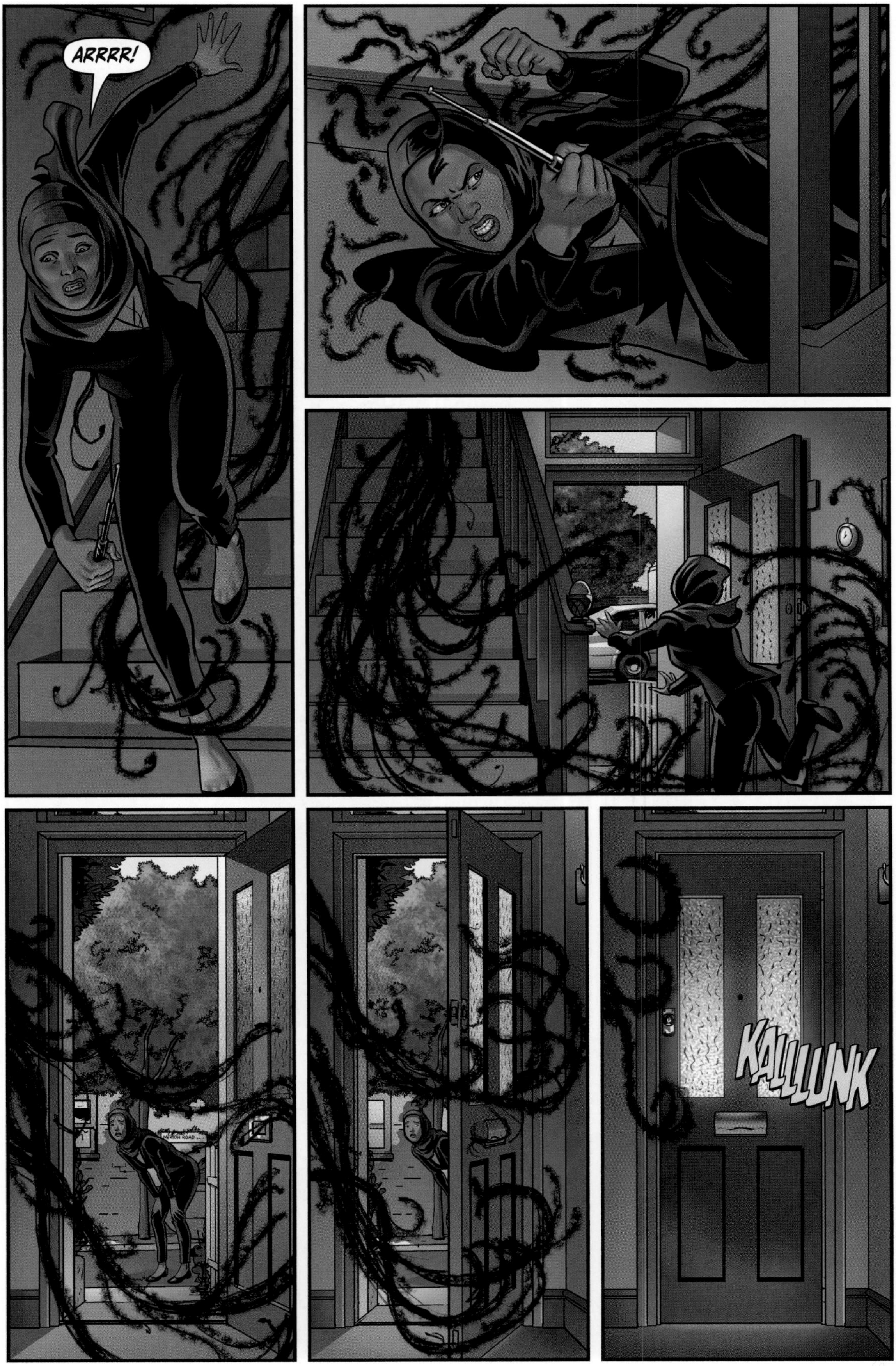
ARRRR!
KALLLUNK

THEY'RE FRIENDS OF THE FAMILY. THEY BOUGHT THE HOUSE AND DID IT UP TO RENT OUT.

BUT NOW THEIR DAUGHTER IS GOING TO UNI IN LONDON, SO THEY'VE HANDED IT OVER TO HER.

VERY NICE.

BUT ABSHIRO, THE DAUGHTER, GOT SO FREAKED OUT ABOUT SOMETHING THAT SHE FLED THE HOUSE AND WON'T GO BACK.

WON'T SAY WHAT'S WRONG.

I THINK THE PARENTS WERE THINKING ALONG THE LINES OF INTIMIDATING NEIGHBOURS. THAT WOULD HAVE BEEN A LOT EASIER TO HANDLE...

NOT TO MENTION WRAP MY HEAD AROUND.

BUT DID THEY SAY ANYTHING ABOUT THE MOULD?

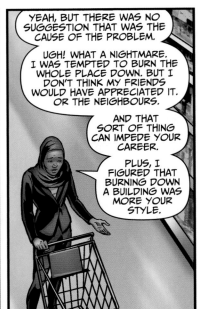

YEAH, BUT THERE WAS NO SUGGESTION THAT WAS THE CAUSE OF THE PROBLEM.

UGH! WHAT A NIGHTMARE. I WAS TEMPTED TO BURN THE WHOLE PLACE DOWN. BUT I DON'T THINK MY FRIENDS WOULD HAVE APPRECIATED IT. OR THE NEIGHBOURS.

AND THAT SORT OF THING CAN IMPEDE YOUR CAREER.

PLUS, I FIGURED THAT BURNING DOWN A BUILDING WAS MORE YOUR STYLE.

NO, NO, THE BUILDING *BLEW UP.*

IT WAS *COVENT GARDEN* THAT BURNT DOWN.

HERE WE GO.

YOU REALLY THINK THIS WILL WORK?

YOU NEED TO TRUST ME WITH ANYTHING OUTSIDE THE REALM OF SCIENTIFIC UNDERSTANDING AND RATIONAL THINKING.

YOU'LL NEED LOTS OF CHIPS TO GO WITH THAT LOT.

AND SALT, TOO, HA HA.

HA. HA.

WE AREN'T GOING AROUND TO ANY OTHER SHOPS BUYING UP ALL THEIR VINEGAR, ARE WE?

NO. NOW WE NEED SOME PLASTIC BUCKETS.

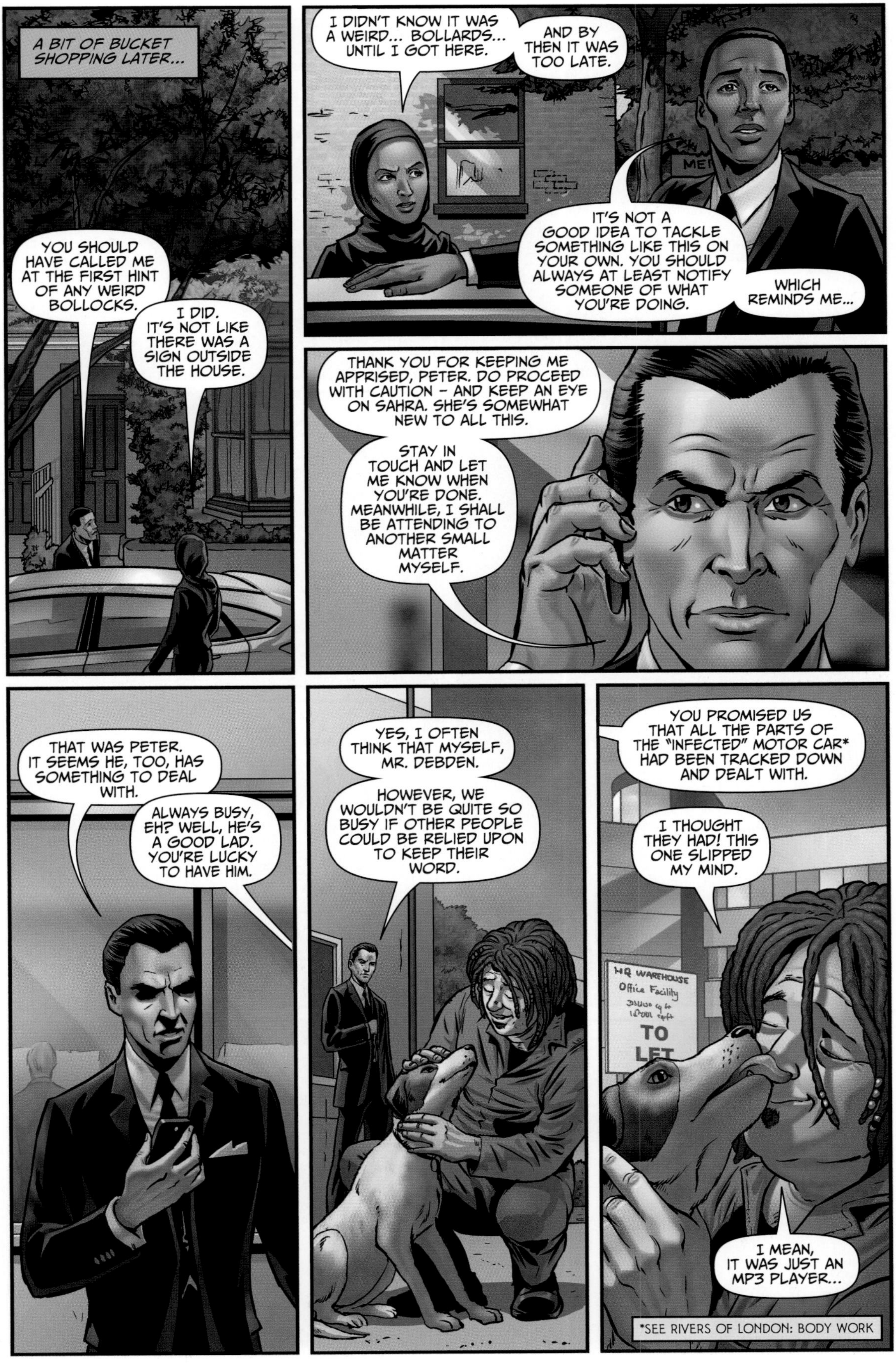
A BIT OF BUCKET SHOPPING LATER...
YOU SHOULD HAVE CALLED ME AT THE FIRST HINT OF ANY WEIRD BOLLOCKS.
I DID. IT'S NOT LIKE THERE WAS A SIGN OUTSIDE THE HOUSE.
I DIDN'T KNOW IT WAS A WEIRD... BOLLARDS... UNTIL I GOT HERE.
AND BY THEN IT WAS TOO LATE.
IT'S NOT A GOOD IDEA TO TACKLE SOMETHING LIKE THIS ON YOUR OWN. YOU SHOULD ALWAYS AT LEAST NOTIFY SOMEONE OF WHAT YOU'RE DOING.
WHICH REMINDS ME...
THANK YOU FOR KEEPING ME APPRISED, PETER. DO PROCEED WITH CAUTION – AND KEEP AN EYE ON SAHRA. SHE'S SOMEWHAT NEW TO ALL THIS.
STAY IN TOUCH AND LET ME KNOW WHEN YOU'RE DONE. MEANWHILE, I SHALL BE ATTENDING TO ANOTHER SMALL MATTER MYSELF.
THAT WAS PETER. IT SEEMS HE, TOO, HAS SOMETHING TO DEAL WITH.
ALWAYS BUSY, EH? WELL, HE'S A GOOD LAD. YOU'RE LUCKY TO HAVE HIM.
YES, I OFTEN THINK THAT MYSELF, MR. DEBDEN.
HOWEVER, WE WOULDN'T BE QUITE SO BUSY IF OTHER PEOPLE COULD BE RELIED UPON TO KEEP THEIR WORD.
YOU PROMISED US THAT ALL THE PARTS OF THE "INFECTED" MOTOR CAR* HAD BEEN TRACKED DOWN AND DEALT WITH.
I THOUGHT THEY HAD! THIS ONE SLIPPED MY MIND.
HQ WAREHOUSE
Office Facility
TO
I MEAN, IT WAS JUST AN MP3 PLAYER...
*SEE RIVERS OF LONDON: BODY WORK

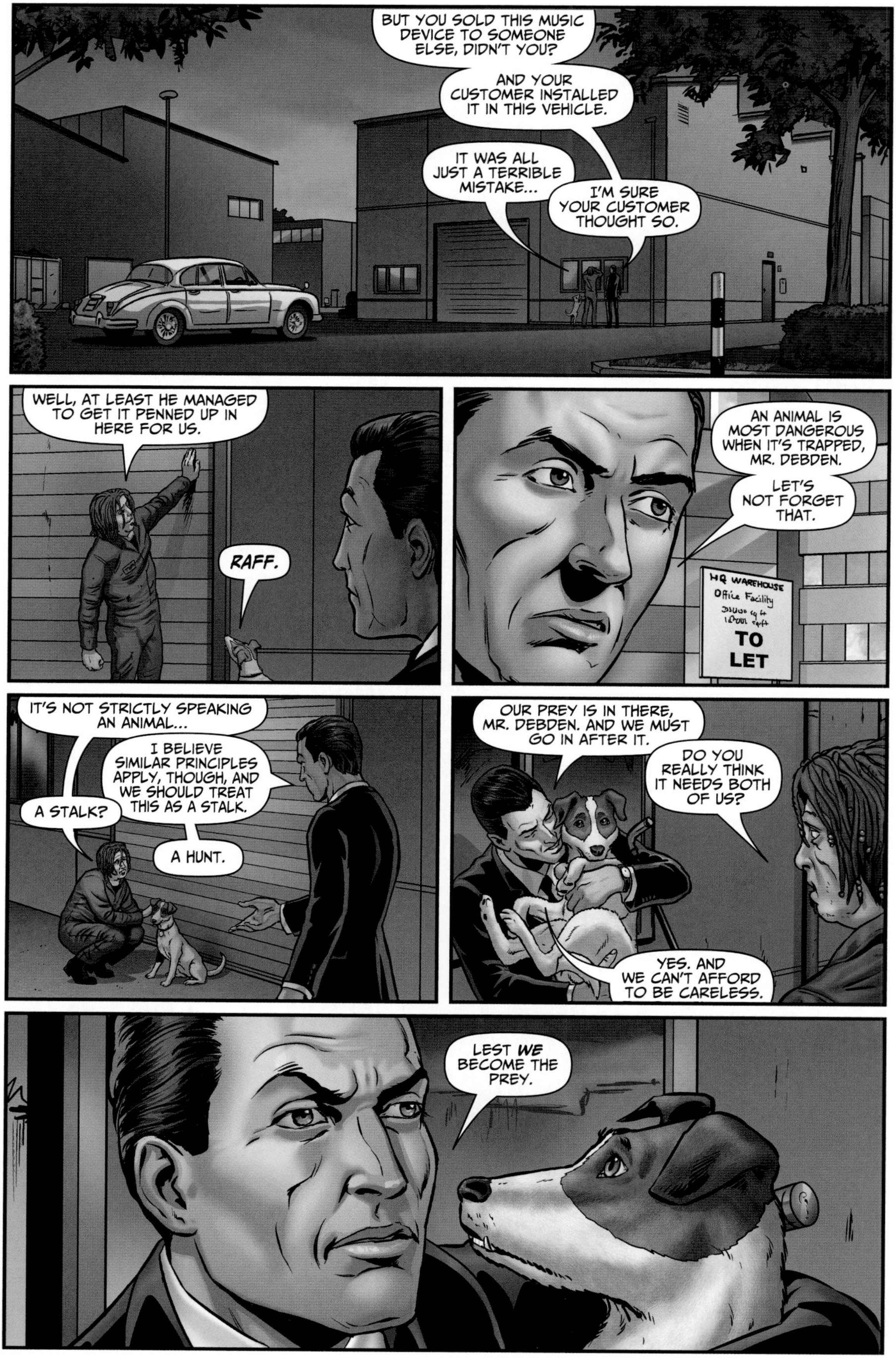

BUT YOU SOLD THIS MUSIC DEVICE TO SOMEONE ELSE, DIDN'T YOU?
AND YOUR CUSTOMER INSTALLED IT IN THIS VEHICLE.
IT WAS ALL JUST A TERRIBLE MISTAKE...
I'M SURE YOUR CUSTOMER THOUGHT SO.
WELL, AT LEAST HE MANAGED TO GET IT PENNED UP IN HERE FOR US.
RAFF.
AN ANIMAL IS MOST DANGEROUS WHEN IT'S TRAPPED, MR. DEBDEN.
LET'S NOT FORGET THAT.
HQ WAREHOUSE
Office Facility
TO LET
IT'S NOT STRICTLY SPEAKING AN ANIMAL...
I BELIEVE SIMILAR PRINCIPLES APPLY, THOUGH, AND WE SHOULD TREAT THIS AS A STALK.
A STALK?
A HUNT.
OUR PREY IS IN THERE, MR. DEBDEN. AND WE MUST GO IN AFTER IT.
DO YOU REALLY THINK IT NEEDS BOTH OF US?
YES. AND WE CAN'T AFFORD TO BE CARELESS.
LEST WE BECOME THE PREY.

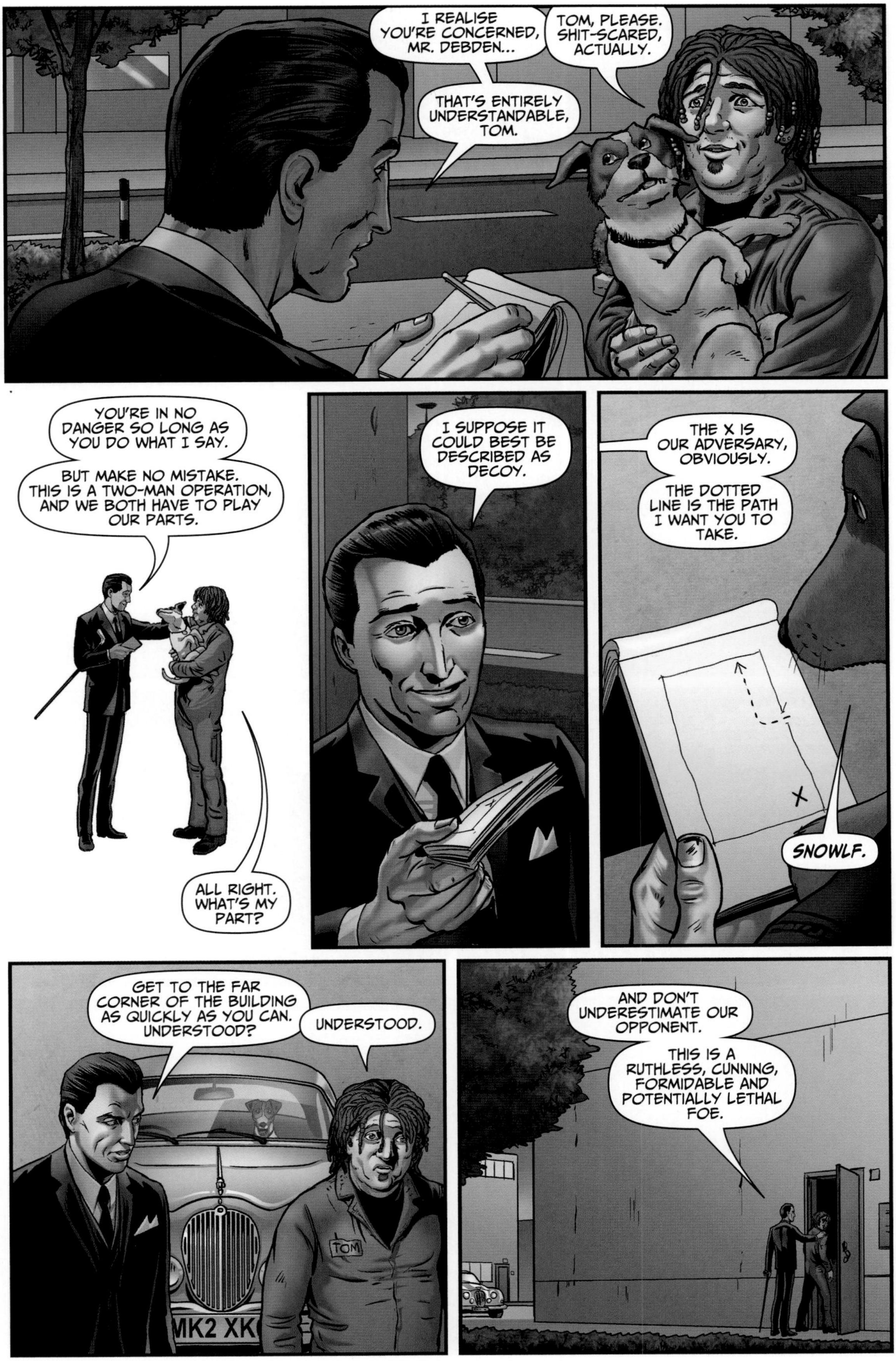
I REALISE YOU'RE CONCERNED, MR. DEBDEN...
TOM, PLEASE. SHIT-SCARED, ACTUALLY.
THAT'S ENTIRELY UNDERSTANDABLE, TOM.
YOU'RE IN NO DANGER SO LONG AS YOU DO WHAT I SAY.
BUT MAKE NO MISTAKE. THIS IS A TWO-MAN OPERATION, AND WE BOTH HAVE TO PLAY OUR PARTS.
ALL RIGHT. WHAT'S MY PART?
I SUPPOSE IT COULD BEST BE DESCRIBED AS DECOY.
THE X IS OUR ADVERSARY, OBVIOUSLY.
THE DOTTED LINE IS THE PATH I WANT YOU TO TAKE.
SNOWLF.
GET TO THE FAR CORNER OF THE BUILDING AS QUICKLY AS YOU CAN. UNDERSTOOD?
UNDERSTOOD.
TOM
AND DON'T UNDERESTIMATE OUR OPPONENT.
THIS IS A RUTHLESS, CUNNING, FORMIDABLE AND POTENTIALLY LETHAL FOE.

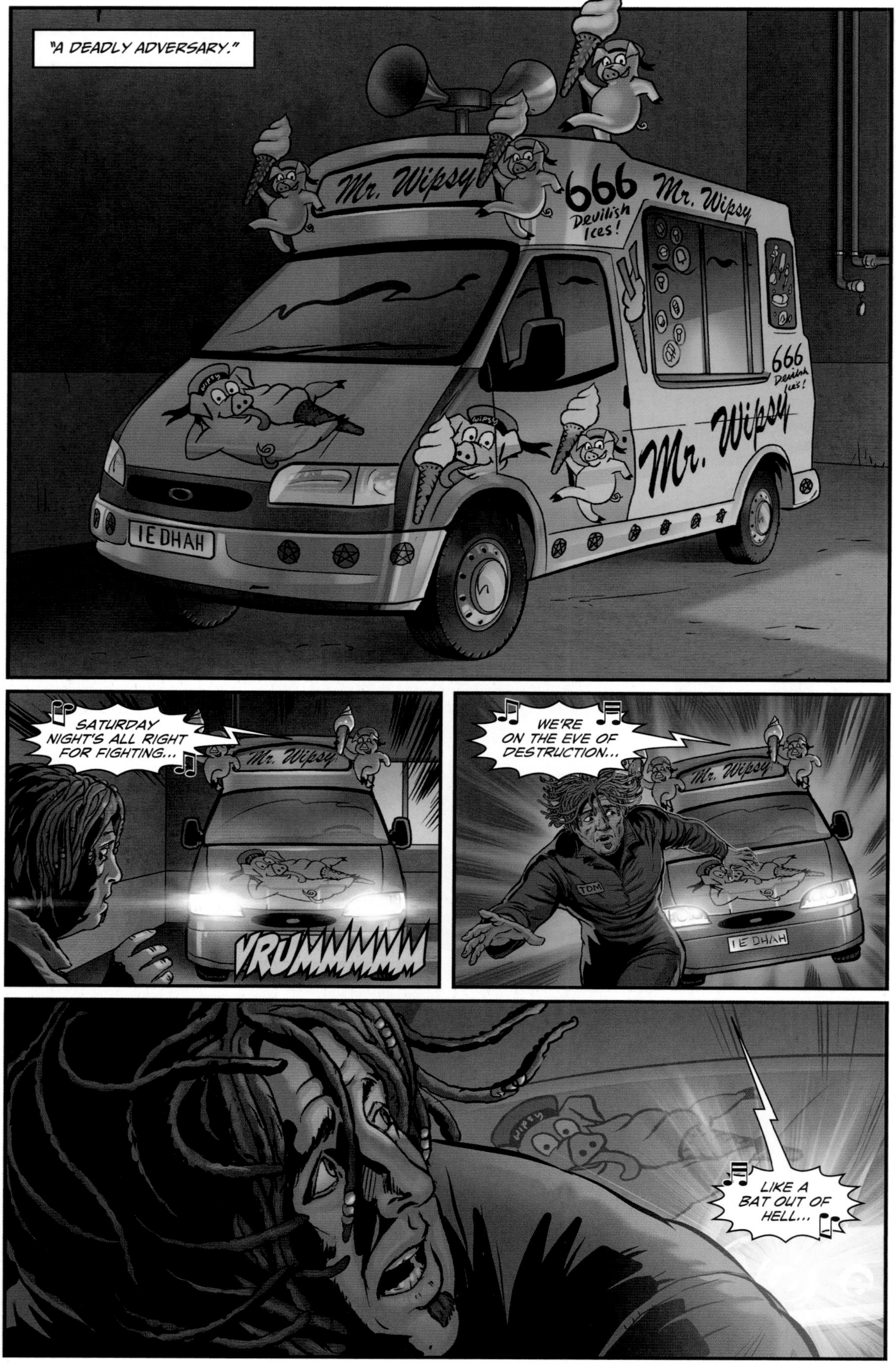
"A DEADLY ADVERSARY."
Mr. Wipsy
666 Devilish Ices!
Mr. Wipsy
IE DHAH
SATURDAY NIGHT'S ALL RIGHT FOR FIGHTING...
VRUMMMMM
WE'RE ON THE EVE OF DESTRUCTION...
TOM
LIKE A BAT OUT OF HELL...

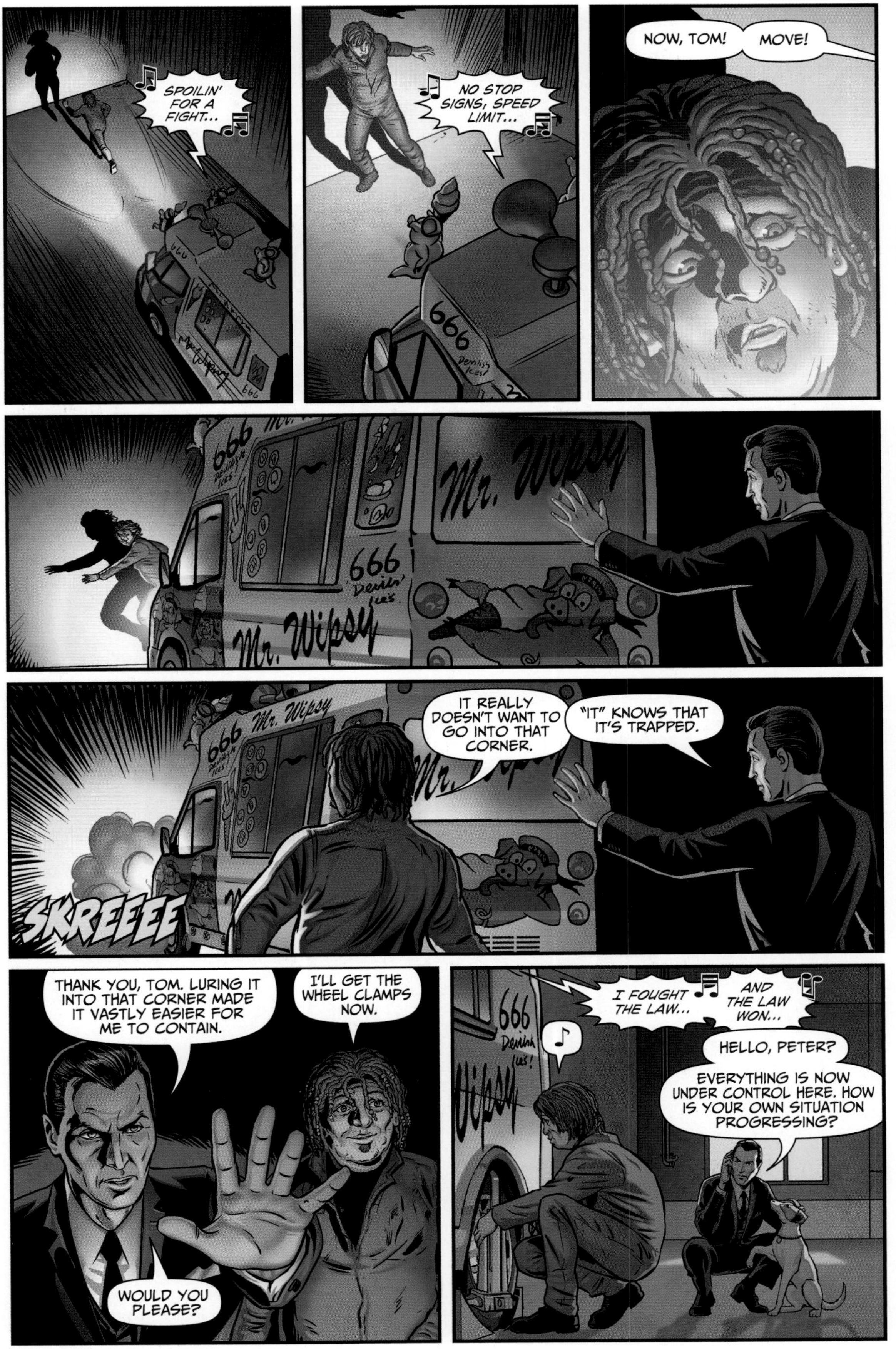

SPOILIN' FOR A FIGHT...
NO STOP SIGNS, SPEED LIMIT...
666
NOW, TOM!
MOVE!
Mr. Wipsy
666
Mr. Wipsy
IT REALLY DOESN'T WANT TO GO INTO THAT CORNER.
"IT" KNOWS THAT IT'S TRAPPED.
SKREEEE
THANK YOU, TOM. LURING IT INTO THAT CORNER MADE IT VASTLY EASIER FOR ME TO CONTAIN.
I'LL GET THE WHEEL CLAMPS NOW.
WOULD YOU PLEASE?
I FOUGHT THE LAW...
AND THE LAW WON...
HELLO, PETER?
EVERYTHING IS NOW UNDER CONTROL HERE. HOW IS YOUR OWN SITUATION PROGRESSING?

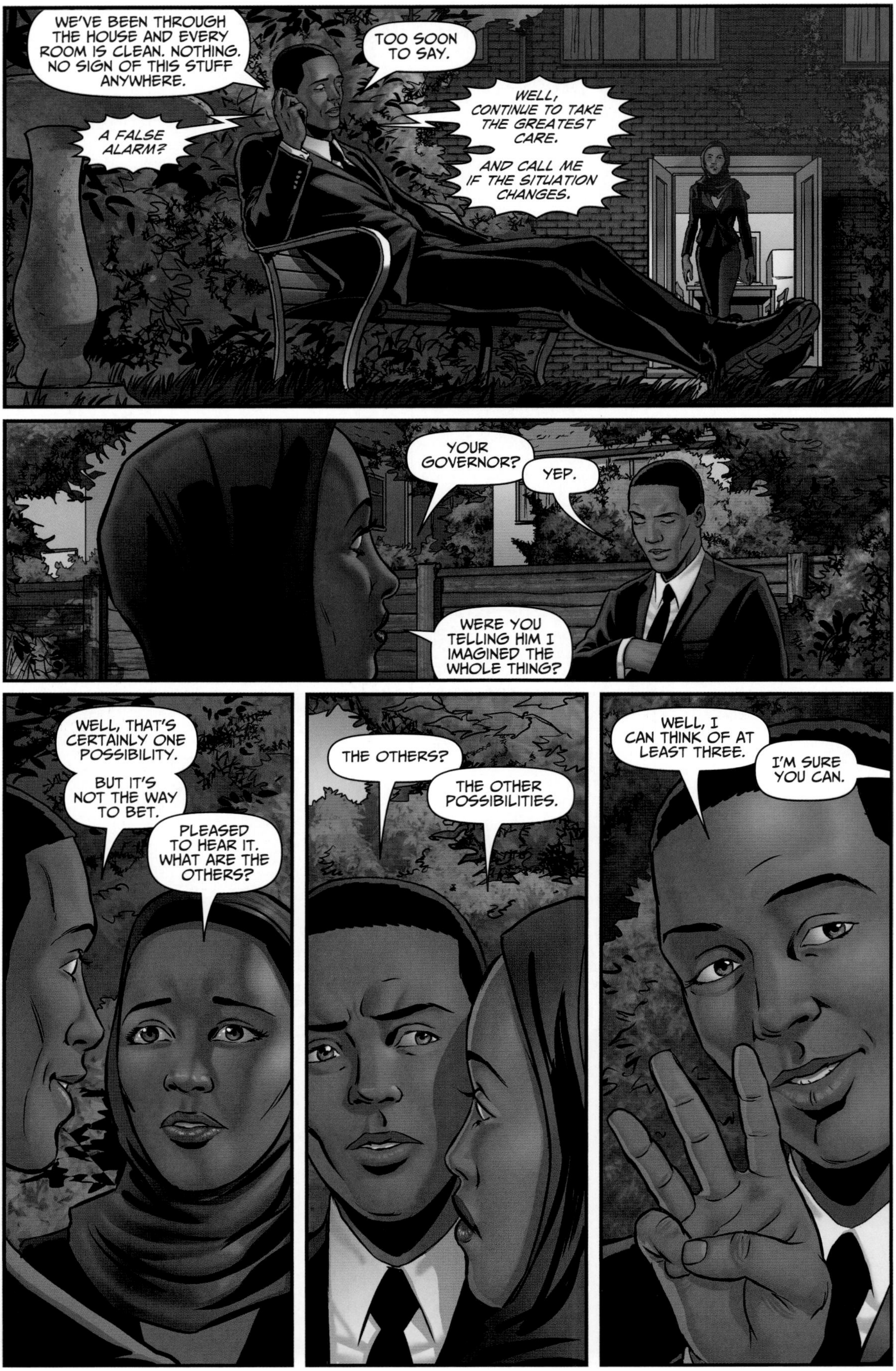
WE'VE BEEN THROUGH THE HOUSE AND EVERY ROOM IS CLEAN. NOTHING. NO SIGN OF THIS STUFF ANYWHERE.
A FALSE ALARM?
TOO SOON TO SAY.
WELL, CONTINUE TO TAKE THE GREATEST CARE.
AND CALL ME IF THE SITUATION CHANGES.
YOUR GOVERNOR?
YEP.
WERE YOU TELLING HIM I IMAGINED THE WHOLE THING?
WELL, THAT'S CERTAINLY ONE POSSIBILITY.
BUT IT'S NOT THE WAY TO BET.
PLEASED TO HEAR IT. WHAT ARE THE OTHERS?
THE OTHERS?
THE OTHER POSSIBILITIES.
WELL, I CAN THINK OF AT LEAST THREE.
I'M SURE YOU CAN.

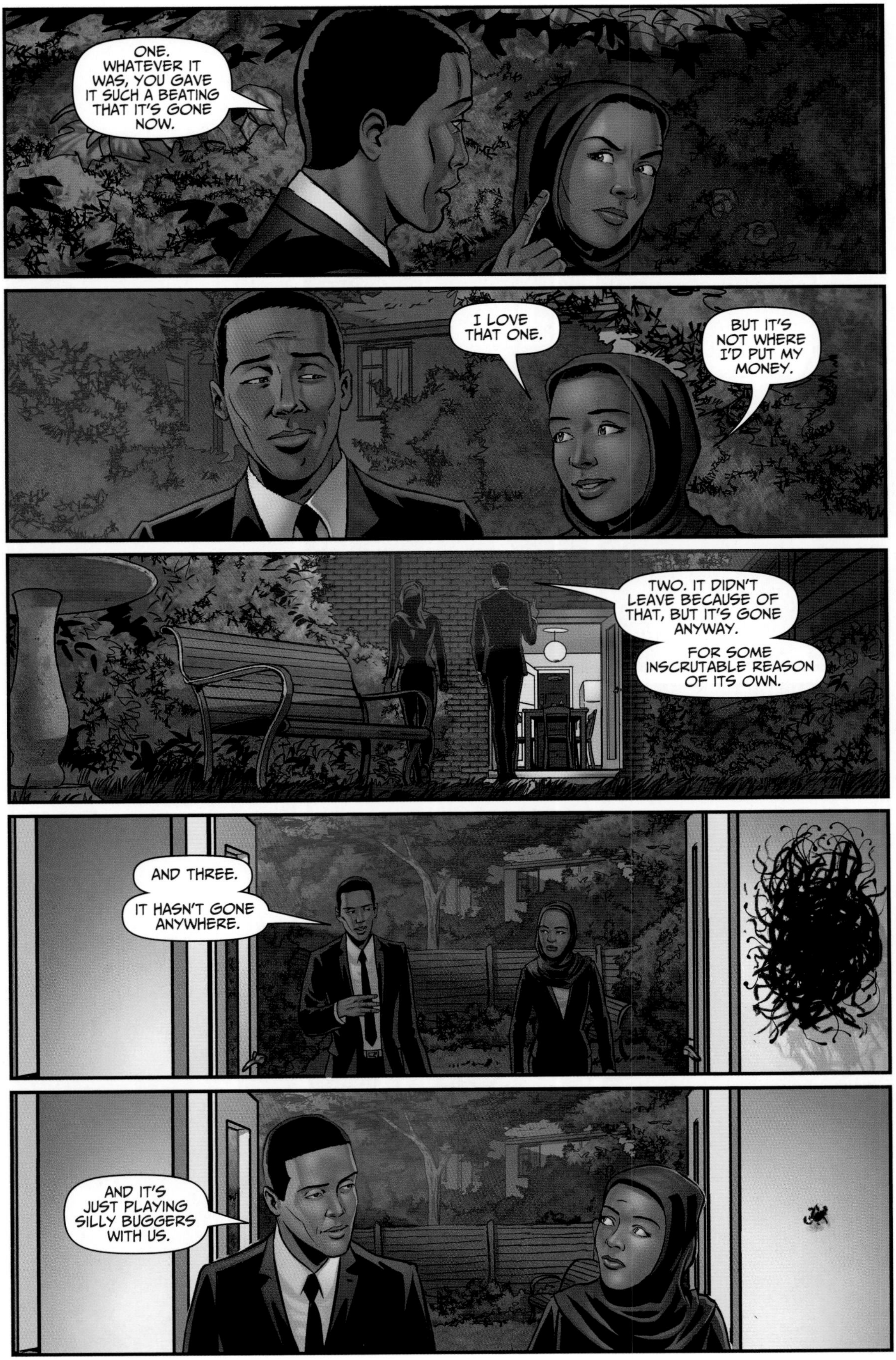
ONE. WHATEVER IT WAS, YOU GAVE IT SUCH A BEATING THAT IT'S GONE NOW.
I LOVE THAT ONE.
BUT IT'S NOT WHERE I'D PUT MY MONEY.
TWO. IT DIDN'T LEAVE BECAUSE OF THAT, BUT IT'S GONE ANYWAY.
FOR SOME INSCRUTABLE REASON OF ITS OWN.
AND THREE.
IT HASN'T GONE ANYWHERE.
AND IT'S JUST PLAYING SILLY BUGGERS WITH US.

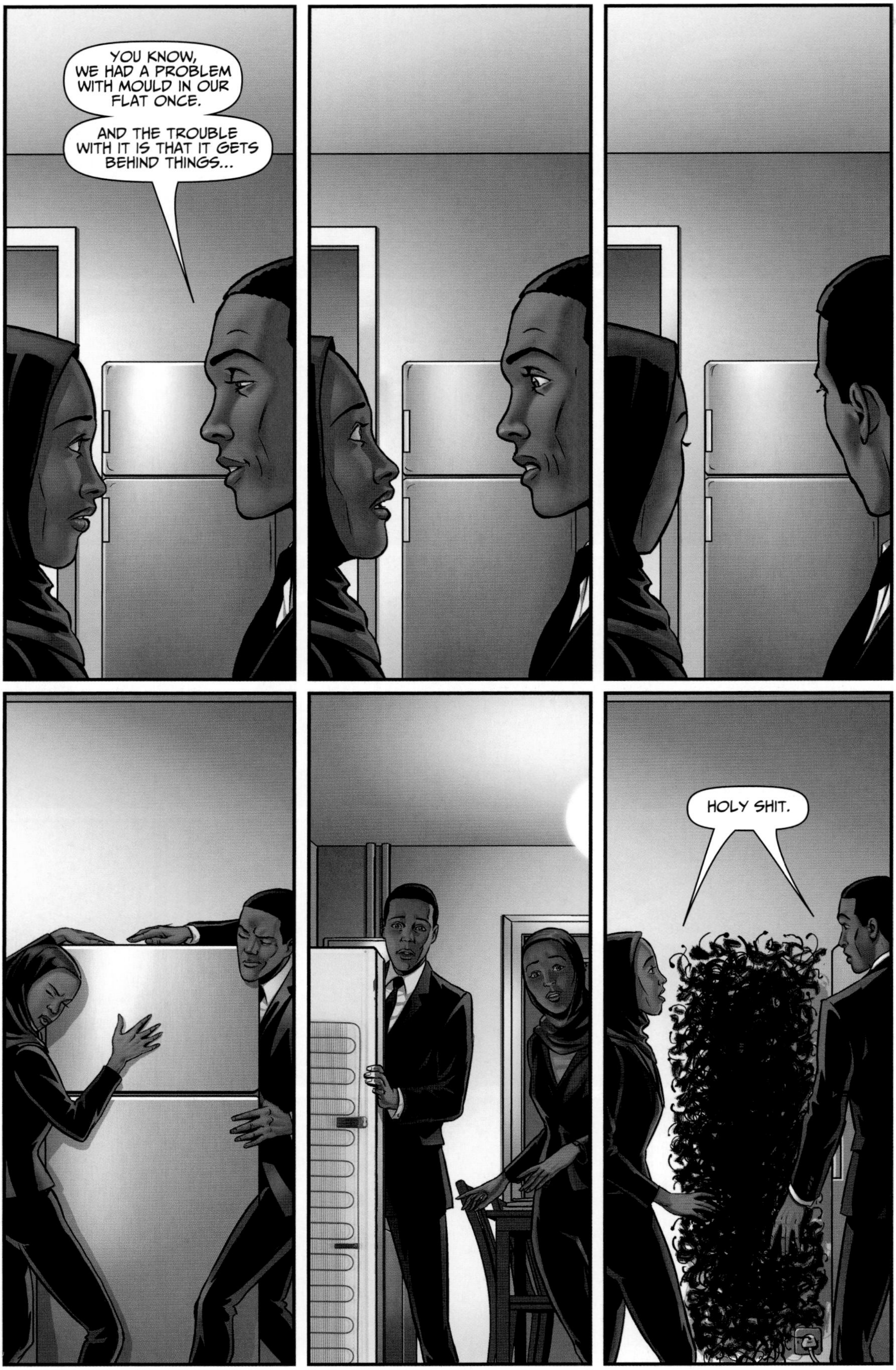
YOU KNOW, WE HAD A PROBLEM WITH MOULD IN OUR FLAT ONCE.
AND THE TROUBLE WITH IT IS THAT IT GETS BEHIND THINGS...
HOLY SHIT.

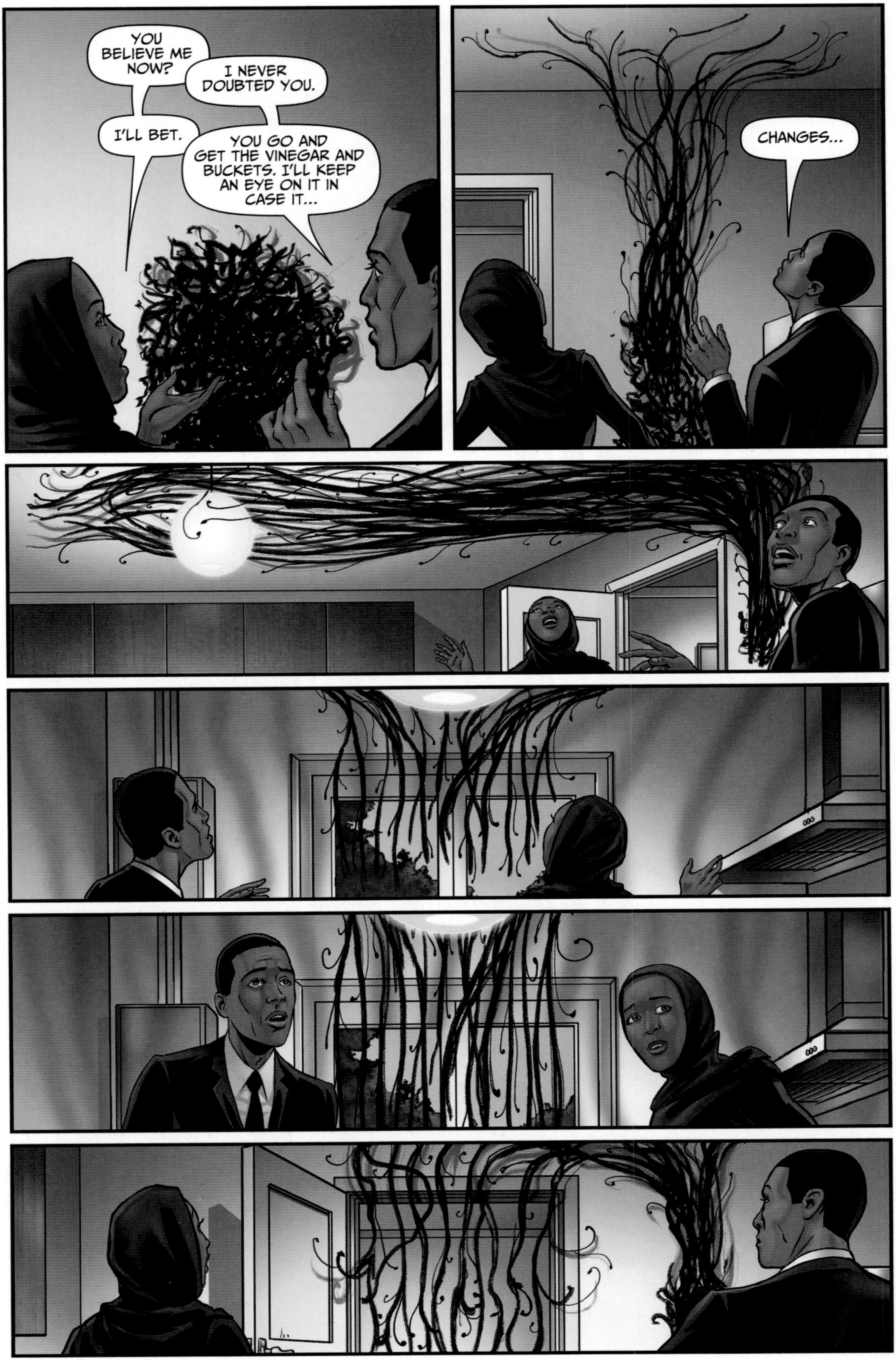
YOU BELIEVE ME NOW?
I NEVER DOUBTED YOU.
I'LL BET.
YOU GO AND GET THE VINEGAR AND BUCKETS. I'LL KEEP AN EYE ON IT IN CASE IT...
CHANGES...

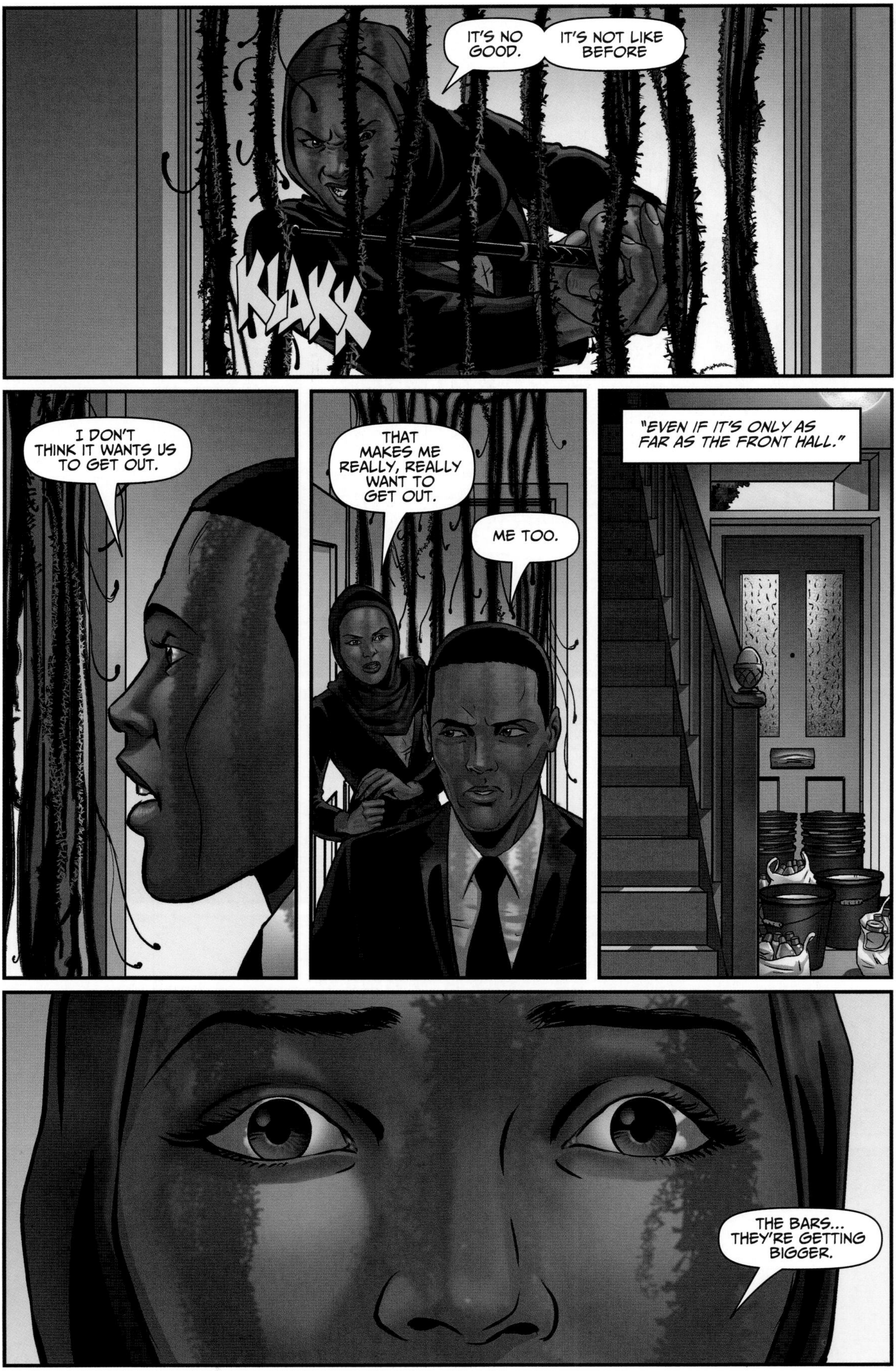
IT'S NO GOOD.
IT'S NOT LIKE BEFORE
KLAKK
I DON'T THINK IT WANTS US TO GET OUT.
THAT MAKES ME REALLY, REALLY WANT TO GET OUT.
ME TOO.
"EVEN IF IT'S ONLY AS FAR AS THE FRONT HALL."
THE BARS... THEY'RE GETTING BIGGER.

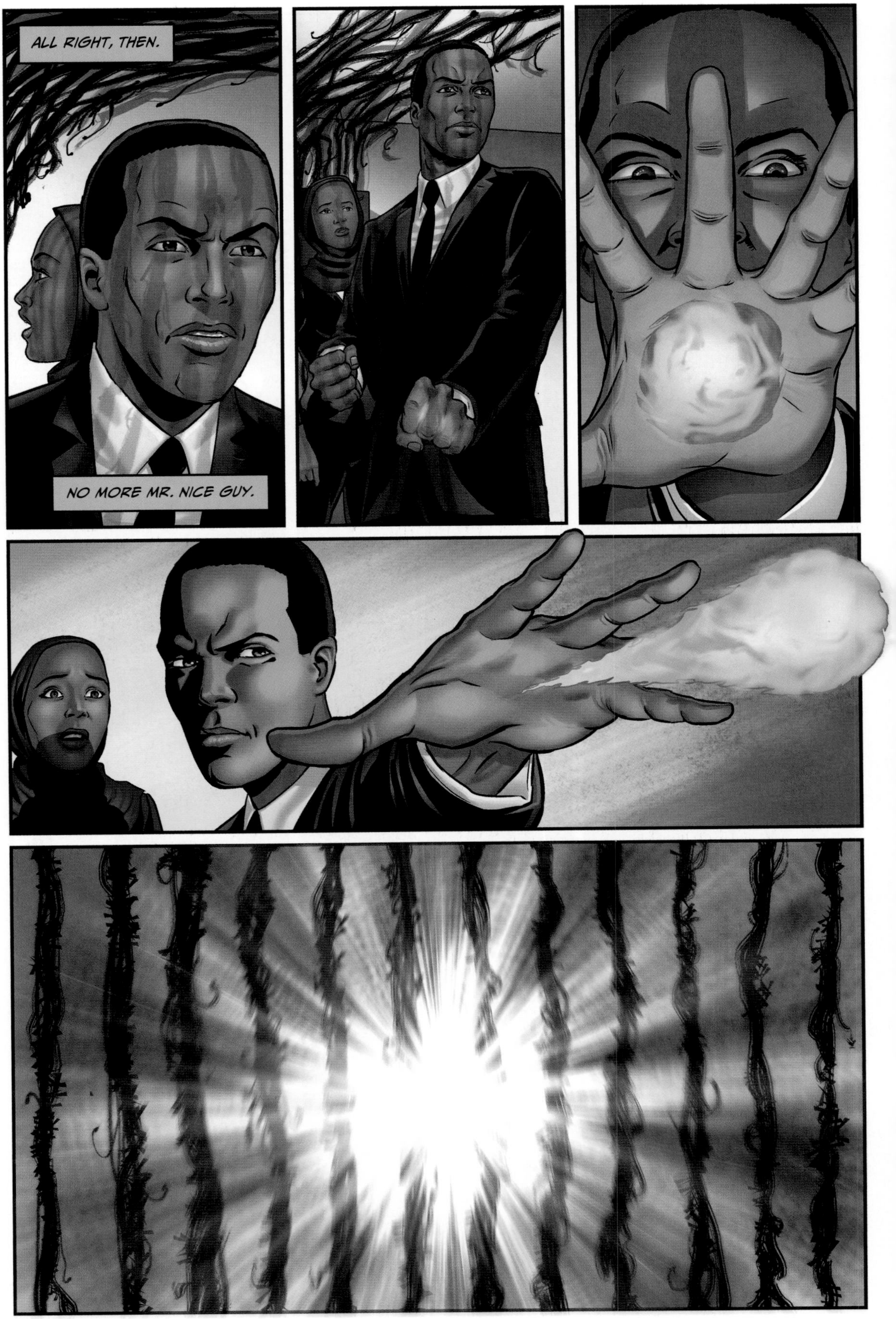
ALL RIGHT, THEN.
NO MORE MR. NICE GUY.

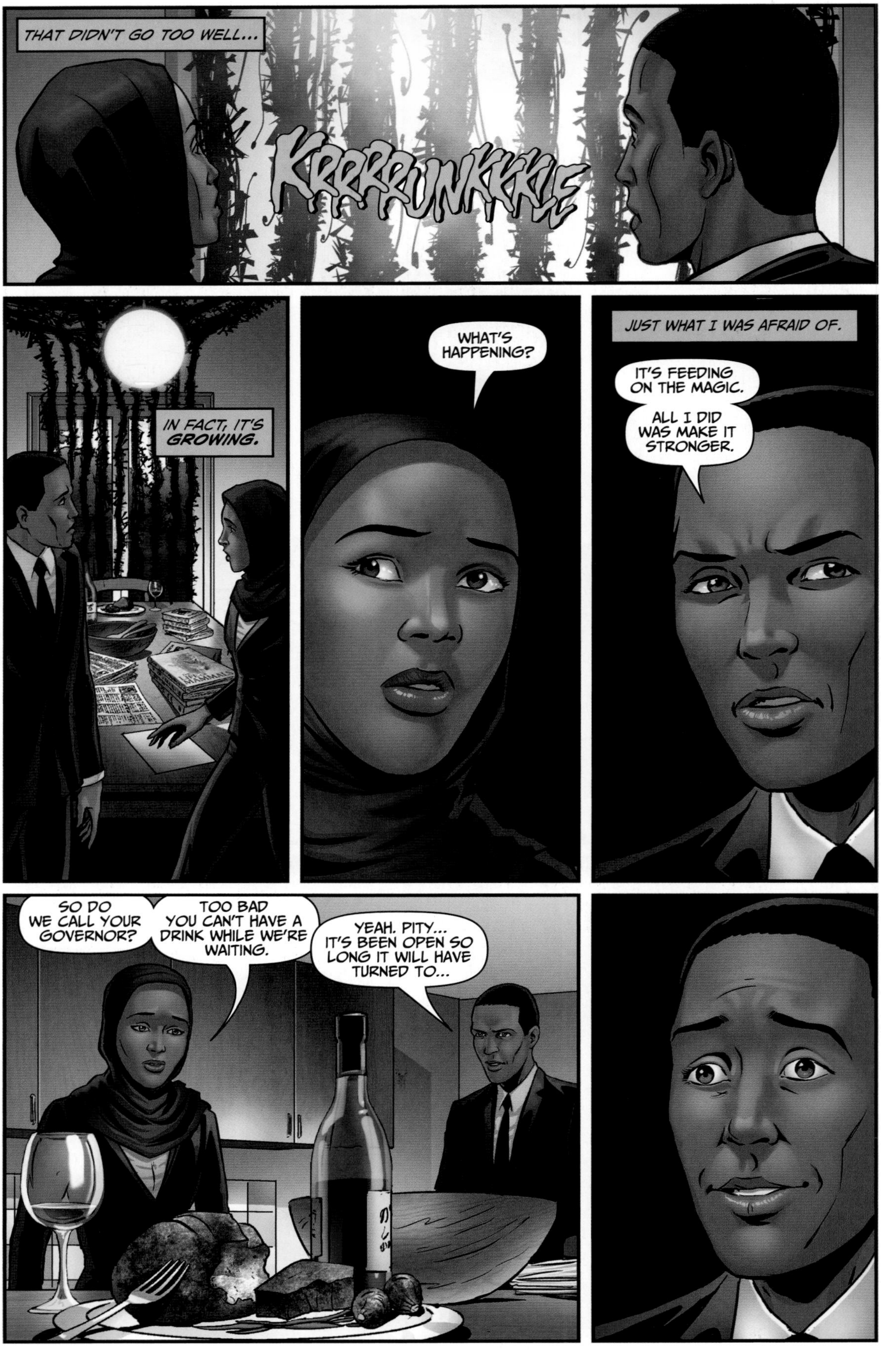
THAT DIDN'T GO TOO WELL...
KRRRRUNKKKLE
IN FACT, IT'S GROWING.
WHAT'S HAPPENING?
JUST WHAT I WAS AFRAID OF.
IT'S FEEDING ON THE MAGIC.
ALL I DID WAS MAKE IT STRONGER.
SO DO WE CALL YOUR GOVERNOR?
TOO BAD YOU CAN'T HAVE A DRINK WHILE WE'RE WAITING.
YEAH. PITY... IT'S BEEN OPEN SO LONG IT WILL HAVE TURNED TO...

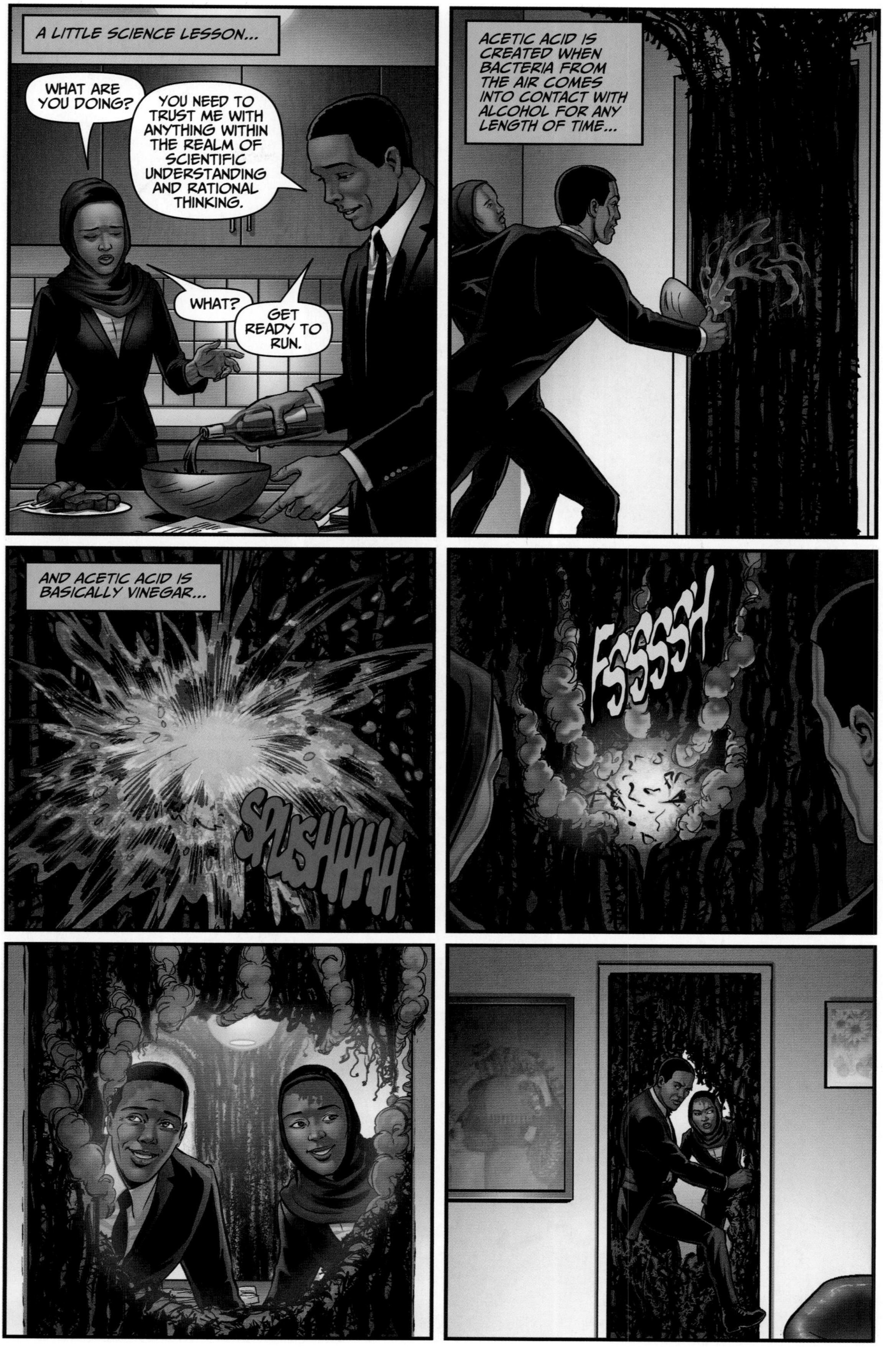
A LITTLE SCIENCE LESSON...
WHAT ARE YOU DOING?
YOU NEED TO TRUST ME WITH ANYTHING WITHIN THE REALM OF SCIENTIFIC UNDERSTANDING AND RATIONAL THINKING.
WHAT?
GET READY TO RUN.
ACETIC ACID IS CREATED WHEN BACTERIA FROM THE AIR COMES INTO CONTACT WITH ALCOHOL FOR ANY LENGTH OF TIME...
AND ACETIC ACID IS BASICALLY VINEGAR...
SPLISHHHH
FSSSSH

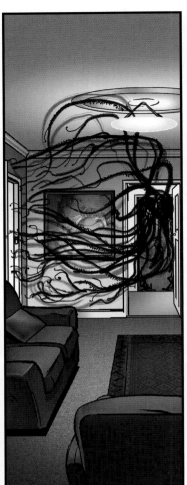

KRIIIIISH

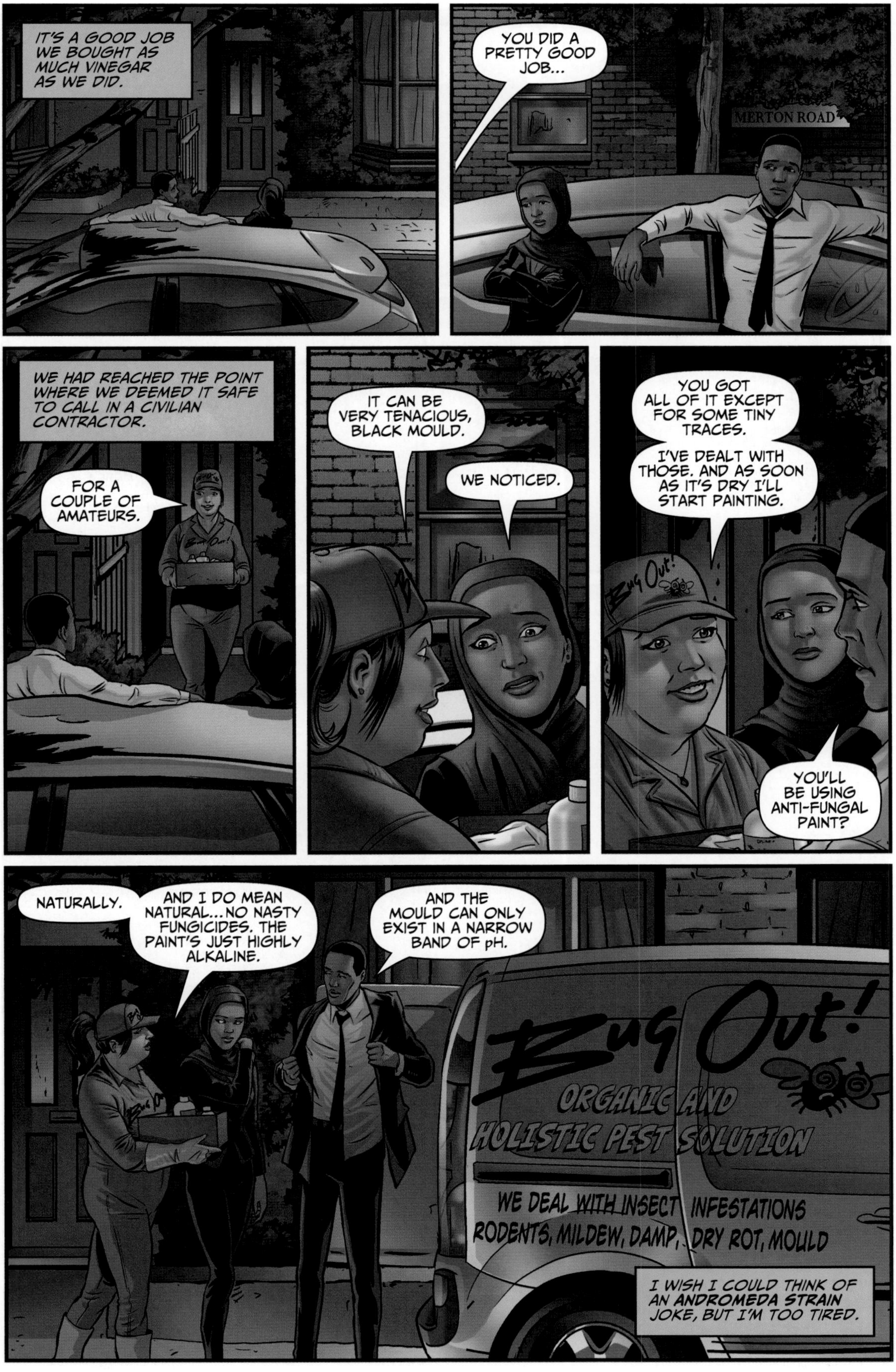
IT'S A GOOD JOB WE BOUGHT AS MUCH VINEGAR AS WE DID.
YOU DID A PRETTY GOOD JOB...
MERTON ROAD
WE HAD REACHED THE POINT WHERE WE DEEMED IT SAFE TO CALL IN A CIVILIAN CONTRACTOR.
FOR A COUPLE OF AMATEURS.
IT CAN BE VERY TENACIOUS, BLACK MOULD.
WE NOTICED.
YOU GOT ALL OF IT EXCEPT FOR SOME TINY TRACES.
I'VE DEALT WITH THOSE. AND AS SOON AS IT'S DRY I'LL START PAINTING.
Bug Out!
YOU'LL BE USING ANTI-FUNGAL PAINT?
NATURALLY.
AND I DO MEAN NATURAL...NO NASTY FUNGICIDES. THE PAINT'S JUST HIGHLY ALKALINE.
AND THE MOULD CAN ONLY EXIST IN A NARROW BAND OF pH.
Bug Out!
ORGANIC AND HOLISTIC PEST SOLUTION
WE DEAL WITH INSECT INFESTATIONS
RODENTS, MILDEW, DAMP, DRY ROT, MOULD
I WISH I COULD THINK OF AN ANDROMEDA STRAIN JOKE, BUT I'M TOO TIRED.

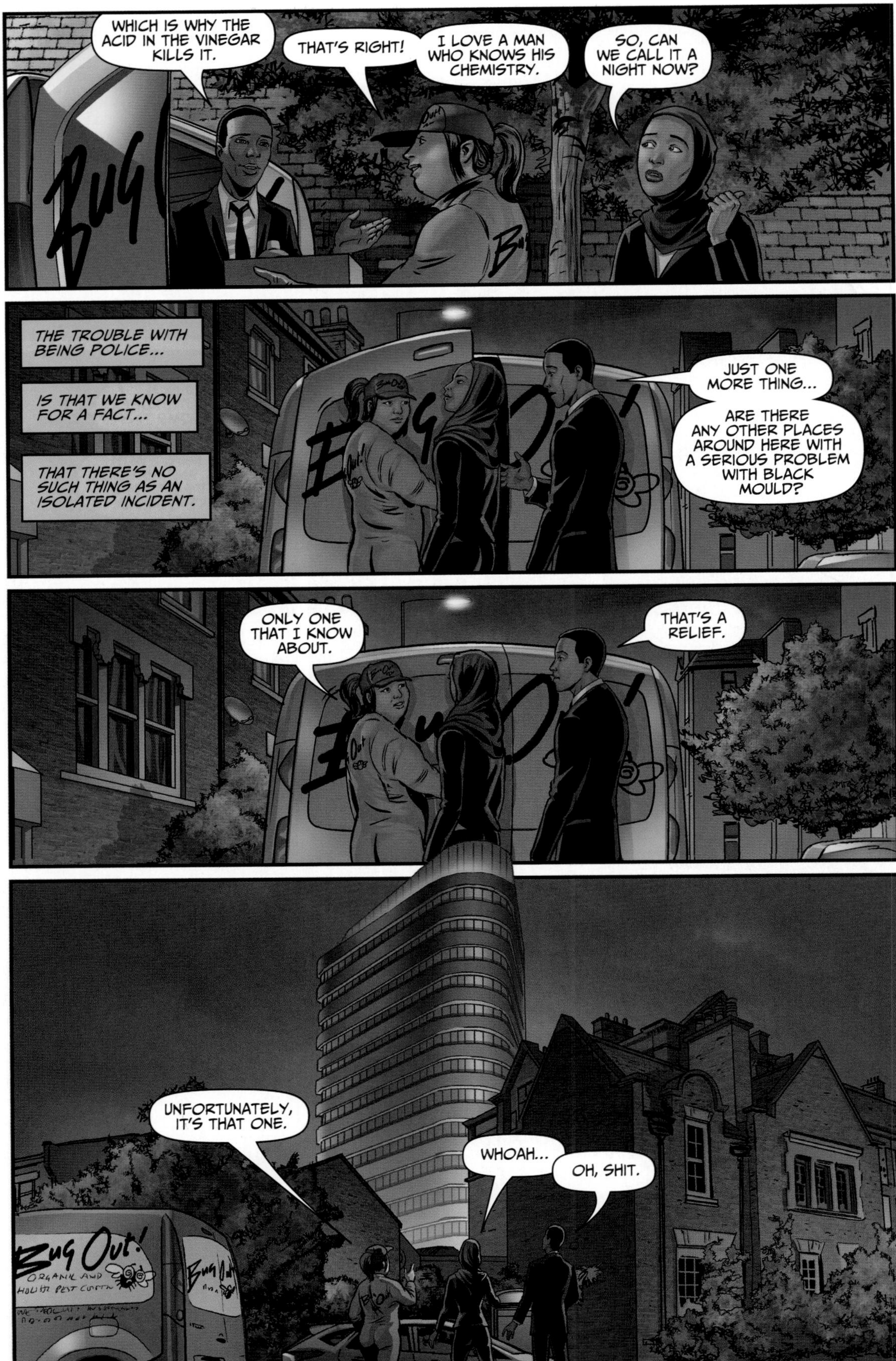
WHICH IS WHY THE ACID IN THE VINEGAR KILLS IT.
THAT'S RIGHT!
I LOVE A MAN WHO KNOWS HIS CHEMISTRY.
SO, CAN WE CALL IT A NIGHT NOW?
THE TROUBLE WITH BEING POLICE...
IS THAT WE KNOW FOR A FACT...
THAT THERE'S NO SUCH THING AS AN ISOLATED INCIDENT.
JUST ONE MORE THING...
ARE THERE ANY OTHER PLACES AROUND HERE WITH A SERIOUS PROBLEM WITH BLACK MOULD?
ONLY ONE THAT I KNOW ABOUT.
THAT'S A RELIEF.
UNFORTUNATELY, IT'S THAT ONE.
WHOAH...
OH, SHIT.
Bug Out!
ORGANIC AND HOLISTIC PEST CONTROL

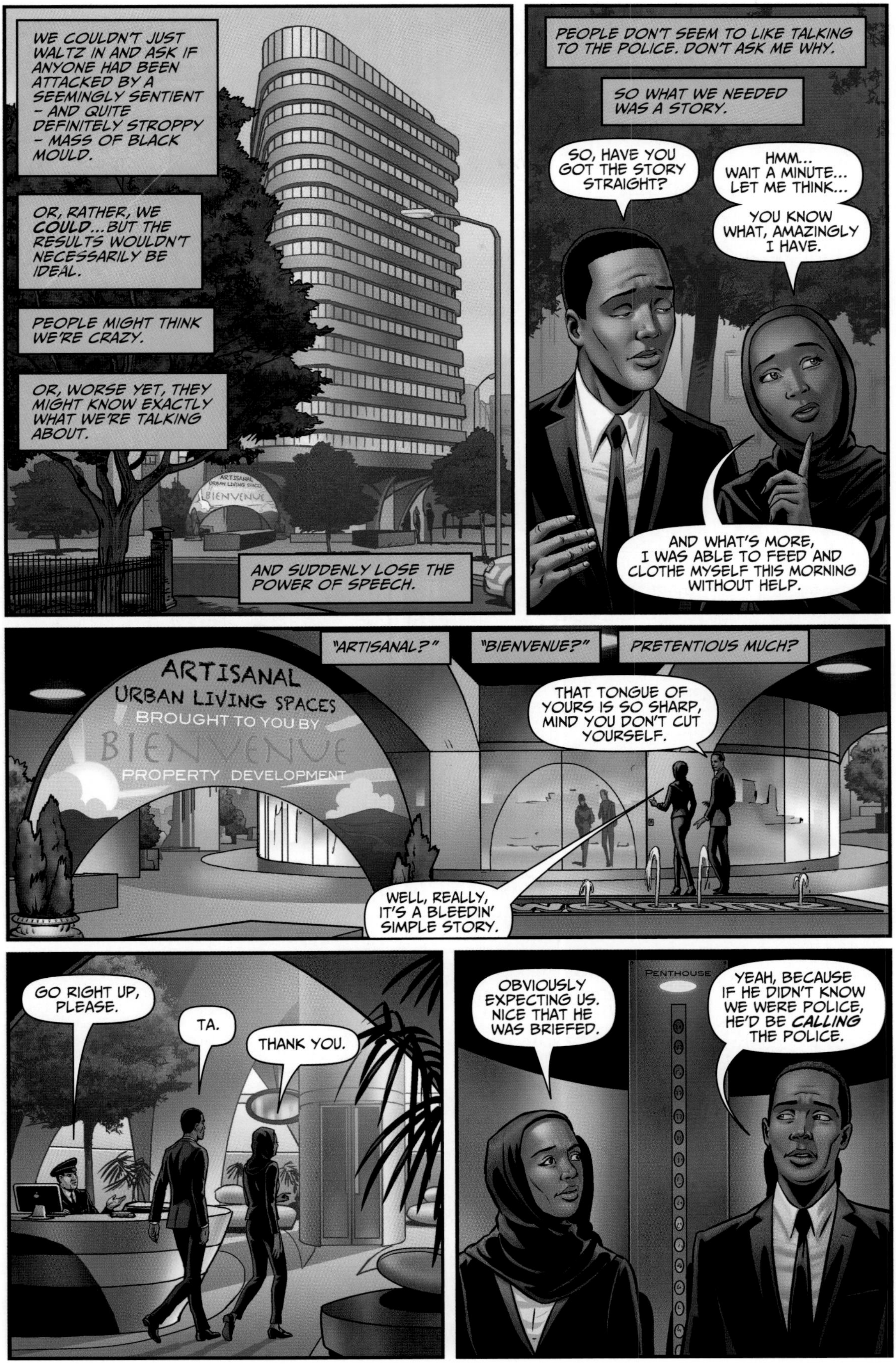
WE COULDN'T JUST WALTZ IN AND ASK IF ANYONE HAD BEEN ATTACKED BY A SEEMINGLY SENTIENT - AND QUITE DEFINITELY STROPPY - MASS OF BLACK MOULD.
OR, RATHER, WE COULD...BUT THE RESULTS WOULDN'T NECESSARILY BE IDEAL.
PEOPLE MIGHT THINK WE'RE CRAZY.
OR, WORSE YET, THEY MIGHT KNOW EXACTLY WHAT WE'RE TALKING ABOUT.
ARTISANAL URBAN LIVING SPACES
BIENVENUE
AND SUDDENLY LOSE THE POWER OF SPEECH.
PEOPLE DON'T SEEM TO LIKE TALKING TO THE POLICE. DON'T ASK ME WHY.
SO WHAT WE NEEDED WAS A STORY.
SO, HAVE YOU GOT THE STORY STRAIGHT?
HMM... WAIT A MINUTE... LET ME THINK...
YOU KNOW WHAT, AMAZINGLY I HAVE.
AND WHAT'S MORE, I WAS ABLE TO FEED AND CLOTHE MYSELF THIS MORNING WITHOUT HELP.
"ARTISANAL?"
"BIENVENUE?"
PRETENTIOUS MUCH?
ARTISANAL URBAN LIVING SPACES BROUGHT TO YOU BY BIENVENUE PROPERTY DEVELOPMENT
THAT TONGUE OF YOURS IS SO SHARP, MIND YOU DON'T CUT YOURSELF.
WELL, REALLY, IT'S A BLEEDIN' SIMPLE STORY.
GO RIGHT UP, PLEASE.
TA.
THANK YOU.
PENTHOUSE
OBVIOUSLY EXPECTING US. NICE THAT HE WAS BRIEFED.
YEAH, BECAUSE IF HE DIDN'T KNOW WE WERE POLICE, HE'D BE CALLING THE POLICE.

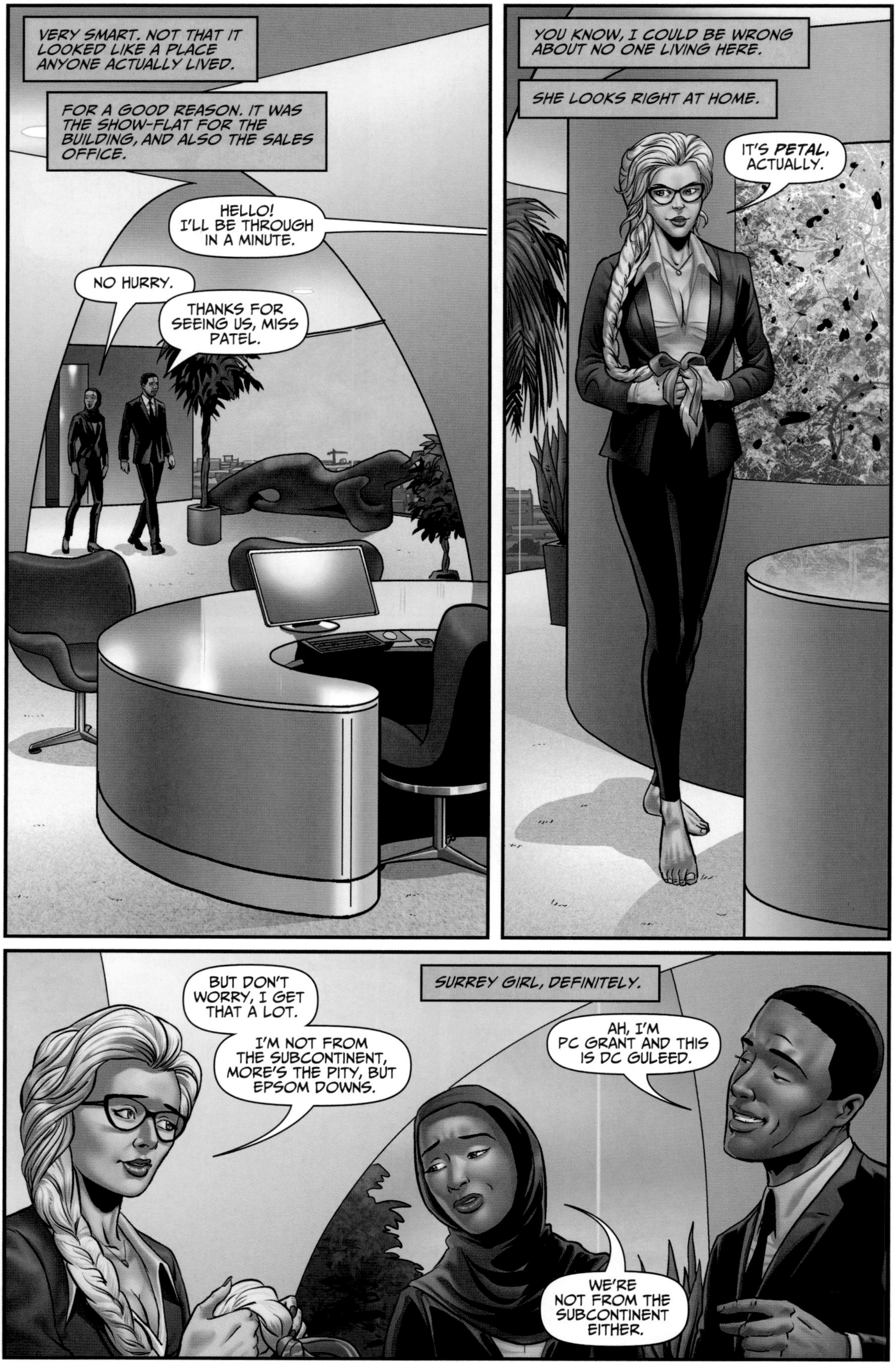
VERY SMART. NOT THAT IT LOOKED LIKE A PLACE ANYONE ACTUALLY LIVED.
FOR A GOOD REASON. IT WAS THE SHOW-FLAT FOR THE BUILDING, AND ALSO THE SALES OFFICE.
HELLO! I'LL BE THROUGH IN A MINUTE.
NO HURRY.
THANKS FOR SEEING US, MISS PATEL.
YOU KNOW, I COULD BE WRONG ABOUT NO ONE LIVING HERE.
SHE LOOKS RIGHT AT HOME.
IT'S PETAL, ACTUALLY.
BUT DON'T WORRY, I GET THAT A LOT.
I'M NOT FROM THE SUBCONTINENT, MORE'S THE PITY, BUT EPSOM DOWNS.
SURREY GIRL, DEFINITELY.
AH, I'M PC GRANT AND THIS IS DC GULEED.
WE'RE NOT FROM THE SUBCONTINENT EITHER.

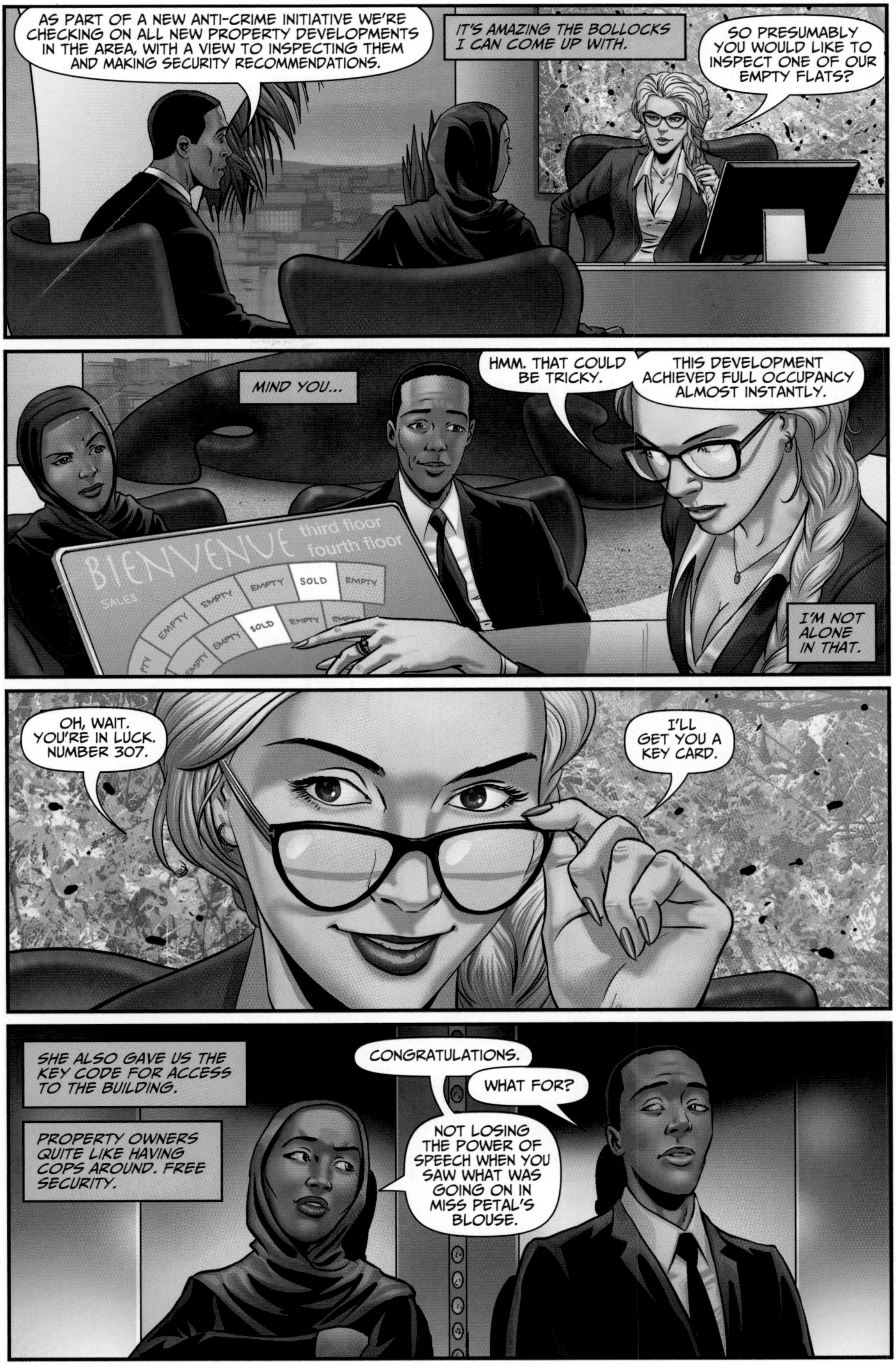
AS PART OF A NEW ANTI-CRIME INITIATIVE WE'RE CHECKING ON ALL NEW PROPERTY DEVELOPMENTS IN THE AREA, WITH A VIEW TO INSPECTING THEM AND MAKING SECURITY RECOMMENDATIONS.
IT'S AMAZING THE BOLLOCKS I CAN COME UP WITH.
SO PRESUMABLY YOU WOULD LIKE TO INSPECT ONE OF OUR EMPTY FLATS?
MIND YOU...
HMM. THAT COULD BE TRICKY.
THIS DEVELOPMENT ACHIEVED FULL OCCUPANCY ALMOST INSTANTLY.
BIENVENUE
third floor
fourth floor
SALES
EMPTY
SOLD
I'M NOT ALONE IN THAT.
OH, WAIT. YOU'RE IN LUCK. NUMBER 307.
I'LL GET YOU A KEY CARD.
SHE ALSO GAVE US THE KEY CODE FOR ACCESS TO THE BUILDING.
PROPERTY OWNERS QUITE LIKE HAVING COPS AROUND. FREE SECURITY.
CONGRATULATIONS.
WHAT FOR?
NOT LOSING THE POWER OF SPEECH WHEN YOU SAW WHAT WAS GOING ON IN MISS PETAL'S BLOUSE.

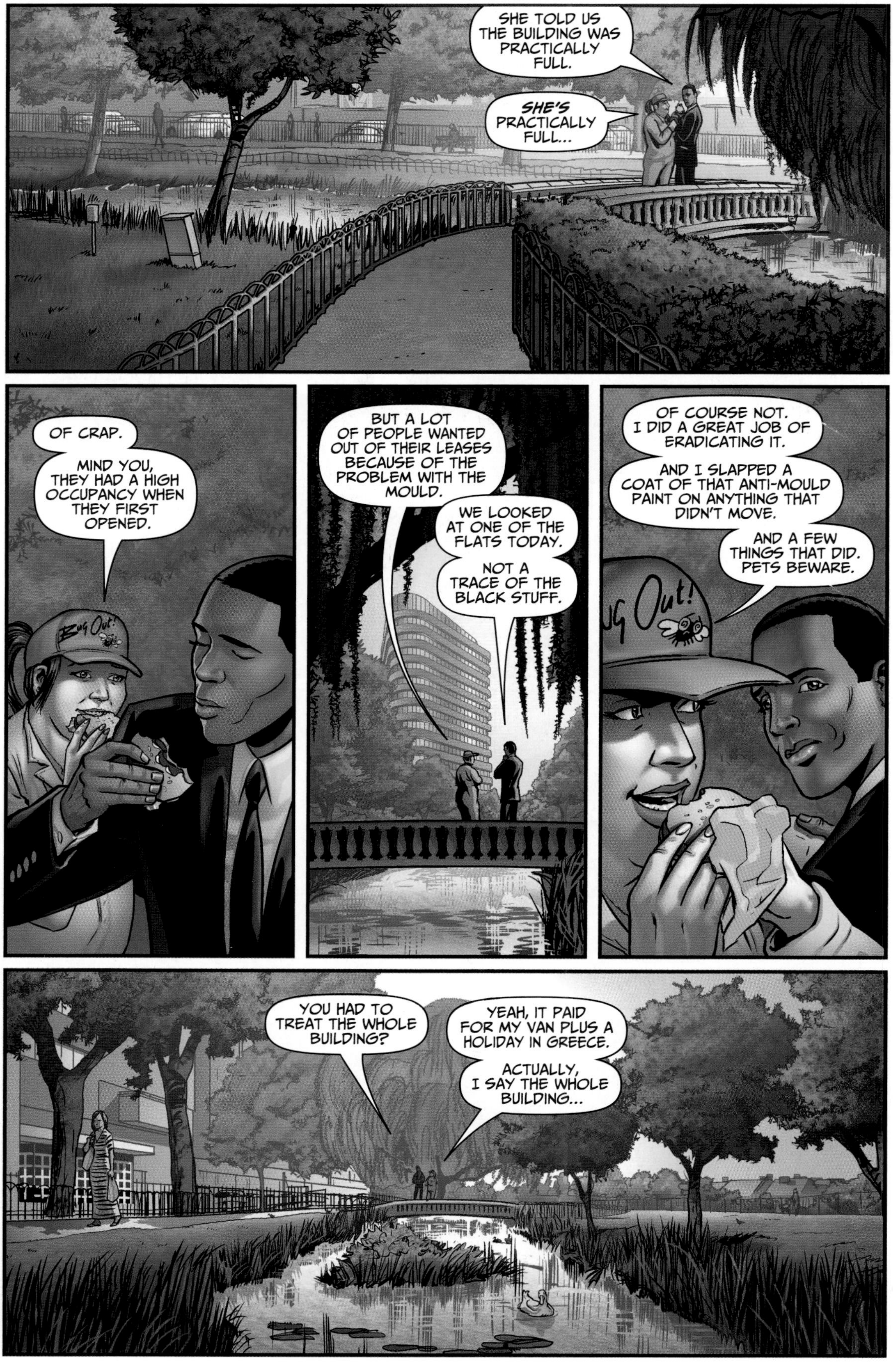
SHE TOLD US THE BUILDING WAS PRACTICALLY FULL.
SHE'S PRACTICALLY FULL...
OF CRAP.
MIND YOU, THEY HAD A HIGH OCCUPANCY WHEN THEY FIRST OPENED.
BUG OUT!
BUT A LOT OF PEOPLE WANTED OUT OF THEIR LEASES BECAUSE OF THE PROBLEM WITH THE MOULD.
WE LOOKED AT ONE OF THE FLATS TODAY.
NOT A TRACE OF THE BLACK STUFF.
OF COURSE NOT. I DID A GREAT JOB OF ERADICATING IT.
AND I SLAPPED A COAT OF THAT ANTI-MOULD PAINT ON ANYTHING THAT DIDN'T MOVE.
AND A FEW THINGS THAT DID. PETS BEWARE.
YOU HAD TO TREAT THE WHOLE BUILDING?
YEAH, IT PAID FOR MY VAN PLUS A HOLIDAY IN GREECE.
ACTUALLY, I SAY THE WHOLE BUILDING...

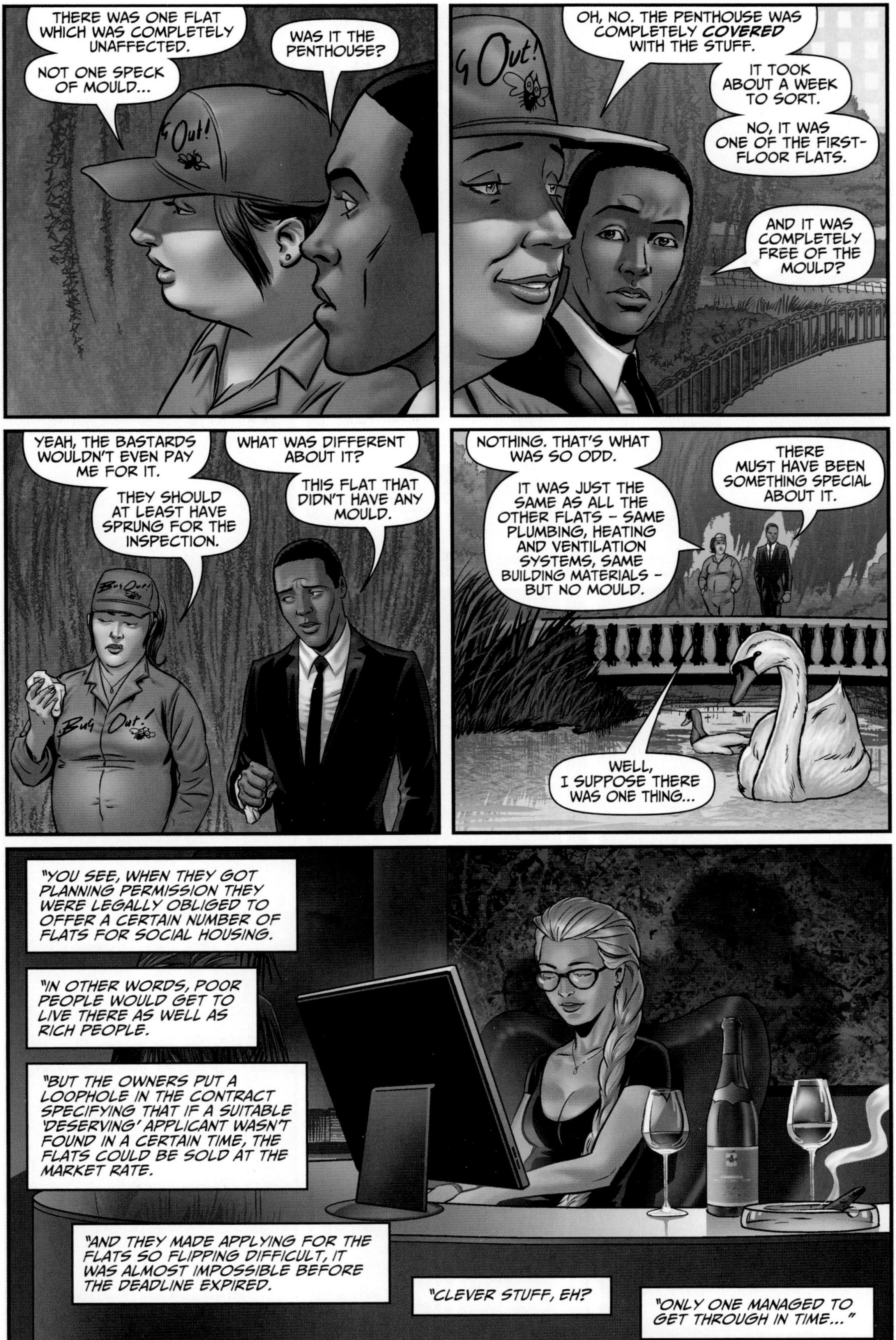
THERE WAS ONE FLAT WHICH WAS COMPLETELY UNAFFECTED.
NOT ONE SPECK OF MOULD...
WAS IT THE PENTHOUSE?
OH, NO. THE PENTHOUSE WAS COMPLETELY COVERED WITH THE STUFF.
IT TOOK ABOUT A WEEK TO SORT.
NO, IT WAS ONE OF THE FIRST-FLOOR FLATS.
AND IT WAS COMPLETELY FREE OF THE MOULD?
YEAH, THE BASTARDS WOULDN'T EVEN PAY ME FOR IT.
THEY SHOULD AT LEAST HAVE SPRUNG FOR THE INSPECTION.
WHAT WAS DIFFERENT ABOUT IT?
THIS FLAT THAT DIDN'T HAVE ANY MOULD.
NOTHING. THAT'S WHAT WAS SO ODD.
IT WAS JUST THE SAME AS ALL THE OTHER FLATS – SAME PLUMBING, HEATING AND VENTILATION SYSTEMS, SAME BUILDING MATERIALS – BUT NO MOULD.
THERE MUST HAVE BEEN SOMETHING SPECIAL ABOUT IT.
WELL, I SUPPOSE THERE WAS ONE THING...
"YOU SEE, WHEN THEY GOT PLANNING PERMISSION THEY WERE LEGALLY OBLIGED TO OFFER A CERTAIN NUMBER OF FLATS FOR SOCIAL HOUSING.
"IN OTHER WORDS, POOR PEOPLE WOULD GET TO LIVE THERE AS WELL AS RICH PEOPLE.
"BUT THE OWNERS PUT A LOOPHOLE IN THE CONTRACT SPECIFYING THAT IF A SUITABLE 'DESERVING' APPLICANT WASN'T FOUND IN A CERTAIN TIME, THE FLATS COULD BE SOLD AT THE MARKET RATE.
"AND THEY MADE APPLYING FOR THE FLATS SO FLIPPING DIFFICULT, IT WAS ALMOST IMPOSSIBLE BEFORE THE DEADLINE EXPIRED.
"CLEVER STUFF, EH?
"ONLY ONE MANAGED TO GET THROUGH IN TIME..."

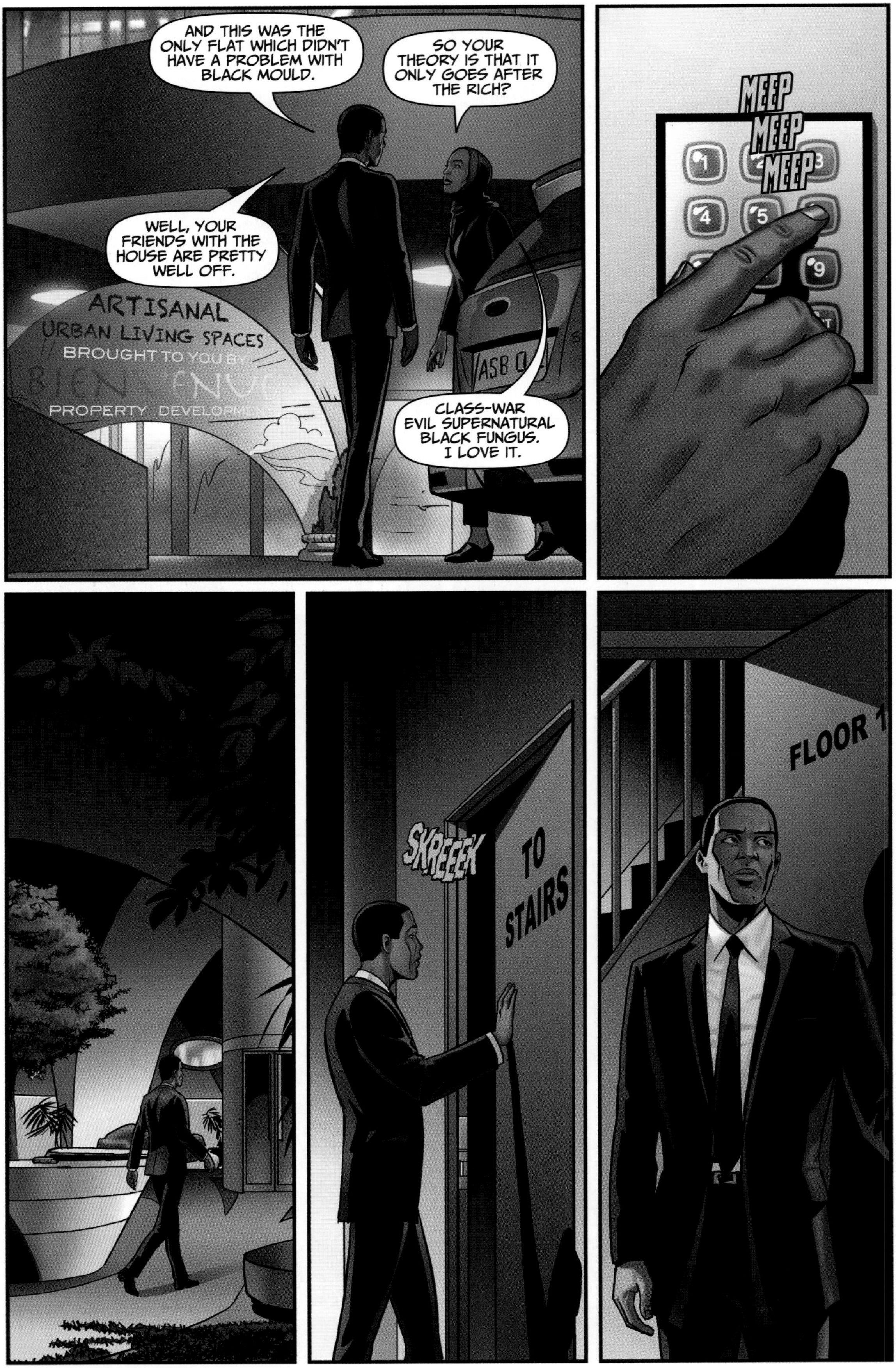
AND THIS WAS THE ONLY FLAT WHICH DIDN'T HAVE A PROBLEM WITH BLACK MOULD.
SO YOUR THEORY IS THAT IT ONLY GOES AFTER THE RICH?
WELL, YOUR FRIENDS WITH THE HOUSE ARE PRETTY WELL OFF.
ARTISANAL URBAN LIVING SPACES BROUGHT TO YOU BY BIENVENUE PROPERTY DEVELOPMENT
ASB O
CLASS-WAR EVIL SUPERNATURAL BLACK FUNGUS. I LOVE IT.
MEEP MEEP MEEP
SKREEEK
TO STAIRS
FLOOR 1

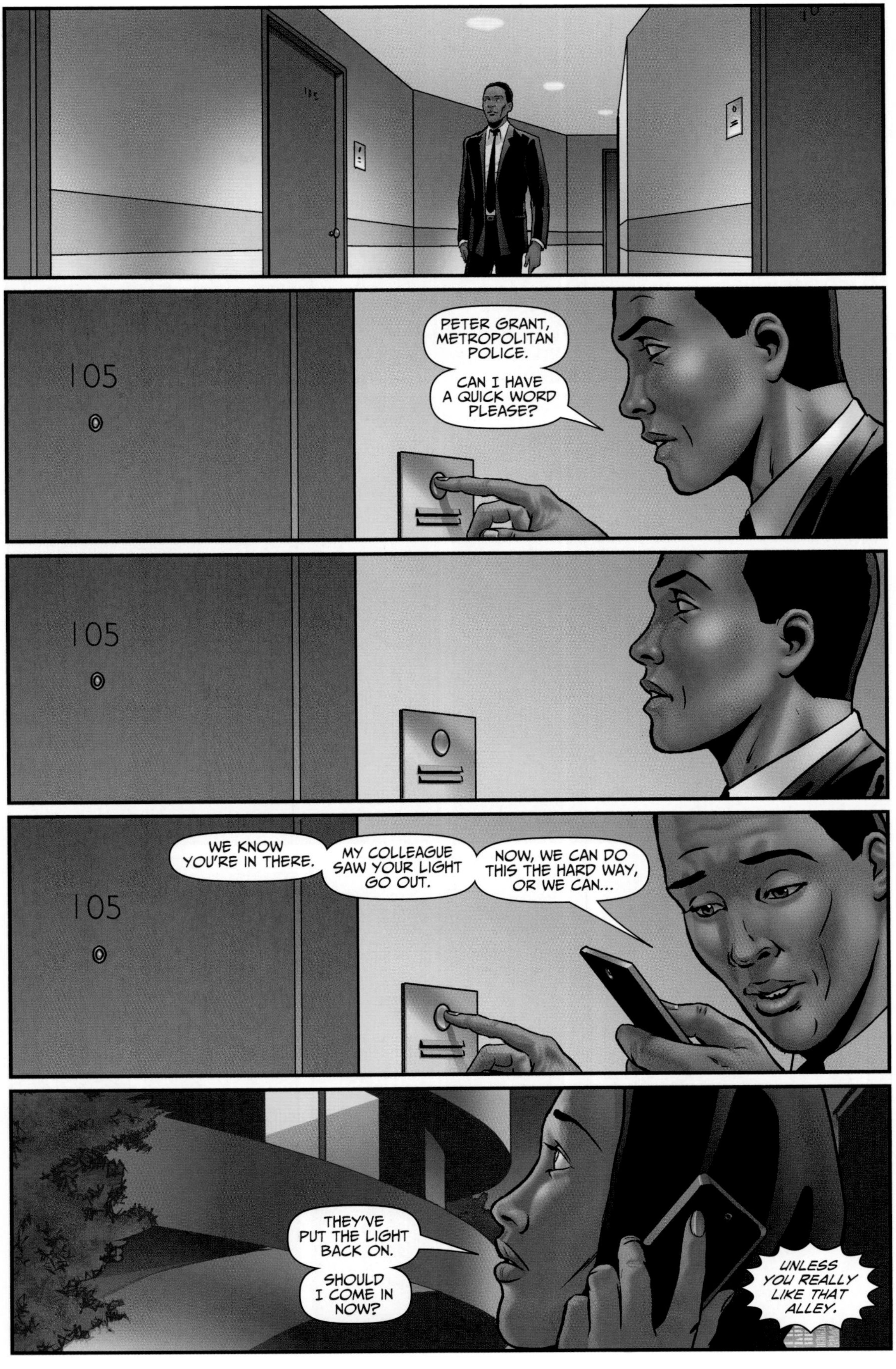
105
PETER GRANT, METROPOLITAN POLICE.
CAN I HAVE A QUICK WORD PLEASE?
105
105
WE KNOW YOU'RE IN THERE.
MY COLLEAGUE SAW YOUR LIGHT GO OUT.
NOW, WE CAN DO THIS THE HARD WAY, OR WE CAN...
THEY'VE PUT THE LIGHT BACK ON.
SHOULD I COME IN NOW?
UNLESS YOU REALLY LIKE THAT ALLEY.

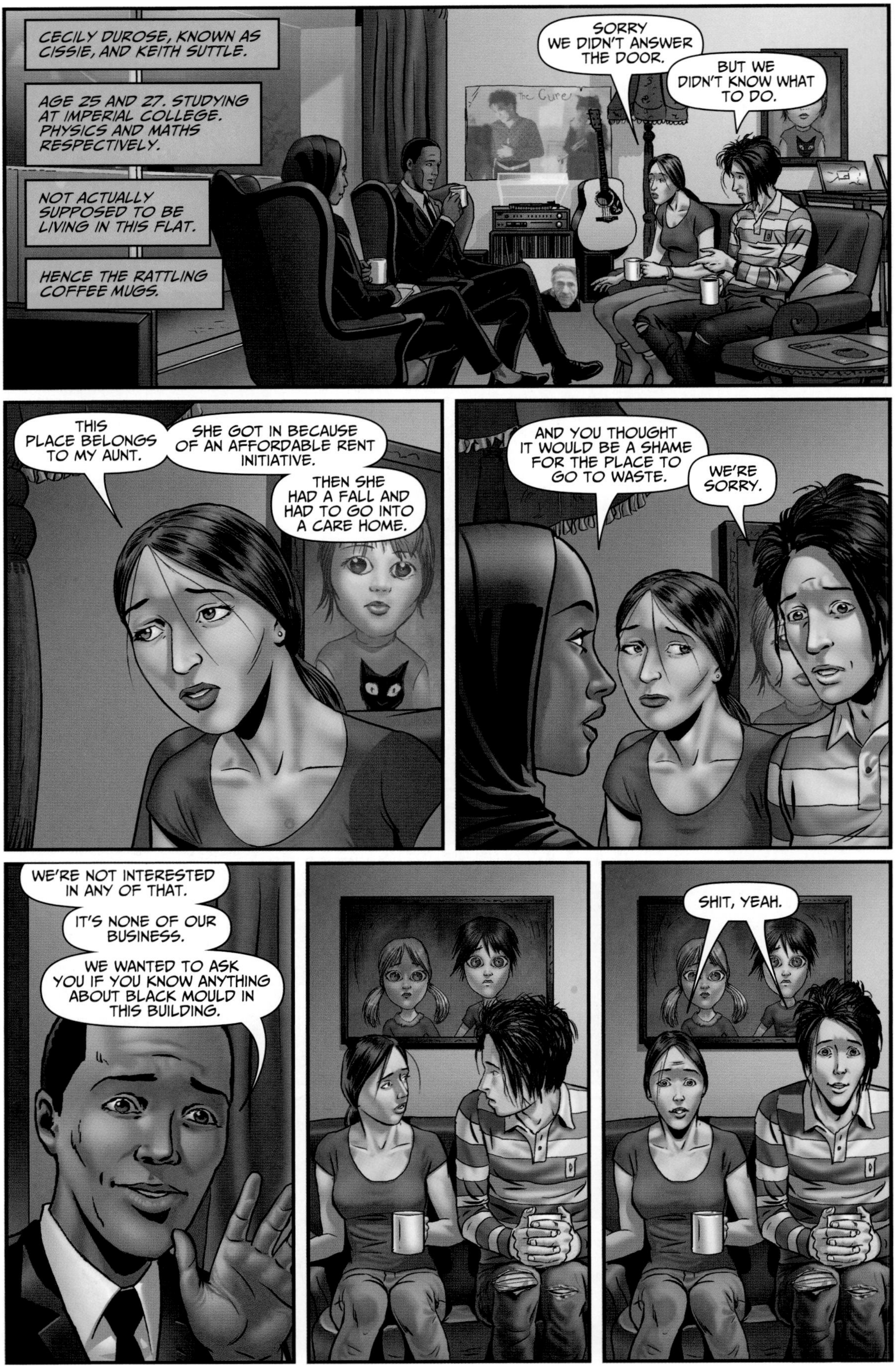
CECILY DUROSE, KNOWN AS CISSIE, AND KEITH SUTTLE.
AGE 25 AND 27. STUDYING AT IMPERIAL COLLEGE. PHYSICS AND MATHS RESPECTIVELY.
NOT ACTUALLY SUPPOSED TO BE LIVING IN THIS FLAT.
HENCE THE RATTLING COFFEE MUGS.
The Cure
SORRY WE DIDN'T ANSWER THE DOOR.
BUT WE DIDN'T KNOW WHAT TO DO.
THIS PLACE BELONGS TO MY AUNT.
SHE GOT IN BECAUSE OF AN AFFORDABLE RENT INITIATIVE.
THEN SHE HAD A FALL AND HAD TO GO INTO A CARE HOME.
AND YOU THOUGHT IT WOULD BE A SHAME FOR THE PLACE TO GO TO WASTE.
WE'RE SORRY.
WE'RE NOT INTERESTED IN ANY OF THAT.
IT'S NONE OF OUR BUSINESS.
WE WANTED TO ASK YOU IF YOU KNOW ANYTHING ABOUT BLACK MOULD IN THIS BUILDING.
SHIT, YEAH.

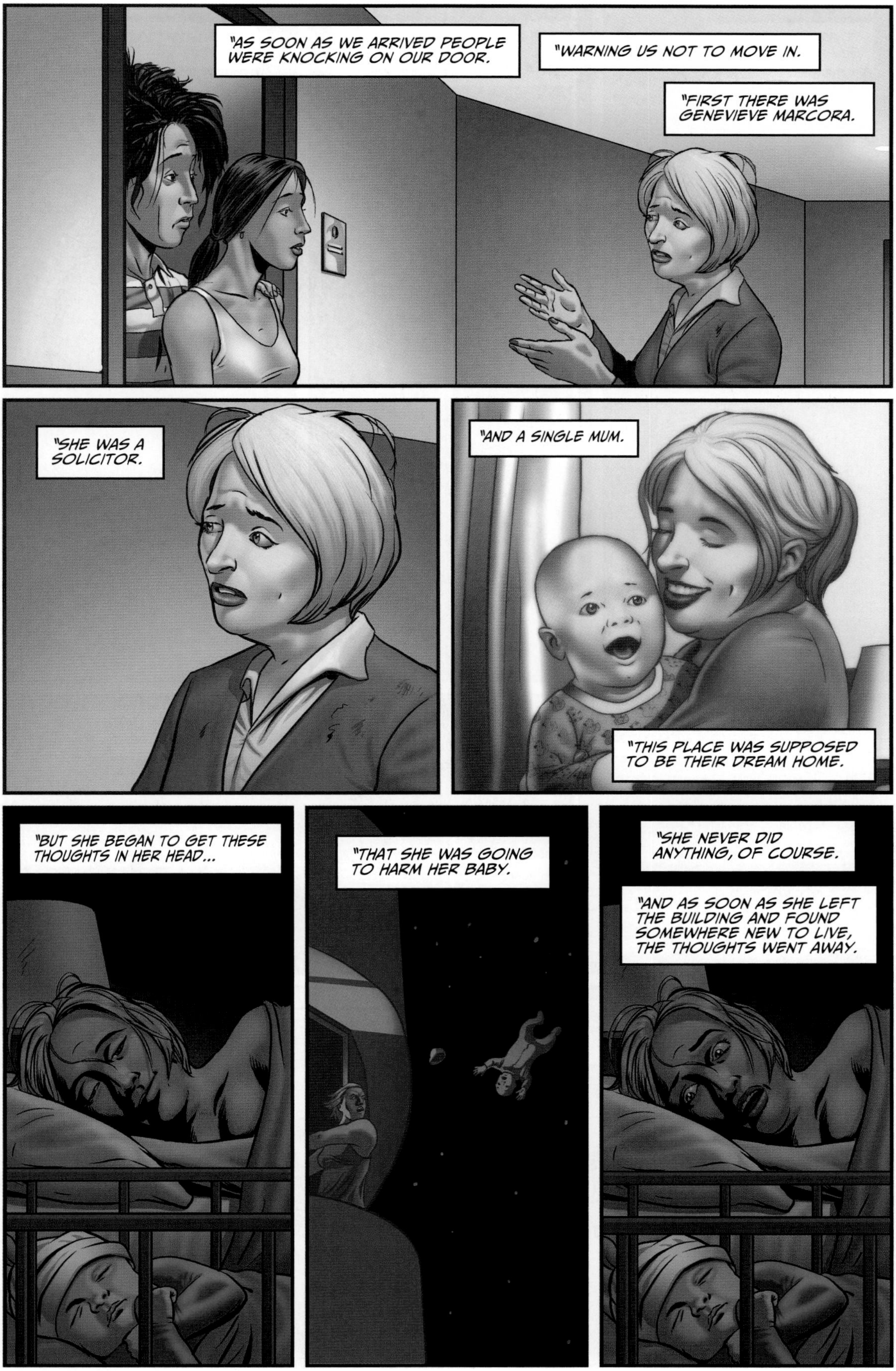
"AS SOON AS WE ARRIVED PEOPLE WERE KNOCKING ON OUR DOOR.
"WARNING US NOT TO MOVE IN.
"FIRST THERE WAS GENEVIEVE MARCORA.
"SHE WAS A SOLICITOR.
"AND A SINGLE MUM.
"THIS PLACE WAS SUPPOSED TO BE THEIR DREAM HOME.
"BUT SHE BEGAN TO GET THESE THOUGHTS IN HER HEAD...
"THAT SHE WAS GOING TO HARM HER BABY.
"SHE NEVER DID ANYTHING, OF COURSE.
"AND AS SOON AS SHE LEFT THE BUILDING AND FOUND SOMEWHERE NEW TO LIVE, THE THOUGHTS WENT AWAY.

"THEN THERE WAS BILLY CONANT.

"HE COULDN'T GET OVER THE IDEA THAT HIS FATHER WAS GOING TO FIND HIM.

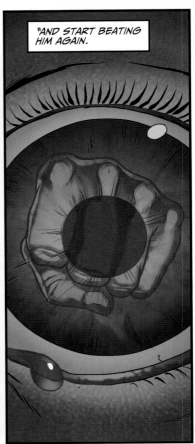

"AND START BEATING HIM AGAIN.

"EVEN THOUGH HE'S BUILT LIKE CHRIS HEMSWORTH...

"AND HIS FATHER HAS BEEN DEAD FOR THIRTY YEARS.

"LIKE THE OTHERS HE WAS IN A LAWSUIT WITH THE OWNERS OF THE BUILDING.

"HE WANTED TO BREAK HIS LEASE.

"HE'D BEEN FINE BEFORE HE MOVED IN HERE."

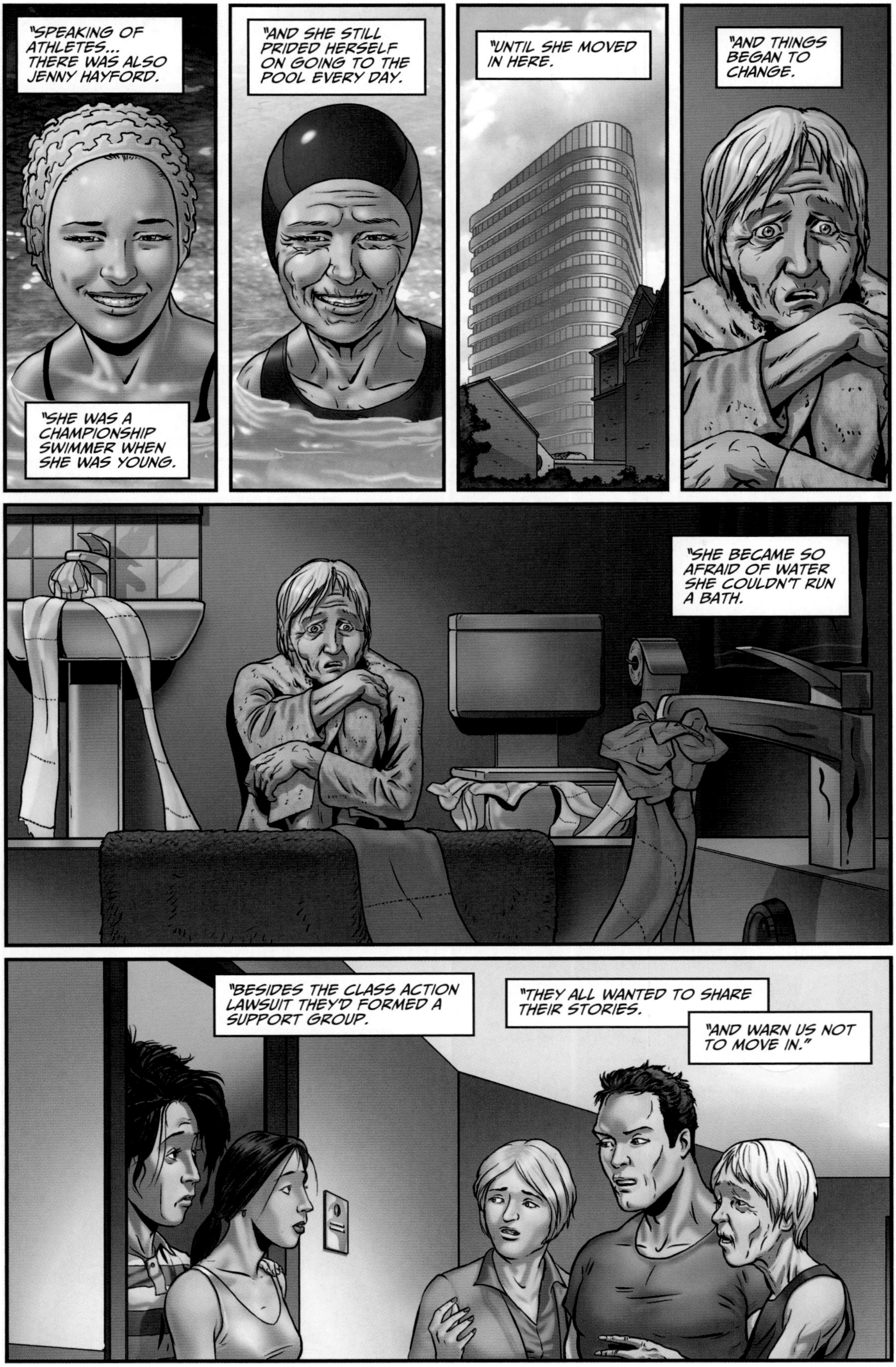
"SPEAKING OF ATHLETES... THERE WAS ALSO JENNY HAYFORD.
"SHE WAS A CHAMPIONSHIP SWIMMER WHEN SHE WAS YOUNG.
"AND SHE STILL PRIDED HERSELF ON GOING TO THE POOL EVERY DAY.
"UNTIL SHE MOVED IN HERE.
"AND THINGS BEGAN TO CHANGE.
"SHE BECAME SO AFRAID OF WATER SHE COULDN'T RUN A BATH.
"BESIDES THE CLASS ACTION LAWSUIT THEY'D FORMED A SUPPORT GROUP.
"THEY ALL WANTED TO SHARE THEIR STORIES.
"AND WARN US NOT TO MOVE IN."

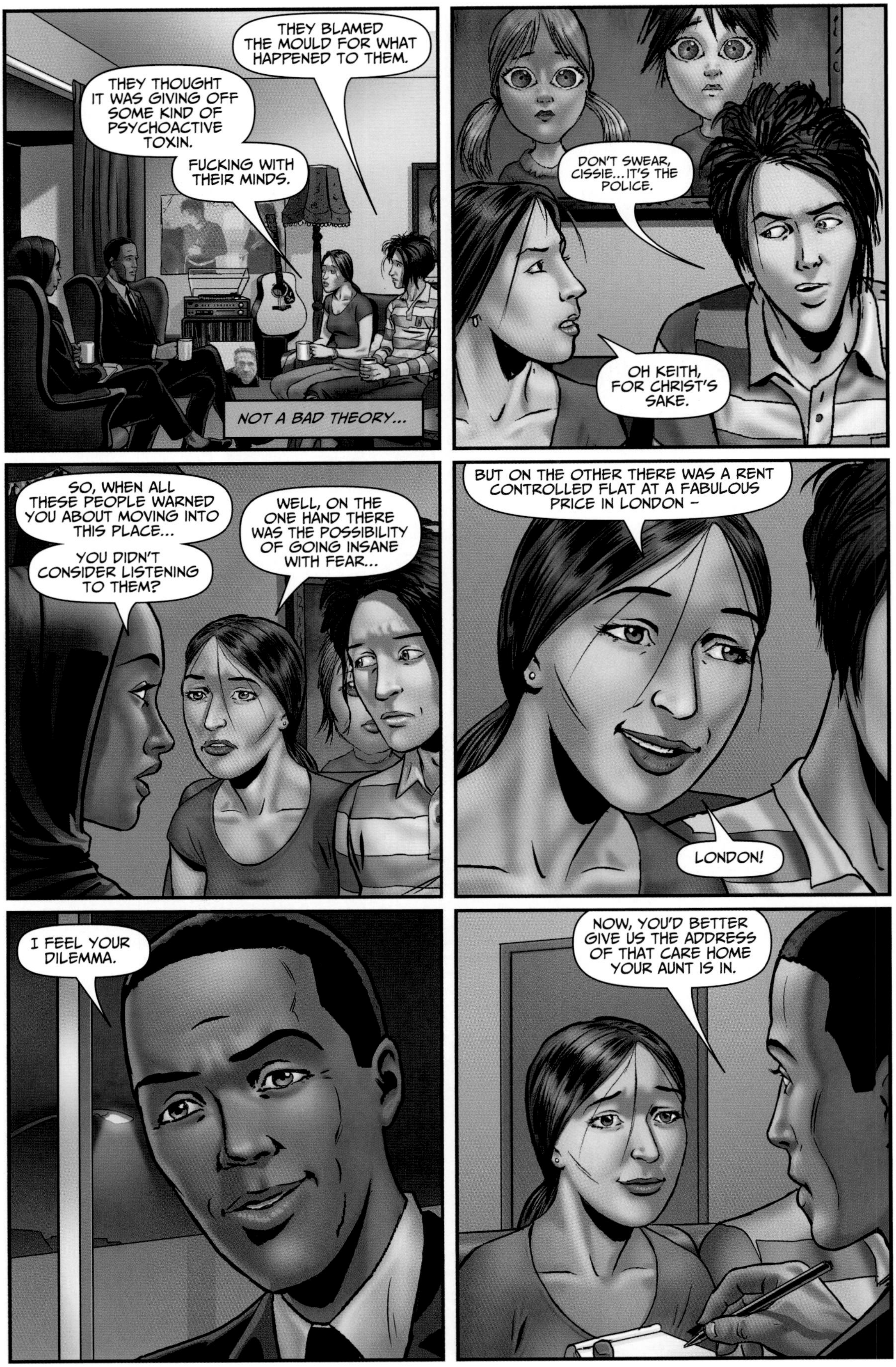
THEY THOUGHT IT WAS GIVING OFF SOME KIND OF PSYCHOACTIVE TOXIN.
THEY BLAMED THE MOULD FOR WHAT HAPPENED TO THEM.
FUCKING WITH THEIR MINDS.
NOT A BAD THEORY...
DON'T SWEAR, CISSIE...IT'S THE POLICE.
OH KEITH, FOR CHRIST'S SAKE.
SO, WHEN ALL THESE PEOPLE WARNED YOU ABOUT MOVING INTO THIS PLACE...
YOU DIDN'T CONSIDER LISTENING TO THEM?
WELL, ON THE ONE HAND THERE WAS THE POSSIBILITY OF GOING INSANE WITH FEAR...
BUT ON THE OTHER THERE WAS A RENT CONTROLLED FLAT AT A FABULOUS PRICE IN LONDON –
LONDON!
I FEEL YOUR DILEMMA.
NOW, YOU'D BETTER GIVE US THE ADDRESS OF THAT CARE HOME YOUR AUNT IS IN.

NICE COUPLE.

HE HAD A FEW TOO MANY CURE ALBUMS FOR MY LIKING.

THOSE STORIES TALLY WITH WHAT MY FRIENDS TOLD ME ABOUT THEIR DAUGHTER.

SHE DIDN'T ACTUALLY GET ATTACKED BY THE STUFF. NEVER *SAW* ANYTHING...

IT WAS ALL PANIC ATTACKS. UNCONTROLLABLE ANXIETY. SHE COULDN'T STUDY, THOUGHT SHE WAS GOING TO FAIL HER EXAMS.

IS SHE NORMALLY A GOOD STUDENT?

ABSOLUTE TOPS. VERY HARD-WORKING AND AMBITIOUS.

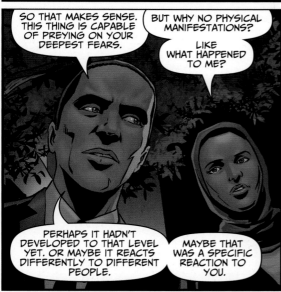

SO THAT MAKES SENSE. THIS THING IS CAPABLE OF PREYING ON YOUR DEEPEST FEARS.

BUT WHY NO PHYSICAL MANIFESTATIONS?

LIKE WHAT HAPPENED TO ME?

PERHAPS IT HADN'T DEVELOPED TO THAT LEVEL YET. OR MAYBE IT REACTS DIFFERENTLY TO DIFFERENT PEOPLE.

MAYBE THAT WAS A SPECIFIC REACTION TO YOU.

LUCKY ME.

BUT WHY DIDN'T IT JUST GO DOWN THE *"DEEPEST FEAR"* ROUTE AND JUST SCARE ME OFF?

I DON'T KNOW. MAYBE IT LIKED YOU.

OH, THANKS!

"DIDN'T YOU SAY IT TRIED TO COP A FEEL?"

"UGH. STOP TALKING. RIGHT NOW."

GET IT? "COP"?

ACTUALLY I PREFERRED THE HORRIFIC SEXUAL SUGGESTION TO THE TERRIBLE PUNS.

FAIR ENOUGH.

"CAN I TAKE THE JAG?"

"FINE PETER, PROVIDING YOU TAKE TOBY, TOO."

"I HAVE A VISITOR TO DEAL WITH."

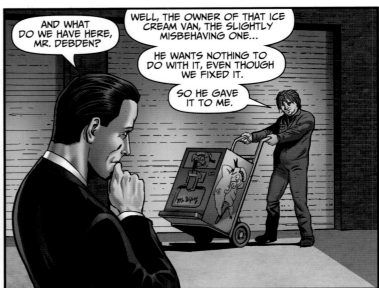

AND WHAT DO WE HAVE HERE, MR. DEBDEN?

WELL, THE OWNER OF THAT ICE CREAM VAN, THE SLIGHTLY MISBEHAVING ONE...

HE WANTS NOTHING TO DO WITH IT, EVEN THOUGH WE FIXED IT.

SO HE GAVE IT TO ME.

BUT I DON'T HAVE ANY USE FOR THE GEAR INSIDE IT.

SO, UH, I WONDERED IF SHE MIGHT HAVE SOME USE FOR IT...

THE LADY WHO LIVES HERE.

MOLLY?

UH, YEAH...

WE GOT OFF ON THE WRONG FOOT LAST TIME.

A BIT.

WOULD YOU LIKE TO GIVE IT TO HER YOURSELF?

OH, NO, NO, NO, NO, NO, NO...

NO THANK YOU.

NO. NOPE.

I'LL JUST WAIT OUT HERE.

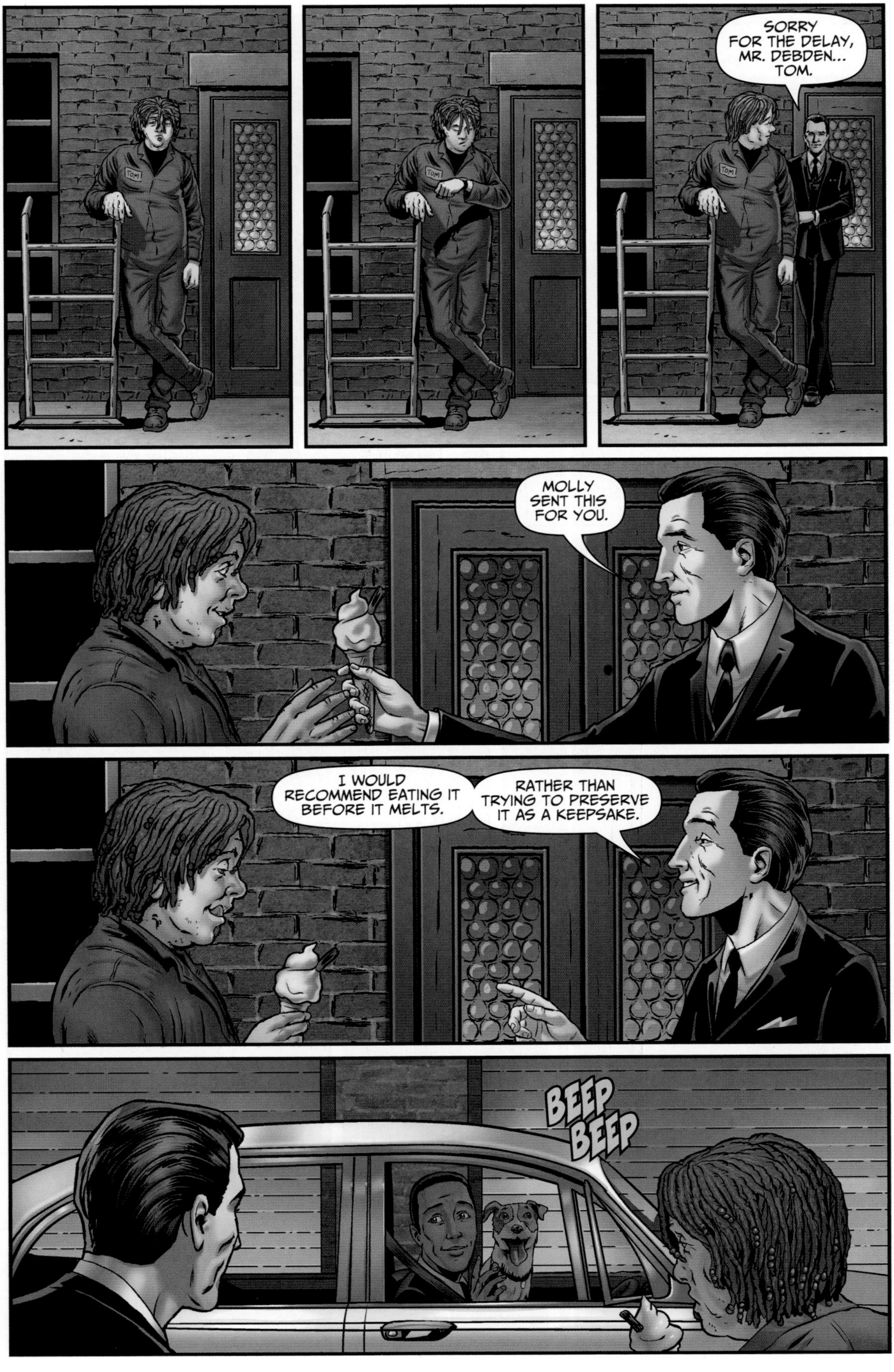
SORRY FOR THE DELAY, MR. DEBDEN... TOM.
MOLLY SENT THIS FOR YOU.
I WOULD RECOMMEND EATING IT BEFORE IT MELTS.
RATHER THAN TRYING TO PRESERVE IT AS A KEEPSAKE.
BEEP BEEP

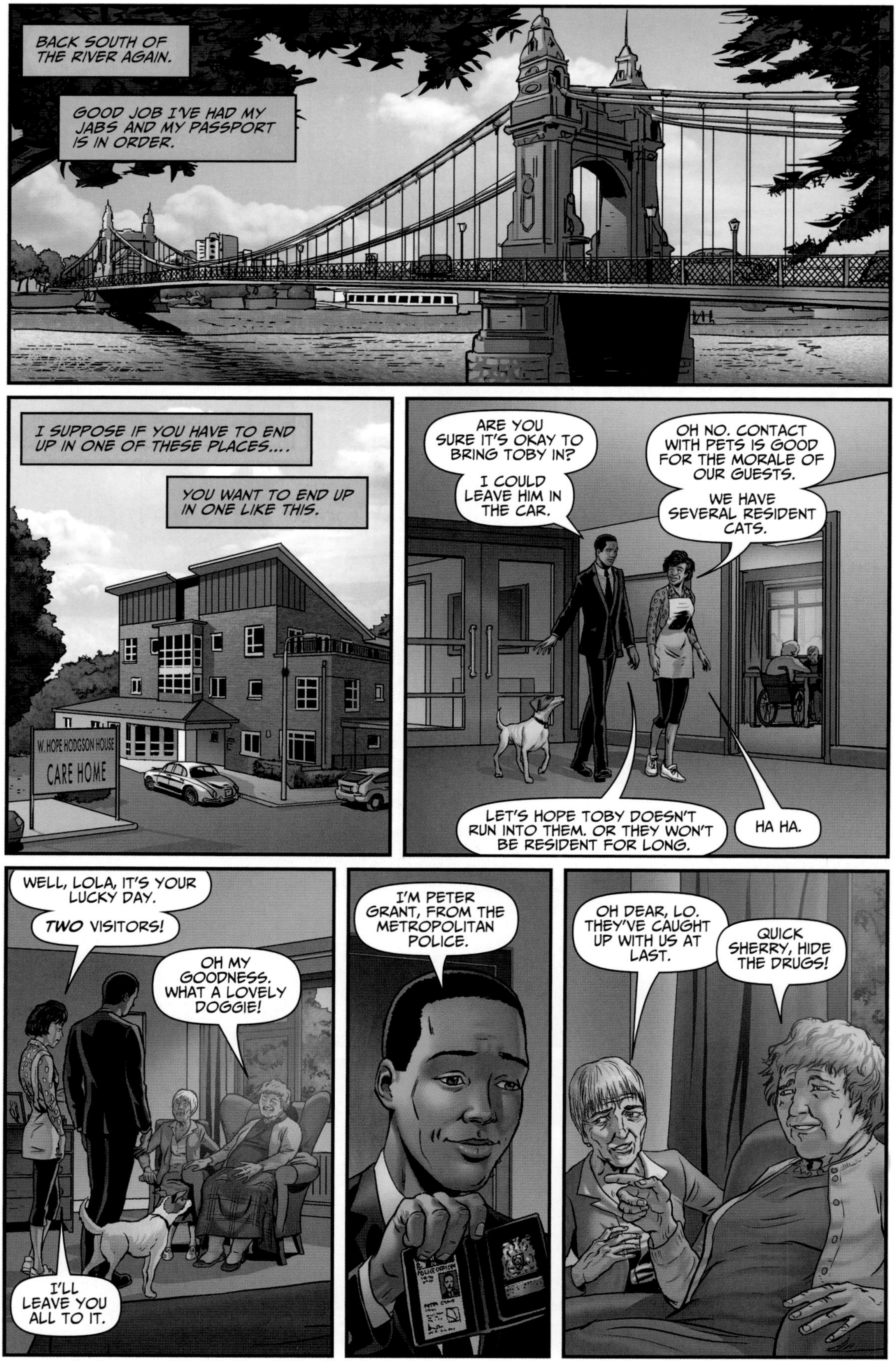
BACK SOUTH OF THE RIVER AGAIN.
GOOD JOB I'VE HAD MY JABS AND MY PASSPORT IS IN ORDER.
I SUPPOSE IF YOU HAVE TO END UP IN ONE OF THESE PLACES....
YOU WANT TO END UP IN ONE LIKE THIS.
W. HOPE HODGSON HOUSE
CARE HOME
ARE YOU SURE IT'S OKAY TO BRING TOBY IN?
I COULD LEAVE HIM IN THE CAR.
OH NO. CONTACT WITH PETS IS GOOD FOR THE MORALE OF OUR GUESTS.
WE HAVE SEVERAL RESIDENT CATS.
LET'S HOPE TOBY DOESN'T RUN INTO THEM. OR THEY WON'T BE RESIDENT FOR LONG.
HA HA.
WELL, LOLA, IT'S YOUR LUCKY DAY.
TWO VISITORS!
OH MY GOODNESS. WHAT A LOVELY DOGGIE!
I'LL LEAVE YOU ALL TO IT.
I'M PETER GRANT, FROM THE METROPOLITAN POLICE.
OH DEAR, LO. THEY'VE CAUGHT UP WITH US AT LAST.
QUICK SHERRY, HIDE THE DRUGS!

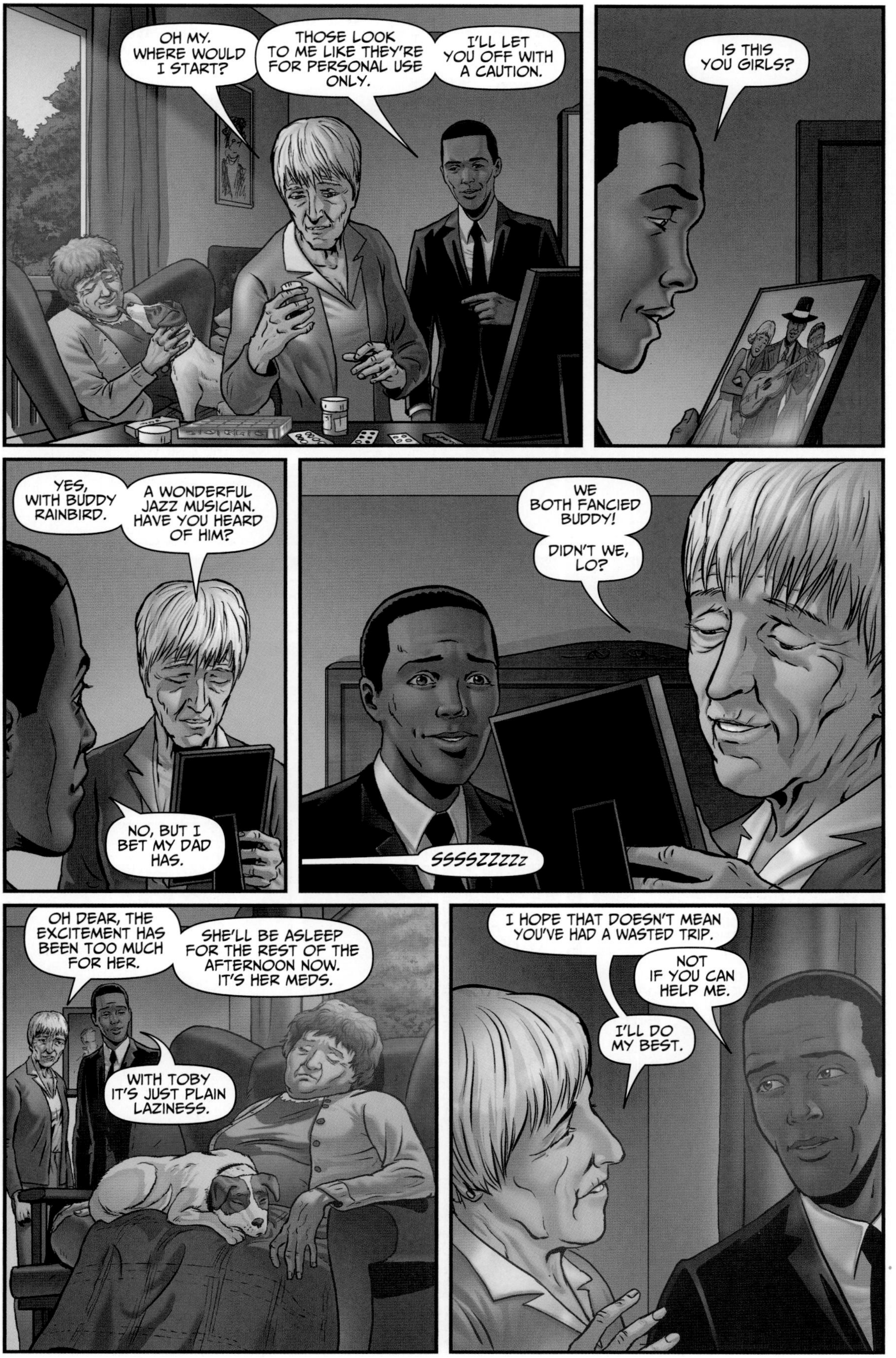
OH MY. WHERE WOULD I START?
THOSE LOOK TO ME LIKE THEY'RE FOR PERSONAL USE ONLY.
I'LL LET YOU OFF WITH A CAUTION.
IS THIS YOU GIRLS?
YES, WITH BUDDY RAINBIRD.
A WONDERFUL JAZZ MUSICIAN. HAVE YOU HEARD OF HIM?
NO, BUT I BET MY DAD HAS.
WE BOTH FANCIED BUDDY!
DIDN'T WE, LO?
SSSSZZZZz
OH DEAR, THE EXCITEMENT HAS BEEN TOO MUCH FOR HER.
SHE'LL BE ASLEEP FOR THE REST OF THE AFTERNOON NOW. IT'S HER MEDS.
WITH TOBY IT'S JUST PLAIN LAZINESS.
I HOPE THAT DOESN'T MEAN YOU'VE HAD A WASTED TRIP.
NOT IF YOU CAN HELP ME.
I'LL DO MY BEST.

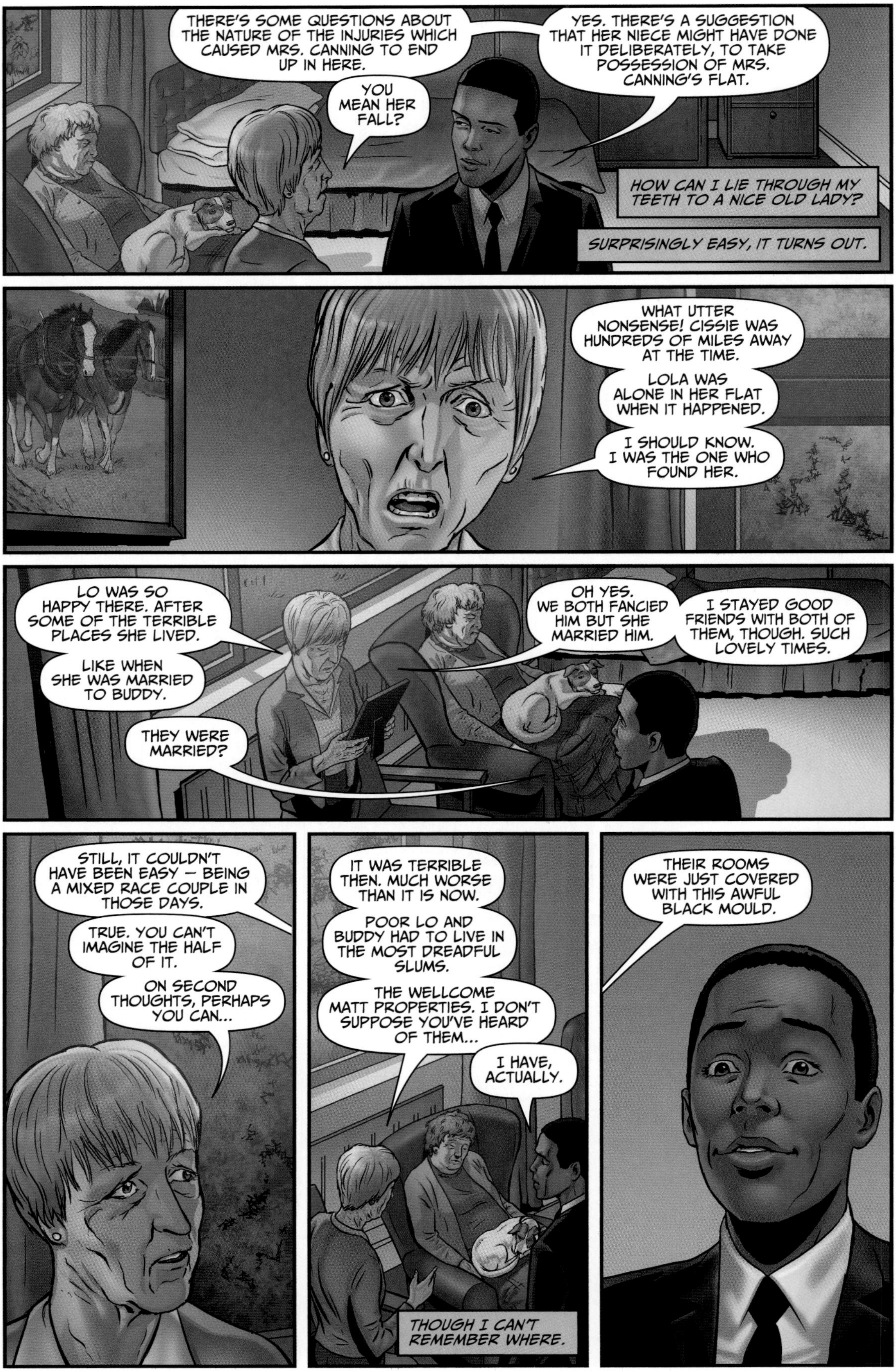

THERE'S SOME QUESTIONS ABOUT THE NATURE OF THE INJURIES WHICH CAUSED MRS. CANNING TO END UP IN HERE.
YOU MEAN HER FALL?
YES. THERE'S A SUGGESTION THAT HER NIECE MIGHT HAVE DONE IT DELIBERATELY, TO TAKE POSSESSION OF MRS. CANNING'S FLAT.
HOW CAN I LIE THROUGH MY TEETH TO A NICE OLD LADY?
SURPRISINGLY EASY, IT TURNS OUT.
WHAT UTTER NONSENSE! CISSIE WAS HUNDREDS OF MILES AWAY AT THE TIME.
LOLA WAS ALONE IN HER FLAT WHEN IT HAPPENED.
I SHOULD KNOW. I WAS THE ONE WHO FOUND HER.
LO WAS SO HAPPY THERE. AFTER SOME OF THE TERRIBLE PLACES SHE LIVED.
LIKE WHEN SHE WAS MARRIED TO BUDDY.
THEY WERE MARRIED?
OH YES. WE BOTH FANCIED HIM BUT SHE MARRIED HIM.
I STAYED GOOD FRIENDS WITH BOTH OF THEM, THOUGH. SUCH LOVELY TIMES.
STILL, IT COULDN'T HAVE BEEN EASY — BEING A MIXED RACE COUPLE IN THOSE DAYS.
TRUE. YOU CAN'T IMAGINE THE HALF OF IT.
ON SECOND THOUGHTS, PERHAPS YOU CAN...
IT WAS TERRIBLE THEN. MUCH WORSE THAN IT IS NOW.
POOR LO AND BUDDY HAD TO LIVE IN THE MOST DREADFUL SLUMS.
THE WELLCOME MATT PROPERTIES. I DON'T SUPPOSE YOU'VE HEARD OF THEM...
I HAVE, ACTUALLY.
THOUGH I CAN'T REMEMBER WHERE.
THEIR ROOMS WERE JUST COVERED WITH THIS AWFUL BLACK MOULD.

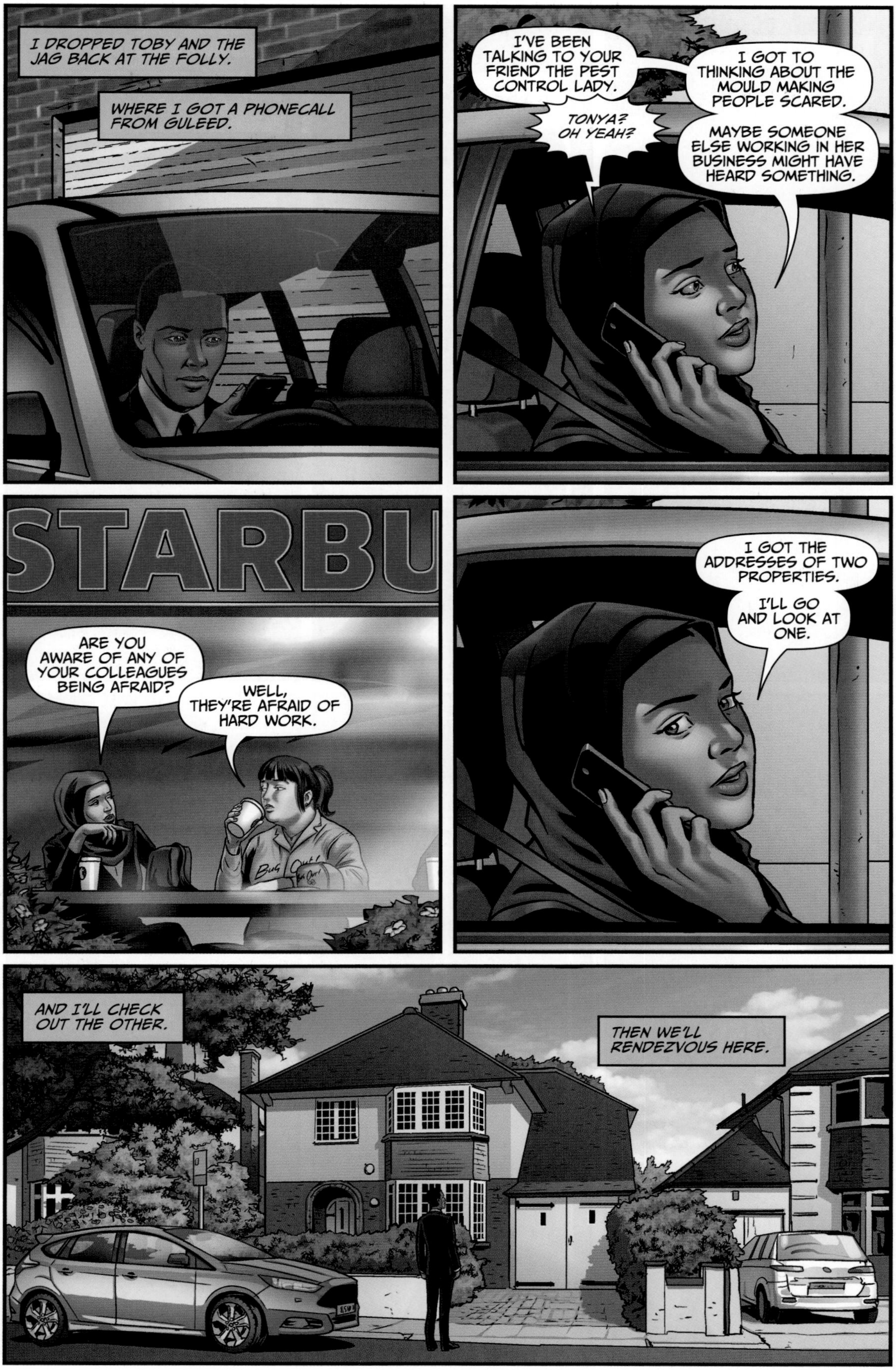
I DROPPED TOBY AND THE JAG BACK AT THE FOLLY.
WHERE I GOT A PHONECALL FROM GULEED.
I'VE BEEN TALKING TO YOUR FRIEND THE PEST CONTROL LADY.
TONYA? OH YEAH?
I GOT TO THINKING ABOUT THE MOULD MAKING PEOPLE SCARED.
MAYBE SOMEONE ELSE WORKING IN HER BUSINESS MIGHT HAVE HEARD SOMETHING.
STARBU
ARE YOU AWARE OF ANY OF YOUR COLLEAGUES BEING AFRAID?
WELL, THEY'RE AFRAID OF HARD WORK.
I GOT THE ADDRESSES OF TWO PROPERTIES.
I'LL GO AND LOOK AT ONE.
AND I'LL CHECK OUT THE OTHER.
THEN WE'LL RENDEZVOUS HERE.

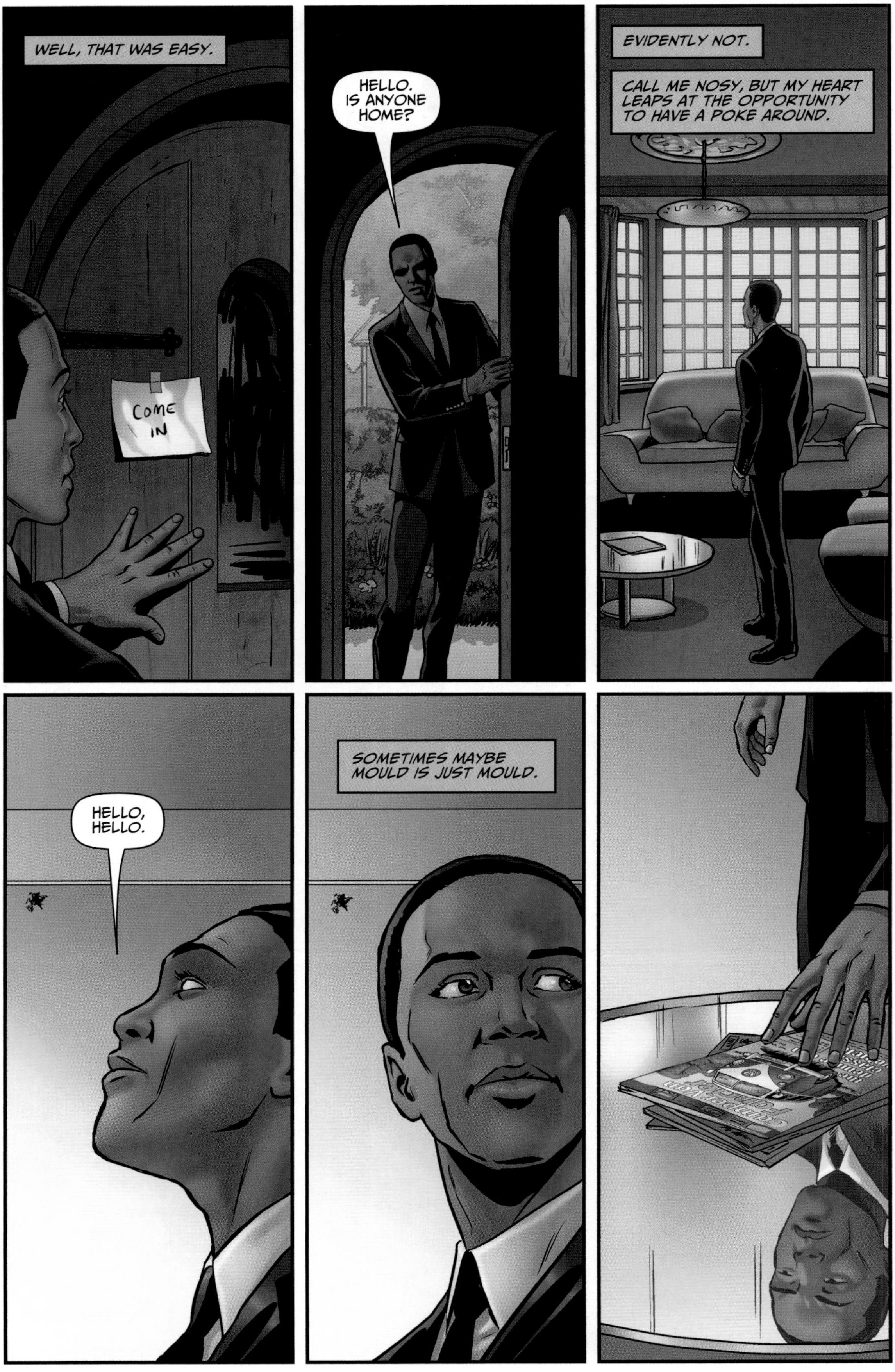
WELL, THAT WAS EASY.
COME IN
HELLO. IS ANYONE HOME?
EVIDENTLY NOT.
CALL ME NOSY, BUT MY HEART LEAPS AT THE OPPORTUNITY TO HAVE A POKE AROUND.
HELLO, HELLO.
SOMETIMES MAYBE MOULD IS JUST MOULD.

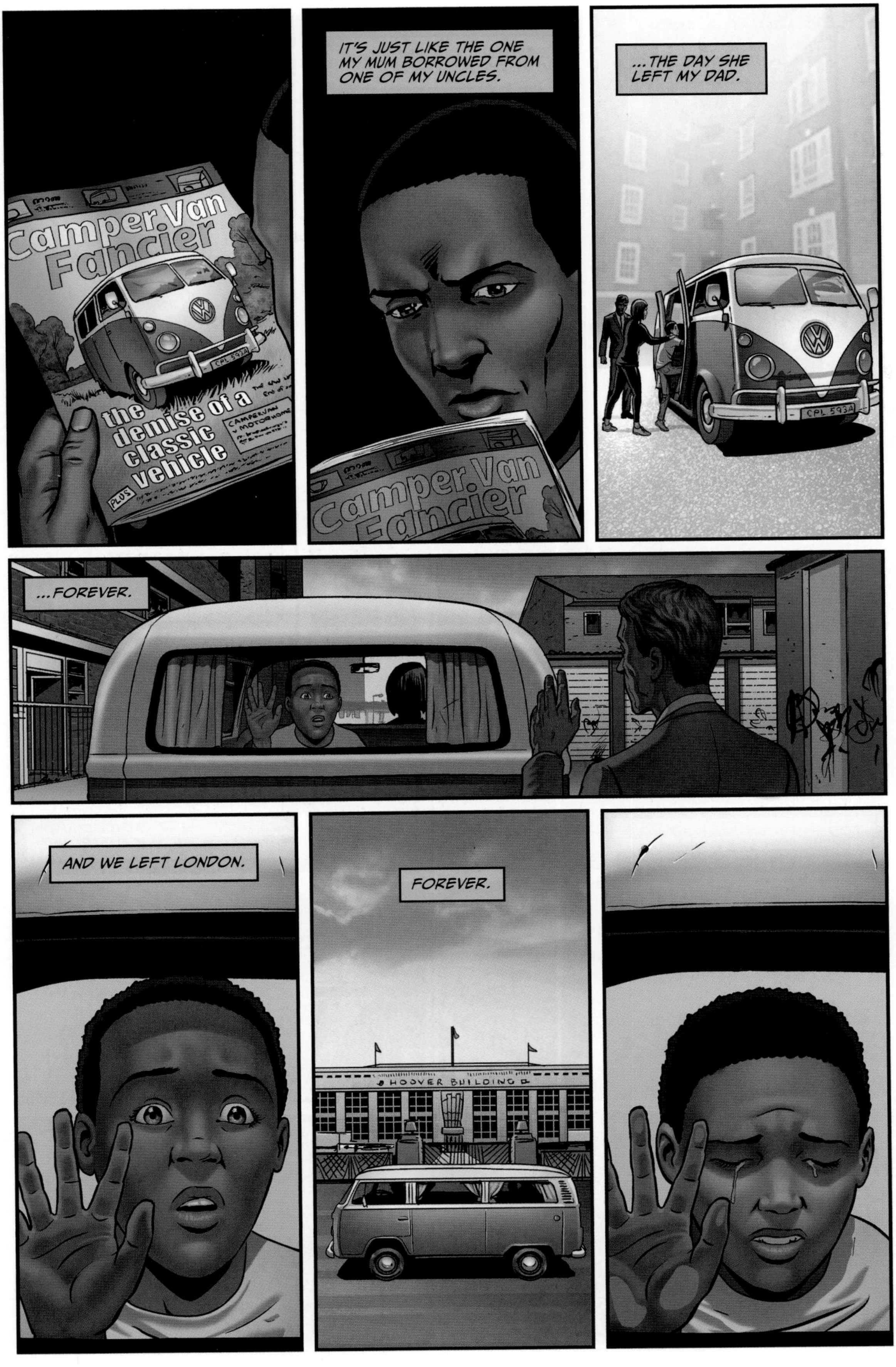
Camper Van Fancier
the demise of a classic vehicle
PLUS
IT'S JUST LIKE THE ONE MY MUM BORROWED FROM ONE OF MY UNCLES.
Camper Van Fancier
...THE DAY SHE LEFT MY DAD.
CPL 593A
...FOREVER.
AND WE LEFT LONDON.
FOREVER.
HOOVER BUILDING

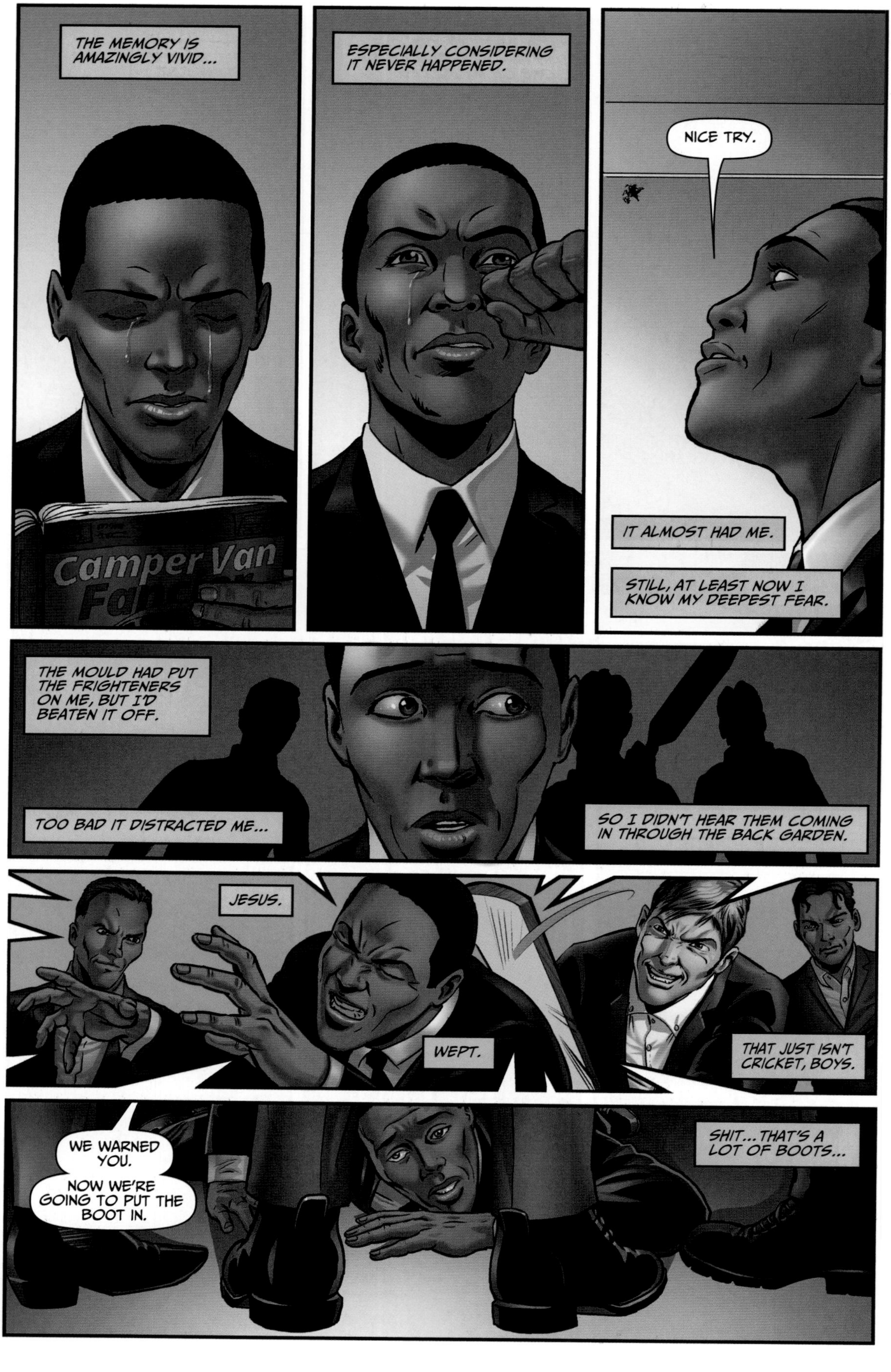
THE MEMORY IS AMAZINGLY VIVID...
Camper Van
ESPECIALLY CONSIDERING IT NEVER HAPPENED.
NICE TRY.
IT ALMOST HAD ME.
STILL, AT LEAST NOW I KNOW MY DEEPEST FEAR.
THE MOULD HAD PUT THE FRIGHTENERS ON ME, BUT I'D BEATEN IT OFF.
TOO BAD IT DISTRACTED ME...
SO I DIDN'T HEAR THEM COMING IN THROUGH THE BACK GARDEN.
JESUS.
WEPT.
THAT JUST ISN'T CRICKET, BOYS.
WE WARNED YOU.
NOW WE'RE GOING TO PUT THE BOOT IN.
SHIT...THAT'S A LOT OF BOOTS...

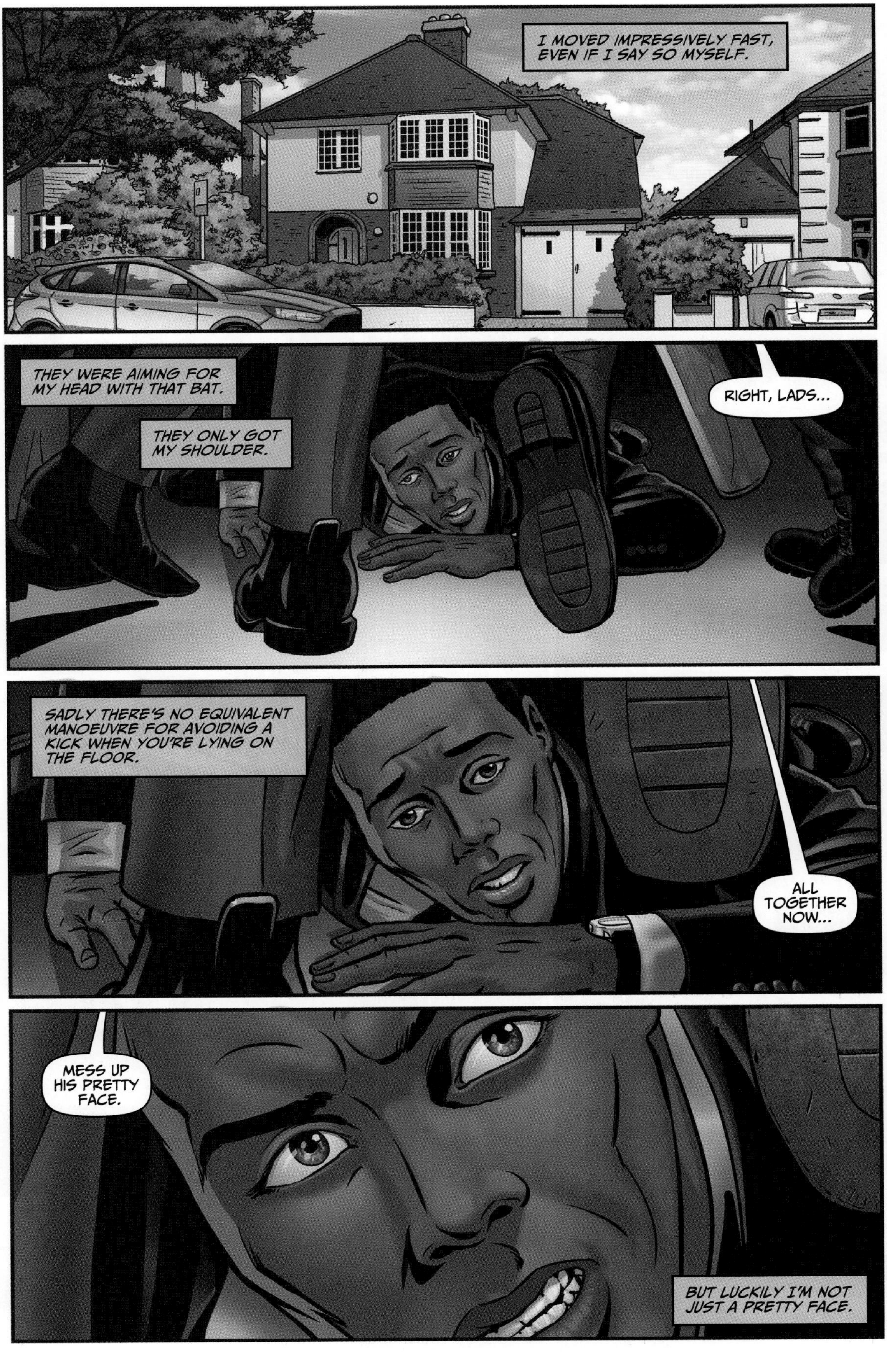
I MOVED IMPRESSIVELY FAST, EVEN IF I SAY SO MYSELF.
THEY WERE AIMING FOR MY HEAD WITH THAT BAT.
THEY ONLY GOT MY SHOULDER.
RIGHT, LADS...
SADLY THERE'S NO EQUIVALENT MANOEUVRE FOR AVOIDING A KICK WHEN YOU'RE LYING ON THE FLOOR.
ALL TOGETHER NOW...
MESS UP HIS PRETTY FACE.
BUT LUCKILY I'M NOT JUST A PRETTY FACE.

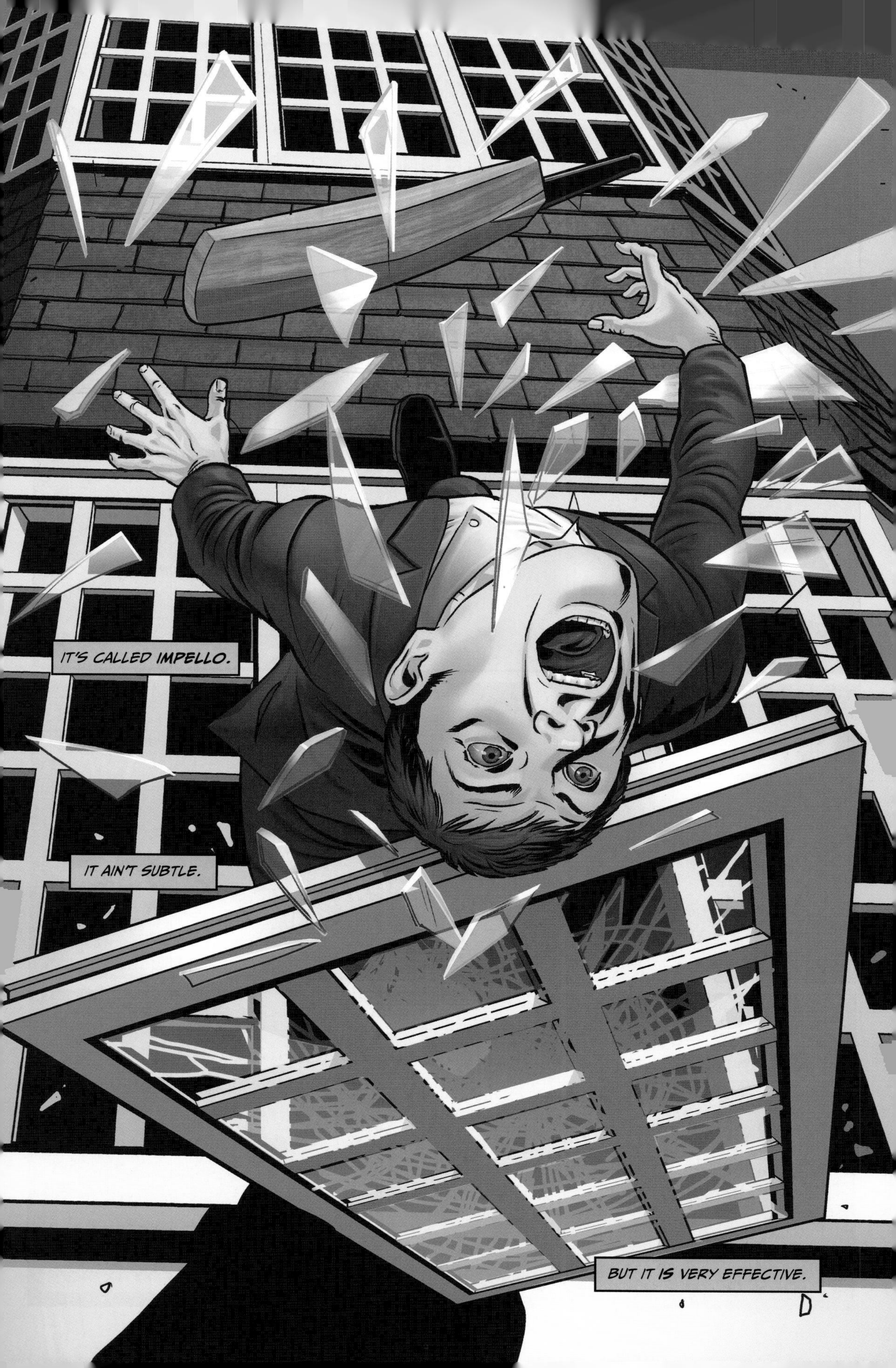
IT'S CALLED IMPELLO.
IT AIN'T SUBTLE.
BUT IT IS VERY EFFECTIVE.

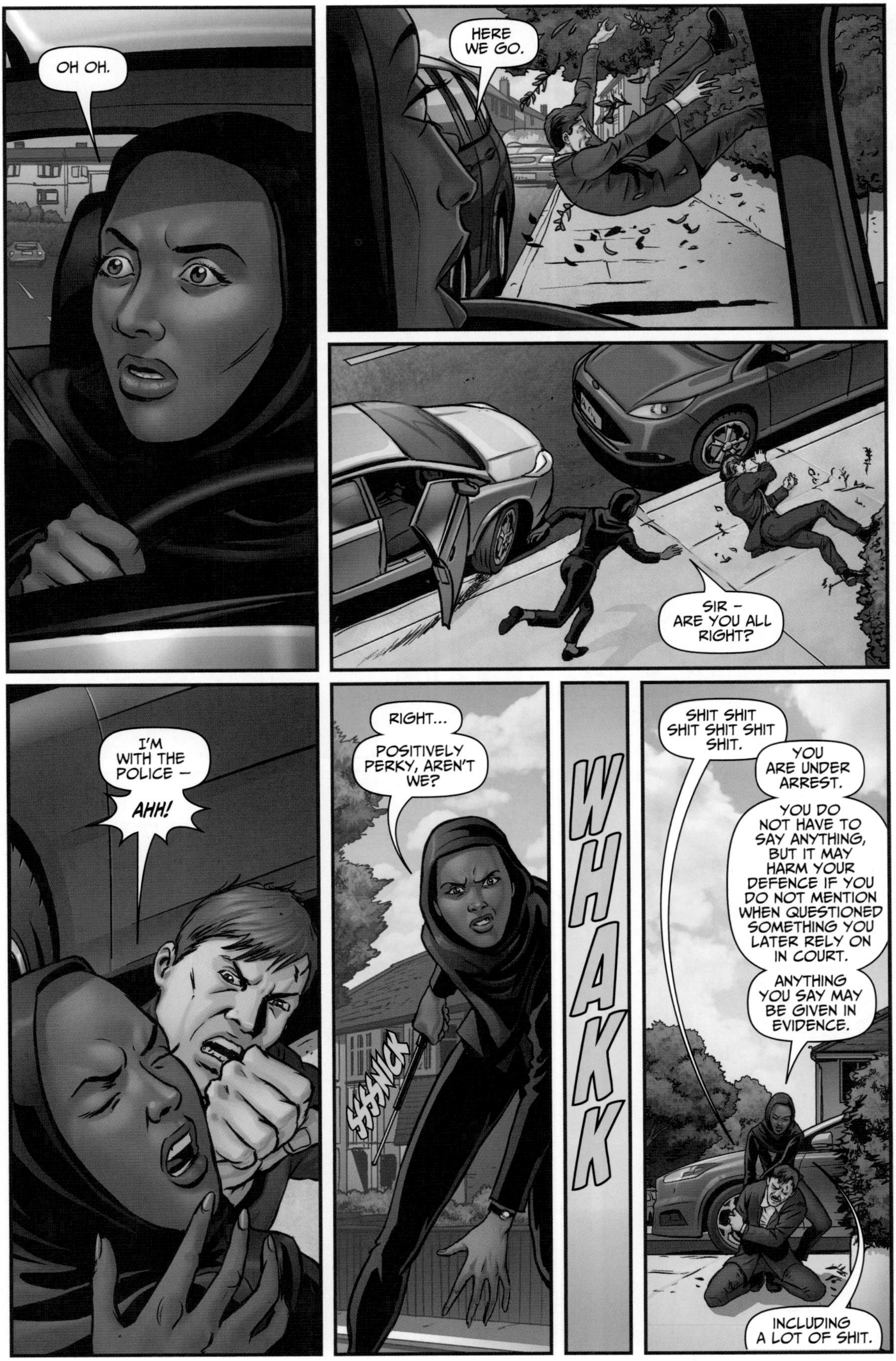
OH OH.
HERE WE GO.
SIR – ARE YOU ALL RIGHT?
I'M WITH THE POLICE –
AHH!
RIGHT...
POSITIVELY PERKY, AREN'T WE?
SHNICK
WHAKK
SHIT SHIT SHIT SHIT SHIT SHIT.
YOU ARE UNDER ARREST.
YOU DO NOT HAVE TO SAY ANYTHING, BUT IT MAY HARM YOUR DEFENCE IF YOU DO NOT MENTION WHEN QUESTIONED SOMETHING YOU LATER RELY ON IN COURT.
ANYTHING YOU SAY MAY BE GIVEN IN EVIDENCE.
INCLUDING A LOT OF SHIT.

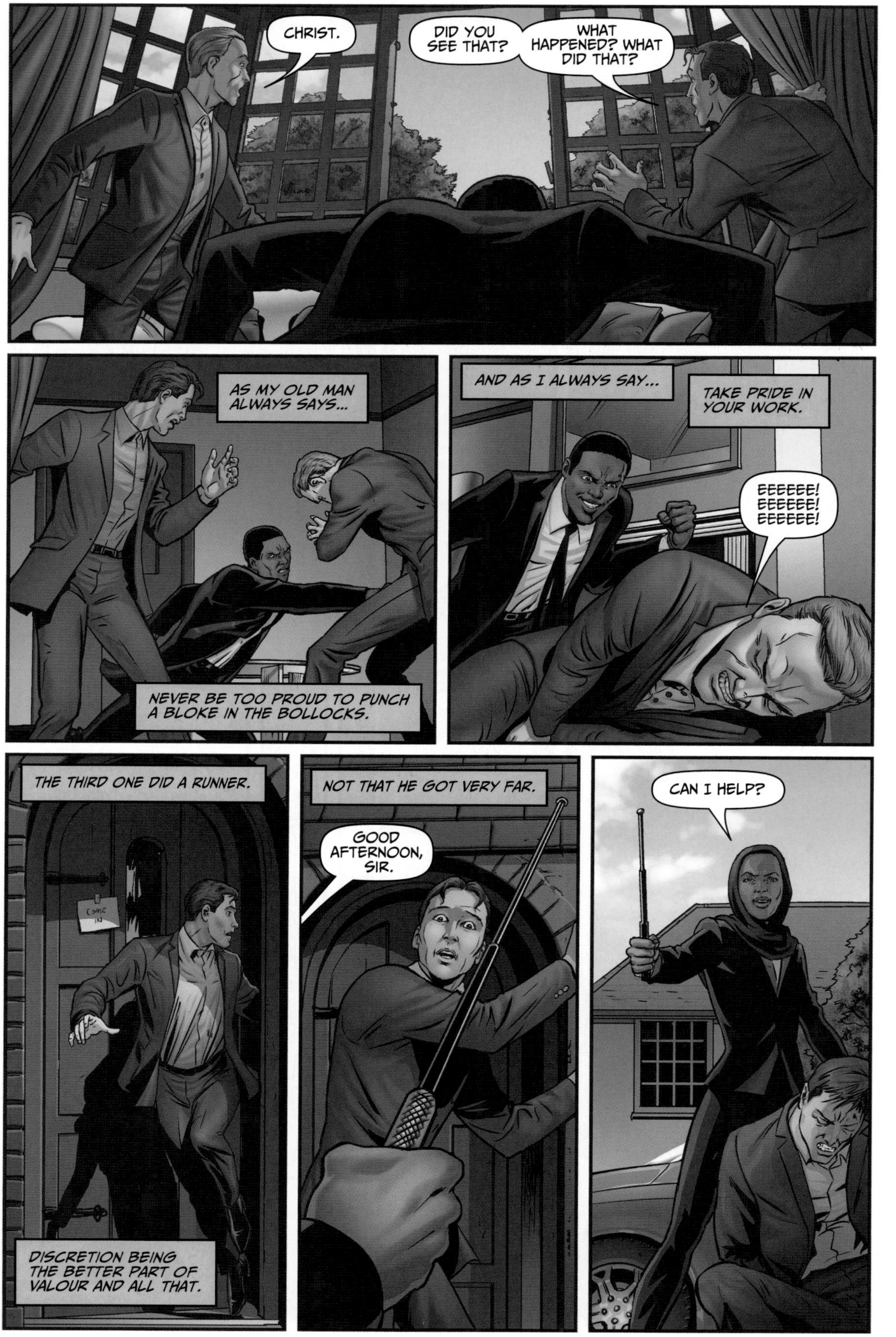
CHRIST.
DID YOU SEE THAT?
WHAT HAPPENED? WHAT DID THAT?
AS MY OLD MAN ALWAYS SAYS...
NEVER BE TOO PROUD TO PUNCH A BLOKE IN THE BOLLOCKS.
AND AS I ALWAYS SAY...
TAKE PRIDE IN YOUR WORK.
EEEEEE! EEEEEE! EEEEEE!
THE THIRD ONE DID A RUNNER.
DISCRETION BEING THE BETTER PART OF VALOUR AND ALL THAT.
NOT THAT HE GOT VERY FAR.
GOOD AFTERNOON, SIR.
CAN I HELP?

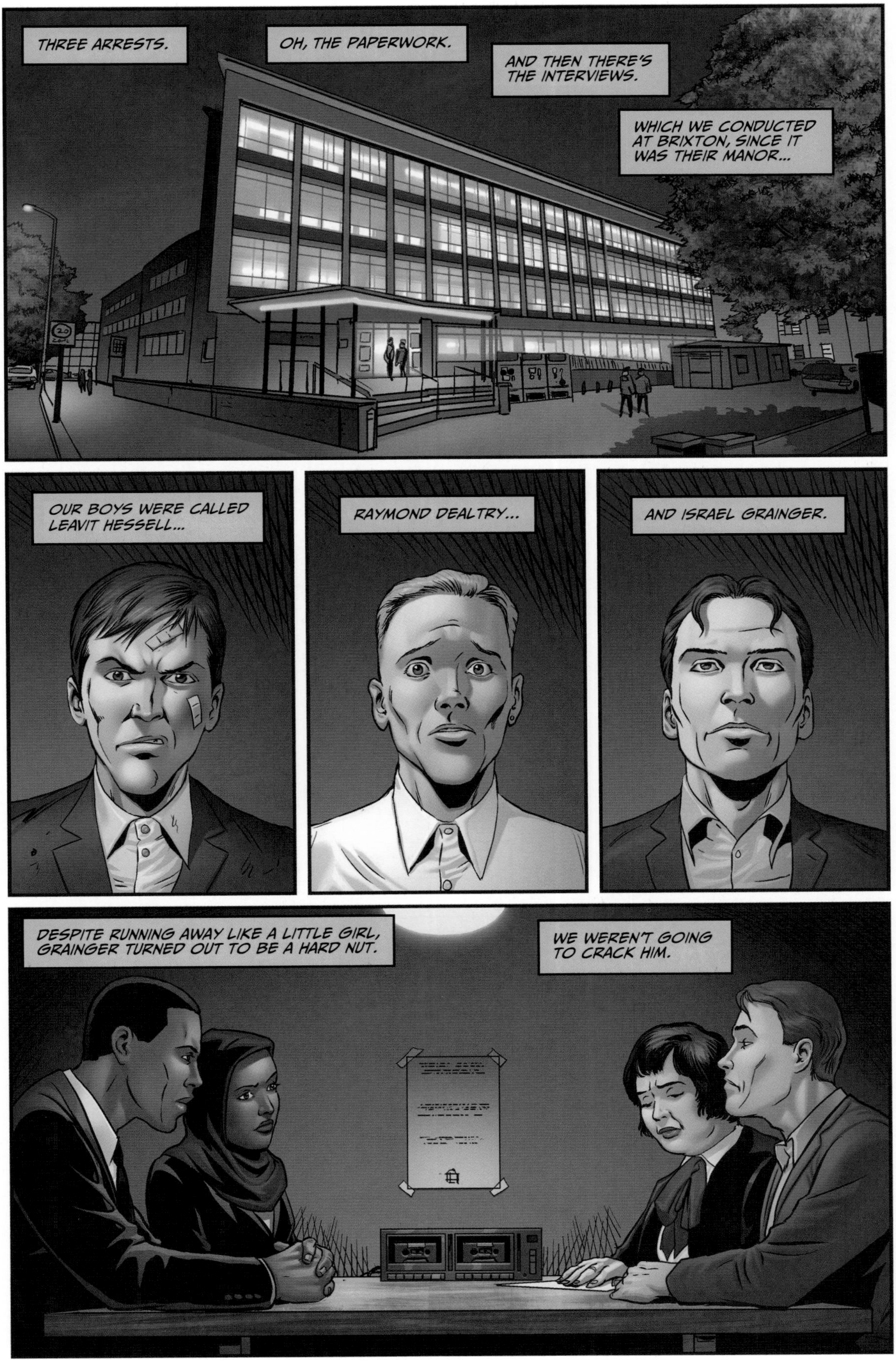
THREE ARRESTS.
OH, THE PAPERWORK.
AND THEN THERE'S THE INTERVIEWS.
WHICH WE CONDUCTED AT BRIXTON, SINCE IT WAS THEIR MANOR...
OUR BOYS WERE CALLED LEAVIT HESSELL...
RAYMOND DEALTRY...
AND ISRAEL GRAINGER.
DESPITE RUNNING AWAY LIKE A LITTLE GIRL, GRAINGER TURNED OUT TO BE A HARD NUT.
WE WEREN'T GOING TO CRACK HIM.

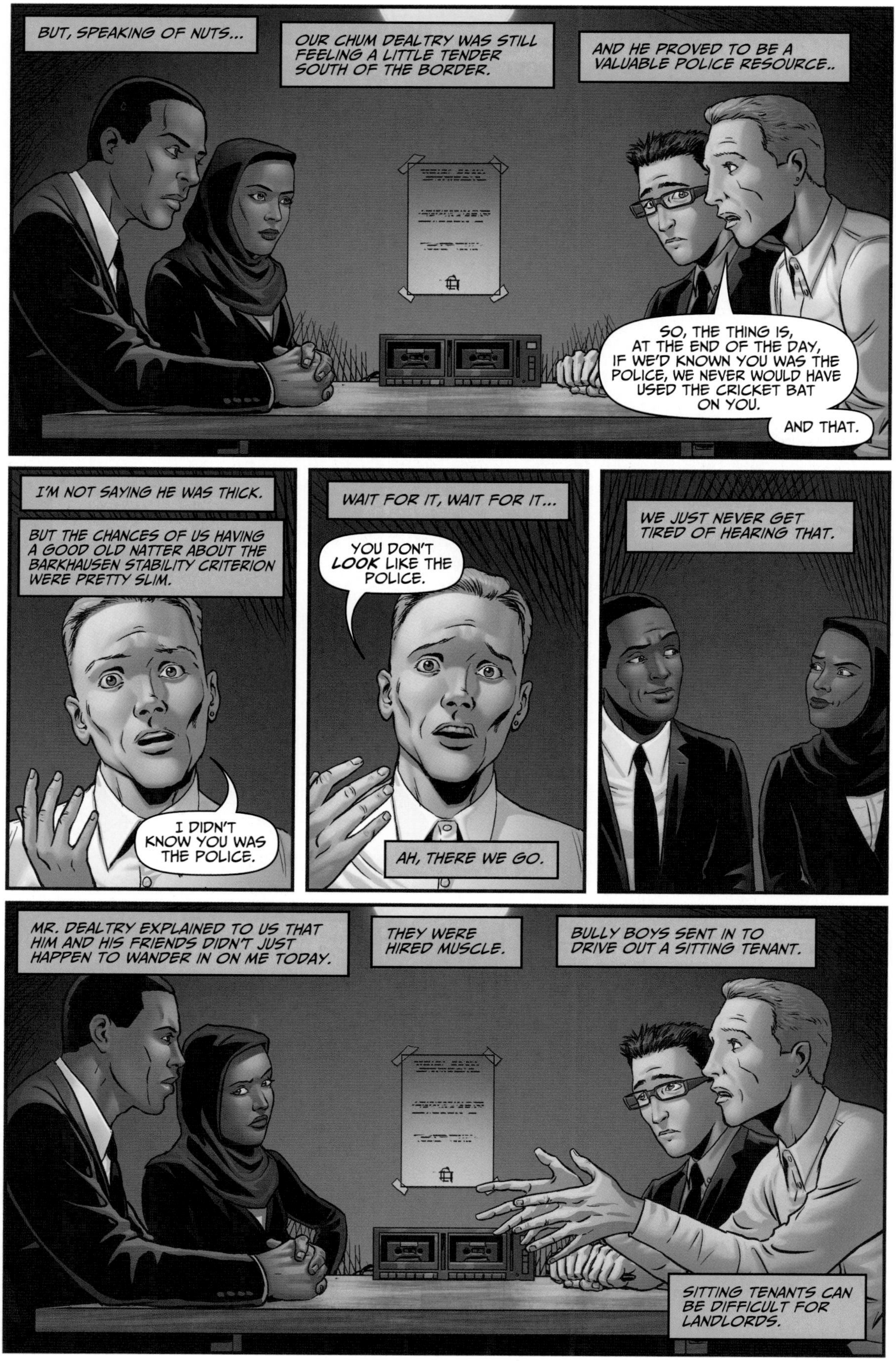
BUT, SPEAKING OF NUTS...
OUR CHUM DEALTRY WAS STILL FEELING A LITTLE TENDER SOUTH OF THE BORDER.
AND HE PROVED TO BE A VALUABLE POLICE RESOURCE..
SO, THE THING IS, AT THE END OF THE DAY, IF WE'D KNOWN YOU WAS THE POLICE, WE NEVER WOULD HAVE USED THE CRICKET BAT ON YOU.
AND THAT.
I'M NOT SAYING HE WAS THICK.
BUT THE CHANCES OF US HAVING A GOOD OLD NATTER ABOUT THE BARKHAUSEN STABILITY CRITERION WERE PRETTY SLIM.
I DIDN'T KNOW YOU WAS THE POLICE.
WAIT FOR IT, WAIT FOR IT...
YOU DON'T LOOK LIKE THE POLICE.
AH, THERE WE GO.
WE JUST NEVER GET TIRED OF HEARING THAT.
MR. DEALTRY EXPLAINED TO US THAT HIM AND HIS FRIENDS DIDN'T JUST HAPPEN TO WANDER IN ON ME TODAY.
THEY WERE HIRED MUSCLE.
BULLY BOYS SENT IN TO DRIVE OUT A SITTING TENANT.
SITTING TENANTS CAN BE DIFFICULT FOR LANDLORDS.

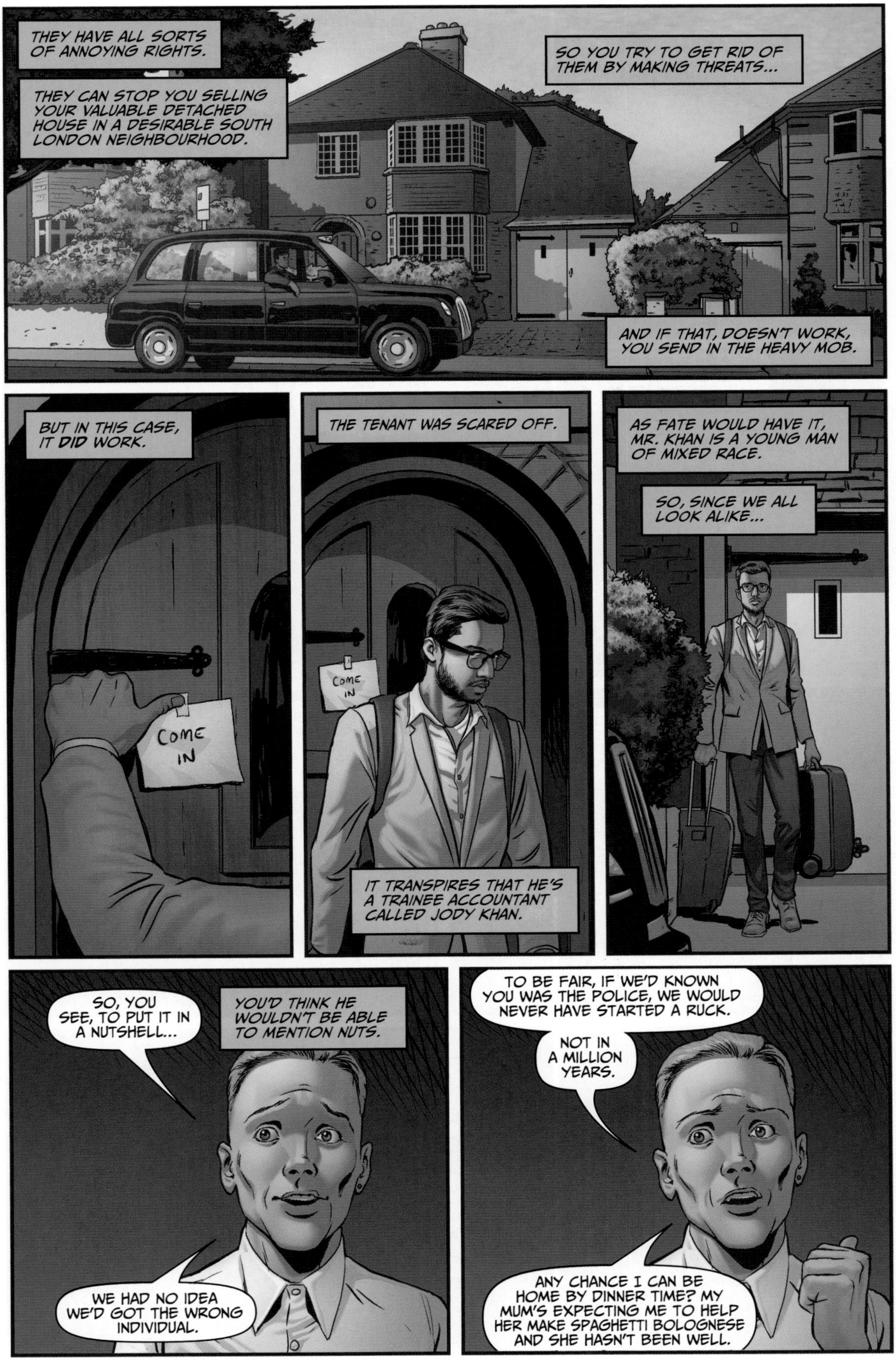
THEY HAVE ALL SORTS OF ANNOYING RIGHTS.
THEY CAN STOP YOU SELLING YOUR VALUABLE DETACHED HOUSE IN A DESIRABLE SOUTH LONDON NEIGHBOURHOOD.
SO YOU TRY TO GET RID OF THEM BY MAKING THREATS...
AND IF THAT, DOESN'T WORK, YOU SEND IN THE HEAVY MOB.
BUT IN THIS CASE, IT DID WORK.
COME IN
THE TENANT WAS SCARED OFF.
COME IN
IT TRANSPIRES THAT HE'S A TRAINEE ACCOUNTANT CALLED JODY KHAN.
AS FATE WOULD HAVE IT, MR. KHAN IS A YOUNG MAN OF MIXED RACE.
SO, SINCE WE ALL LOOK ALIKE...
SO, YOU SEE, TO PUT IT IN A NUTSHELL...
YOU'D THINK HE WOULDN'T BE ABLE TO MENTION NUTS.
WE HAD NO IDEA WE'D GOT THE WRONG INDIVIDUAL.
TO BE FAIR, IF WE'D KNOWN YOU WAS THE POLICE, WE WOULD NEVER HAVE STARTED A RUCK.
NOT IN A MILLION YEARS.
ANY CHANCE I CAN BE HOME BY DINNER TIME? MY MUM'S EXPECTING ME TO HELP HER MAKE SPAGHETTI BOLOGNESE AND SHE HASN'T BEEN WELL.

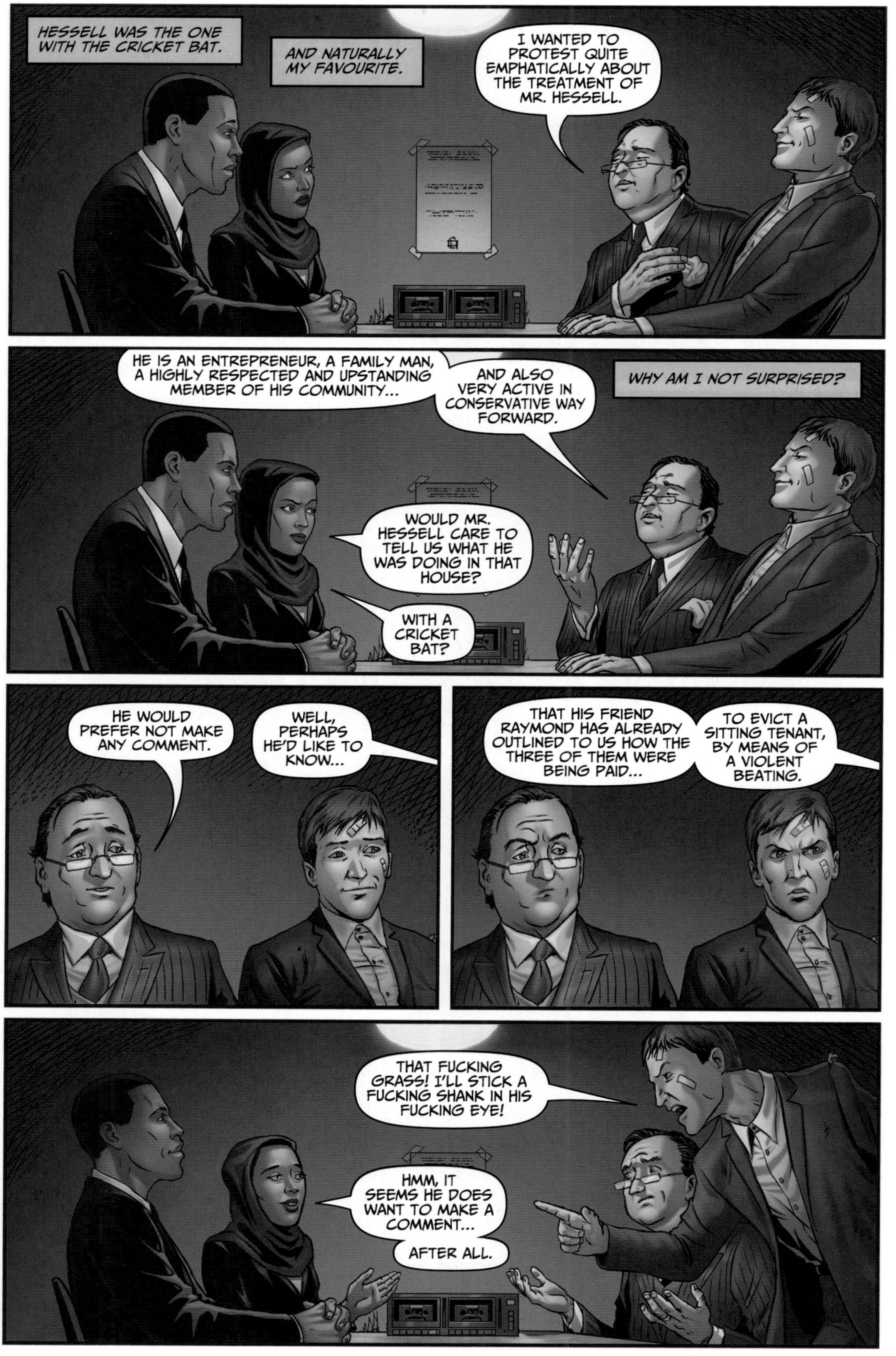
HESSELL WAS THE ONE WITH THE CRICKET BAT.
AND NATURALLY MY FAVOURITE.
I WANTED TO PROTEST QUITE EMPHATICALLY ABOUT THE TREATMENT OF MR. HESSELL.
HE IS AN ENTREPRENEUR, A FAMILY MAN, A HIGHLY RESPECTED AND UPSTANDING MEMBER OF HIS COMMUNITY...
AND ALSO VERY ACTIVE IN CONSERVATIVE WAY FORWARD.
WHY AM I NOT SURPRISED?
WOULD MR. HESSELL CARE TO TELL US WHAT HE WAS DOING IN THAT HOUSE?
WITH A CRICKET BAT?
HE WOULD PREFER NOT MAKE ANY COMMENT.
WELL, PERHAPS HE'D LIKE TO KNOW...
THAT HIS FRIEND RAYMOND HAS ALREADY OUTLINED TO US HOW THE THREE OF THEM WERE BEING PAID...
TO EVICT A SITTING TENANT, BY MEANS OF A VIOLENT BEATING.
THAT FUCKING GRASS! I'LL STICK A FUCKING SHANK IN HIS FUCKING EYE!
HMM, IT SEEMS HE DOES WANT TO MAKE A COMMENT...
AFTER ALL.

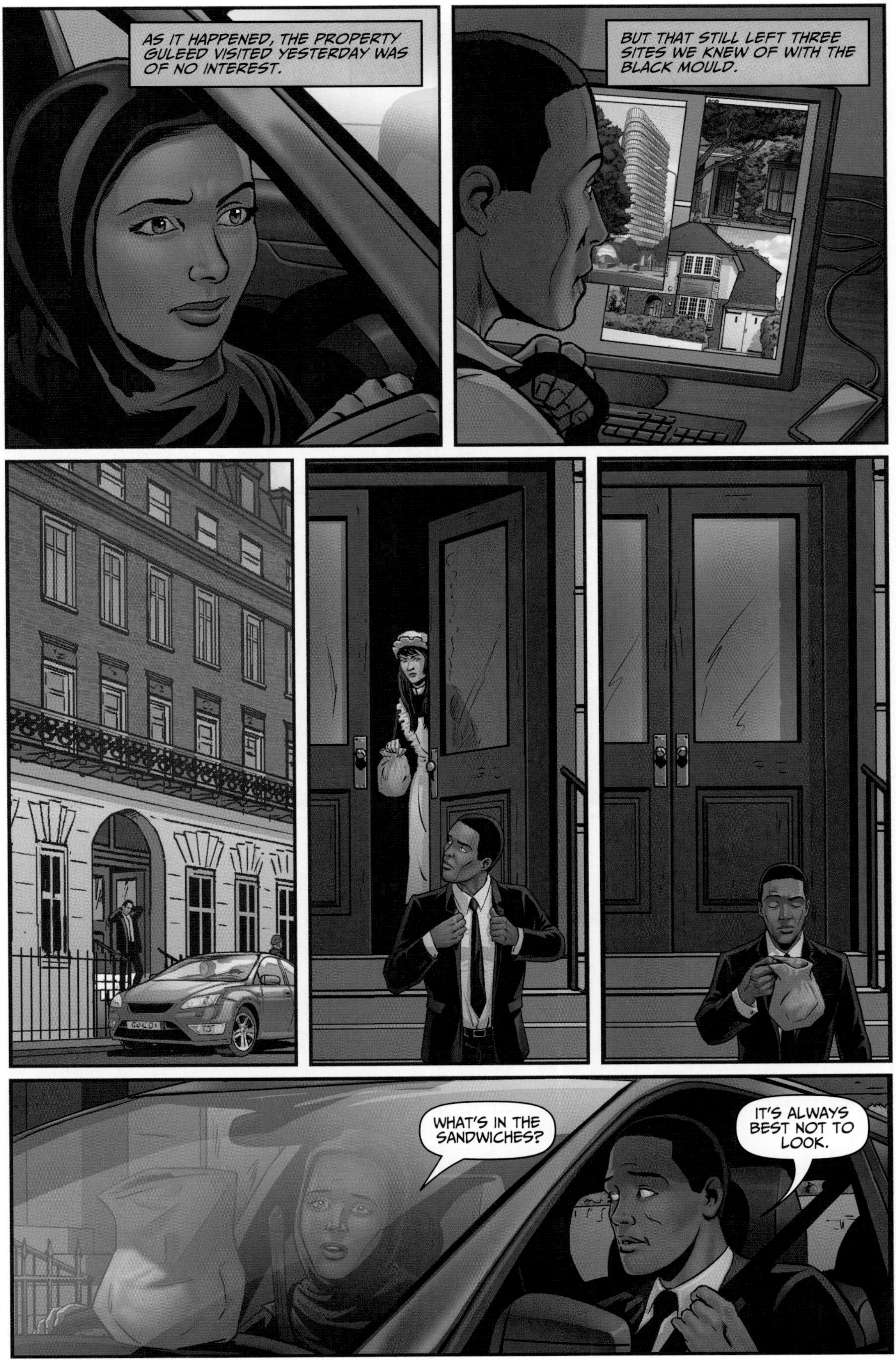

AS IT HAPPENED, THE PROPERTY GULEED VISITED YESTERDAY WAS OF NO INTEREST.
BUT THAT STILL LEFT THREE SITES WE KNEW OF WITH THE BLACK MOULD.
WHAT'S IN THE SANDWICHES?
IT'S ALWAYS BEST NOT TO LOOK.

WE WERE ON OUR WAY TO DARKEST MAYFAIR TO HAVE A LITTLE WORD WITH THE LANDLORD OF THE PROPERTY RENTED BY THE UNFORTUNATE MR. KHAN.

AND VISITED BY THE ALMOST VERY UNFORTUNATE PC GRANT.

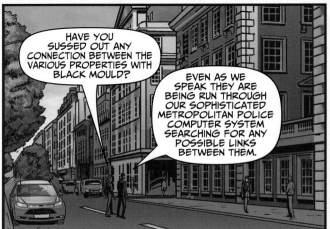

HAVE YOU SUSSED OUT ANY CONNECTION BETWEEN THE VARIOUS PROPERTIES WITH BLACK MOULD?

EVEN AS WE SPEAK THEY ARE BEING RUN THROUGH OUR SOPHISTICATED METROPOLITAN POLICE COMPUTER SYSTEM SEARCHING FOR ANY POSSIBLE LINKS BETWEEN THEM.

WE SHOULD KNOW BY TOMORROW.

BEM VINDO PROPERTIES

OR MAYBE SOONER.

OH. HELLO AGAIN.

PCs GULEED AND GRANT, ISN'T IT?

BEM VINDO

UH...YES.

DC, ACTUALLY.

FULL MARKS FOR GETTING THE NAMES RIGHT, THOUGH.

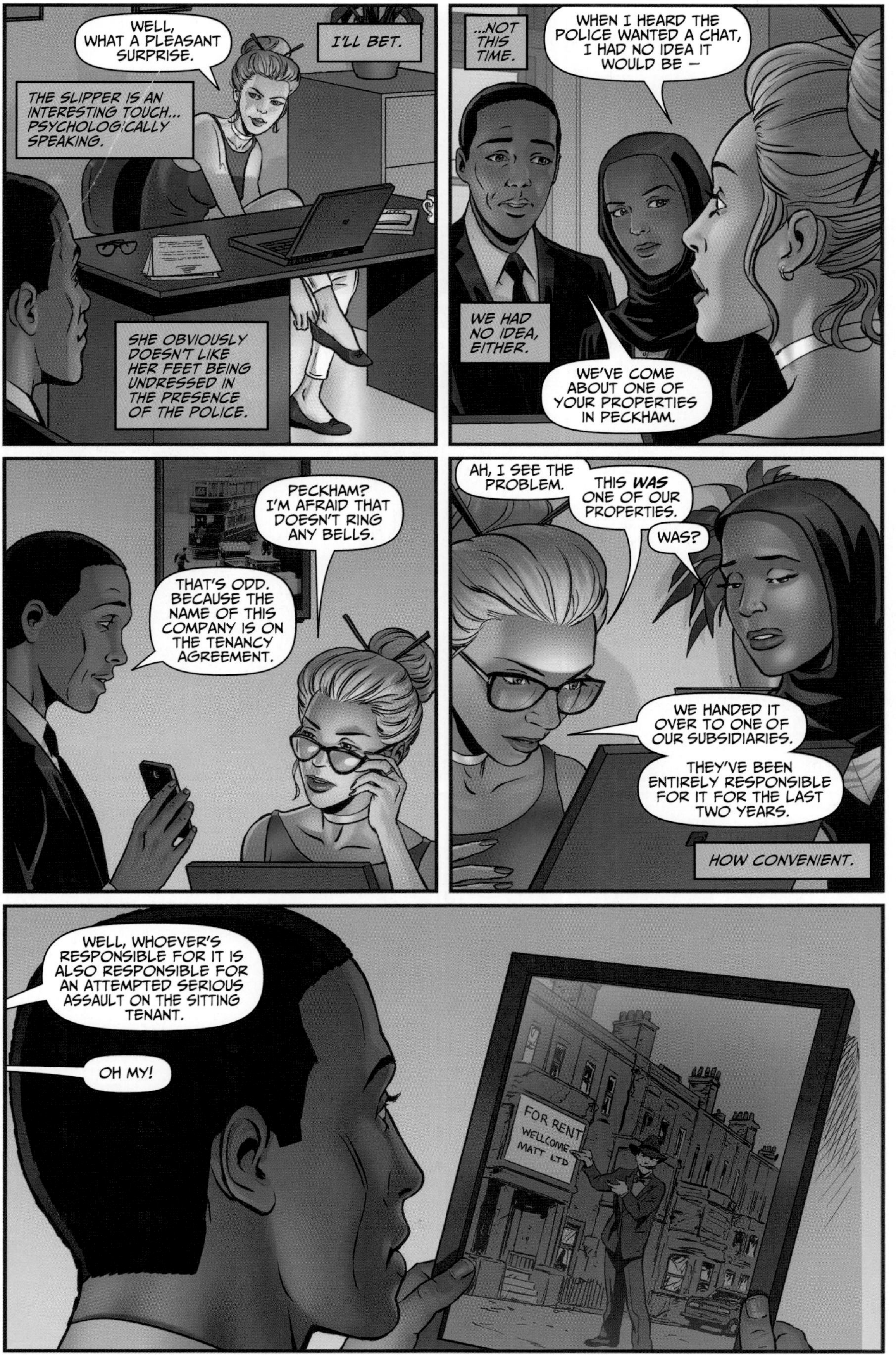
WELL, WHAT A PLEASANT SURPRISE.
I'LL BET.
THE SLIPPER IS AN INTERESTING TOUCH... PSYCHOLOGICALLY SPEAKING.
SHE OBVIOUSLY DOESN'T LIKE HER FEET BEING UNDRESSED IN THE PRESENCE OF THE POLICE.
...NOT THIS TIME.
WHEN I HEARD THE POLICE WANTED A CHAT, I HAD NO IDEA IT WOULD BE —
WE HAD NO IDEA, EITHER.
WE'VE COME ABOUT ONE OF YOUR PROPERTIES IN PECKHAM.
PECKHAM? I'M AFRAID THAT DOESN'T RING ANY BELLS.
THAT'S ODD. BECAUSE THE NAME OF THIS COMPANY IS ON THE TENANCY AGREEMENT.
AH, I SEE THE PROBLEM.
THIS WAS ONE OF OUR PROPERTIES.
WAS?
WE HANDED IT OVER TO ONE OF OUR SUBSIDIARIES.
THEY'VE BEEN ENTIRELY RESPONSIBLE FOR IT FOR THE LAST TWO YEARS.
HOW CONVENIENT.
WELL, WHOEVER'S RESPONSIBLE FOR IT IS ALSO RESPONSIBLE FOR AN ATTEMPTED SERIOUS ASSAULT ON THE SITTING TENANT.
OH MY!
FOR RENT
WELLCOME MATT LTD

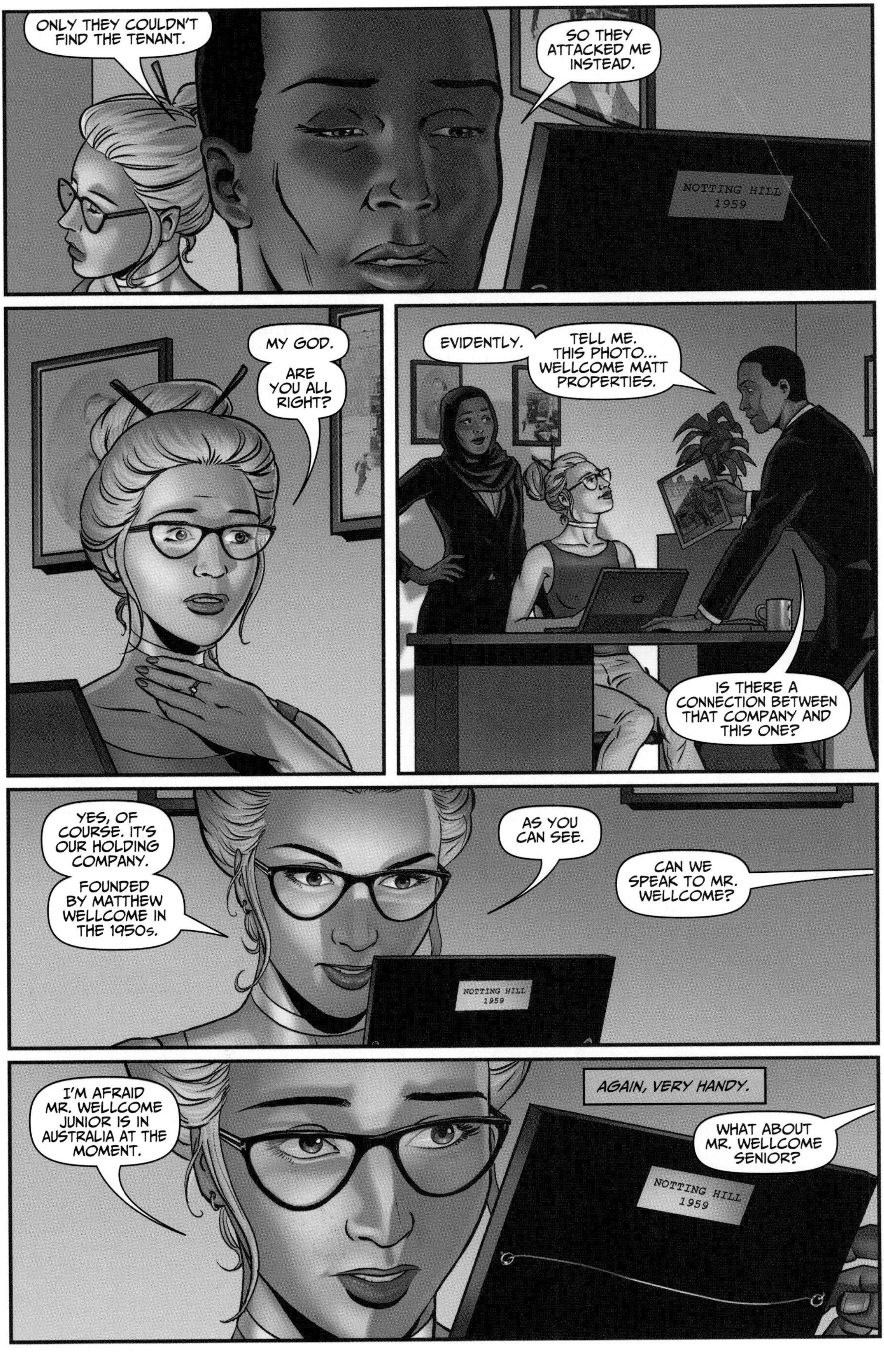
ONLY THEY COULDN'T FIND THE TENANT.
SO THEY ATTACKED ME INSTEAD.
NOTTING HILL 1959
MY GOD.
ARE YOU ALL RIGHT?
EVIDENTLY.
TELL ME. THIS PHOTO... WELLCOME MATT PROPERTIES.
IS THERE A CONNECTION BETWEEN THAT COMPANY AND THIS ONE?
YES, OF COURSE. IT'S OUR HOLDING COMPANY.
FOUNDED BY MATTHEW WELLCOME IN THE 1950s.
AS YOU CAN SEE.
CAN WE SPEAK TO MR. WELLCOME?
NOTTING HILL 1959
I'M AFRAID MR. WELLCOME JUNIOR IS IN AUSTRALIA AT THE MOMENT.
AGAIN, VERY HANDY.
WHAT ABOUT MR. WELLCOME SENIOR?
NOTTING HILL 1959

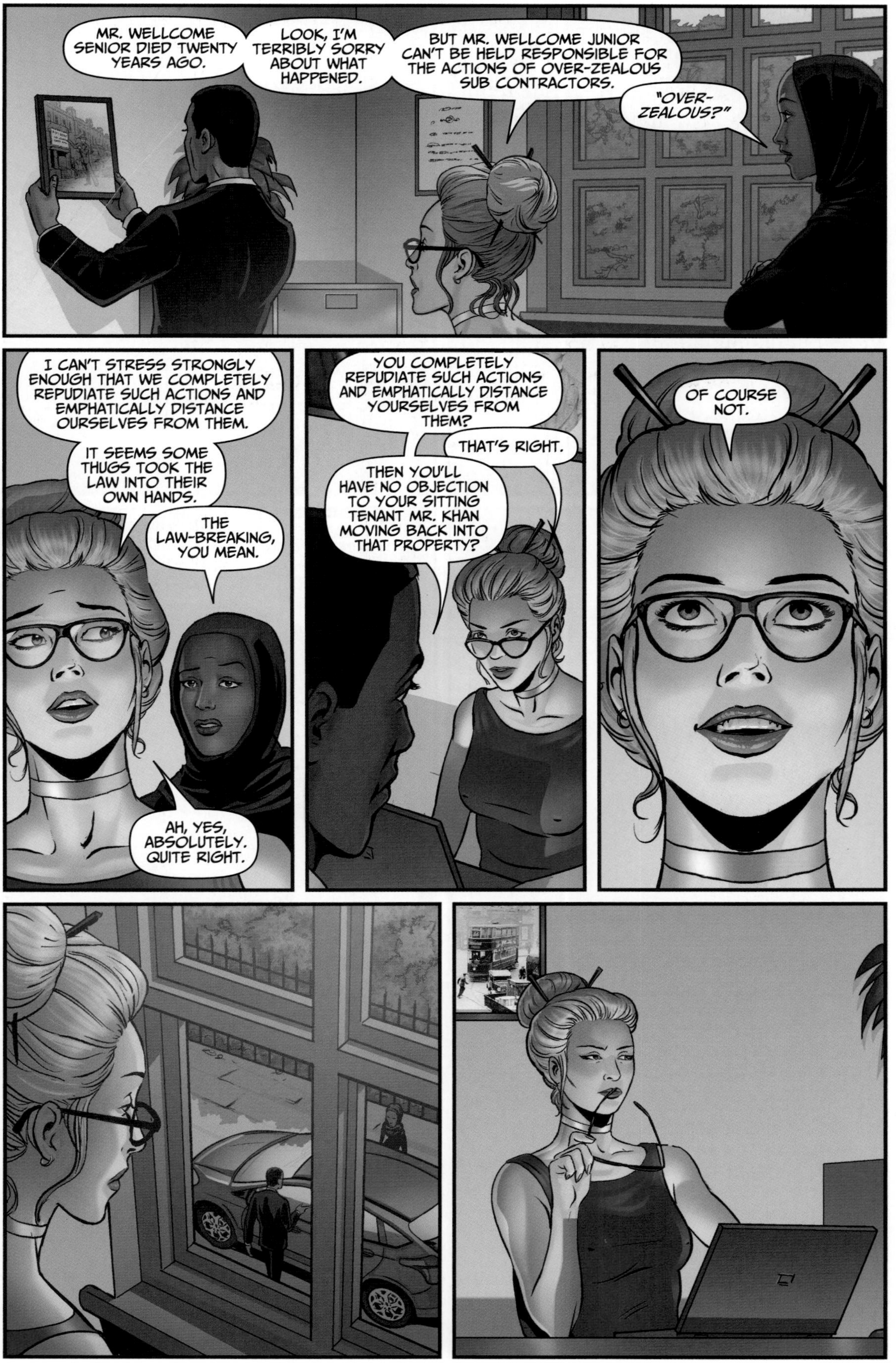
MR. WELLCOME SENIOR DIED TWENTY YEARS AGO.
LOOK, I'M TERRIBLY SORRY ABOUT WHAT HAPPENED.
BUT MR. WELLCOME JUNIOR CAN'T BE HELD RESPONSIBLE FOR THE ACTIONS OF OVER-ZEALOUS SUB CONTRACTORS.
"OVER-ZEALOUS?"
I CAN'T STRESS STRONGLY ENOUGH THAT WE COMPLETELY REPUDIATE SUCH ACTIONS AND EMPHATICALLY DISTANCE OURSELVES FROM THEM.
IT SEEMS SOME THUGS TOOK THE LAW INTO THEIR OWN HANDS.
THE LAW-BREAKING, YOU MEAN.
AH, YES, ABSOLUTELY. QUITE RIGHT.
YOU COMPLETELY REPUDIATE SUCH ACTIONS AND EMPHATICALLY DISTANCE YOURSELVES FROM THEM?
THAT'S RIGHT.
THEN YOU'LL HAVE NO OBJECTION TO YOUR SITTING TENANT MR. KHAN MOVING BACK INTO THAT PROPERTY?
OF COURSE NOT.

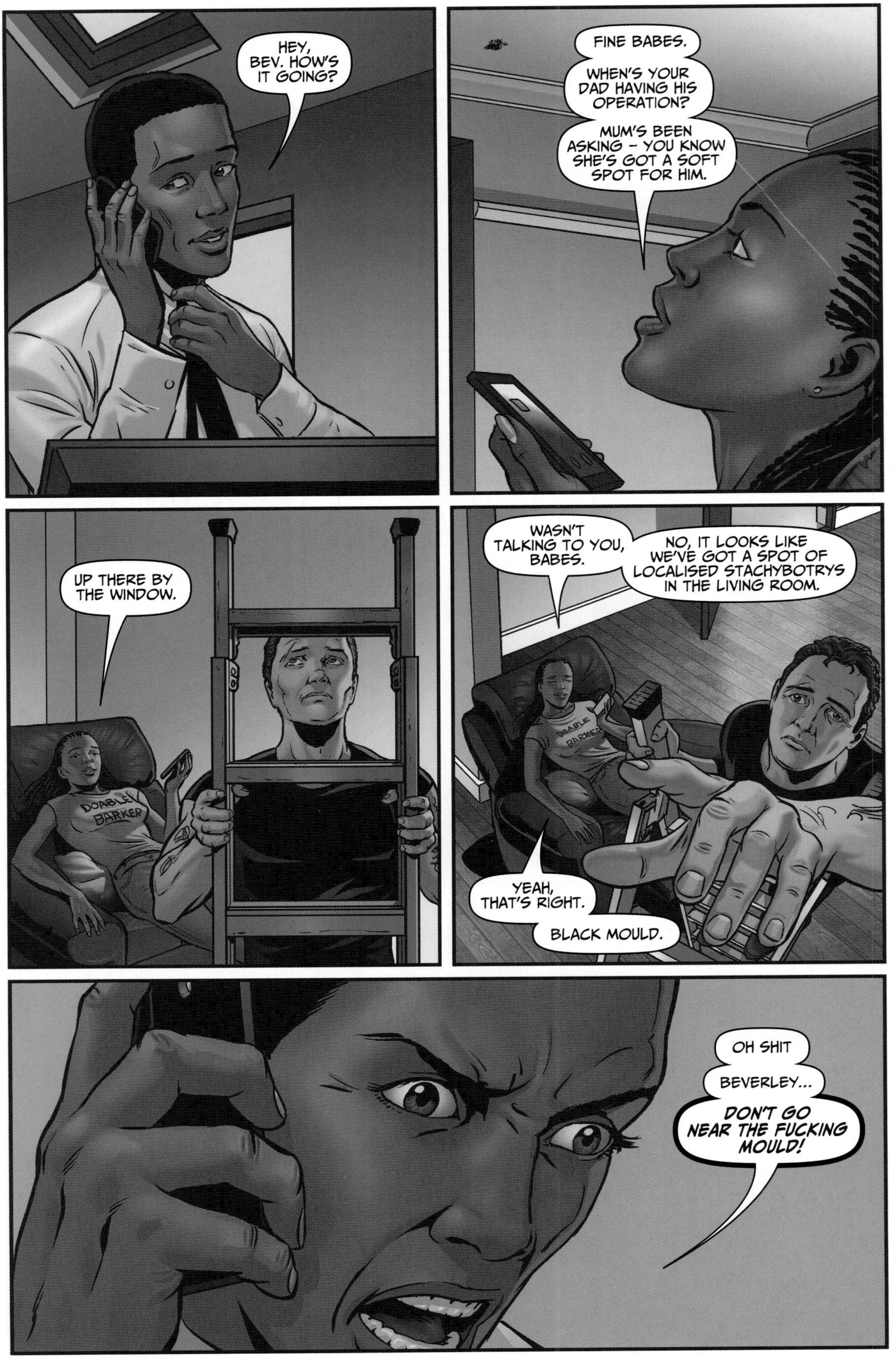
HEY, BEV. HOW'S IT GOING?
FINE BABES.
WHEN'S YOUR DAD HAVING HIS OPERATION?
MUM'S BEEN ASKING – YOU KNOW SHE'S GOT A SOFT SPOT FOR HIM.
UP THERE BY THE WINDOW.
WASN'T TALKING TO YOU, BABES.
NO, IT LOOKS LIKE WE'VE GOT A SPOT OF LOCALISED STACHYBOTRYS IN THE LIVING ROOM.
DOABLE BARKER
YEAH, THAT'S RIGHT.
BLACK MOULD.
OH SHIT
BEVERLEY...
DON'T GO NEAR THE FUCKING MOULD!

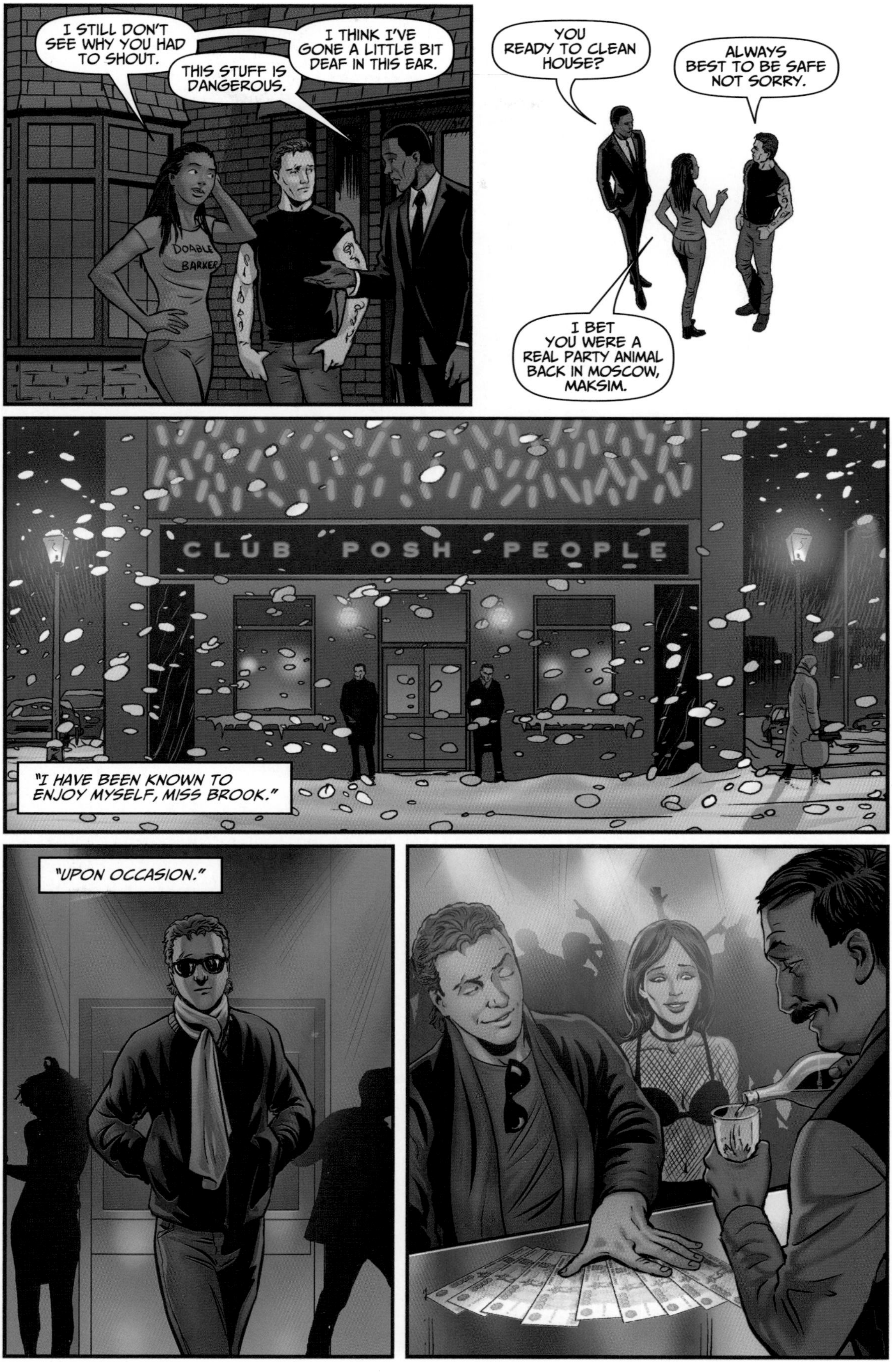
I STILL DON'T SEE WHY YOU HAD TO SHOUT.
I THINK I'VE GONE A LITTLE BIT DEAF IN THIS EAR.
THIS STUFF IS DANGEROUS.
DOABLE BARKER
YOU READY TO CLEAN HOUSE?
ALWAYS BEST TO BE SAFE NOT SORRY.
I BET YOU WERE A REAL PARTY ANIMAL BACK IN MOSCOW, MAKSIM.
CLUB POSH PEOPLE
"I HAVE BEEN KNOWN TO ENJOY MYSELF, MISS BROOK."
"UPON OCCASION."

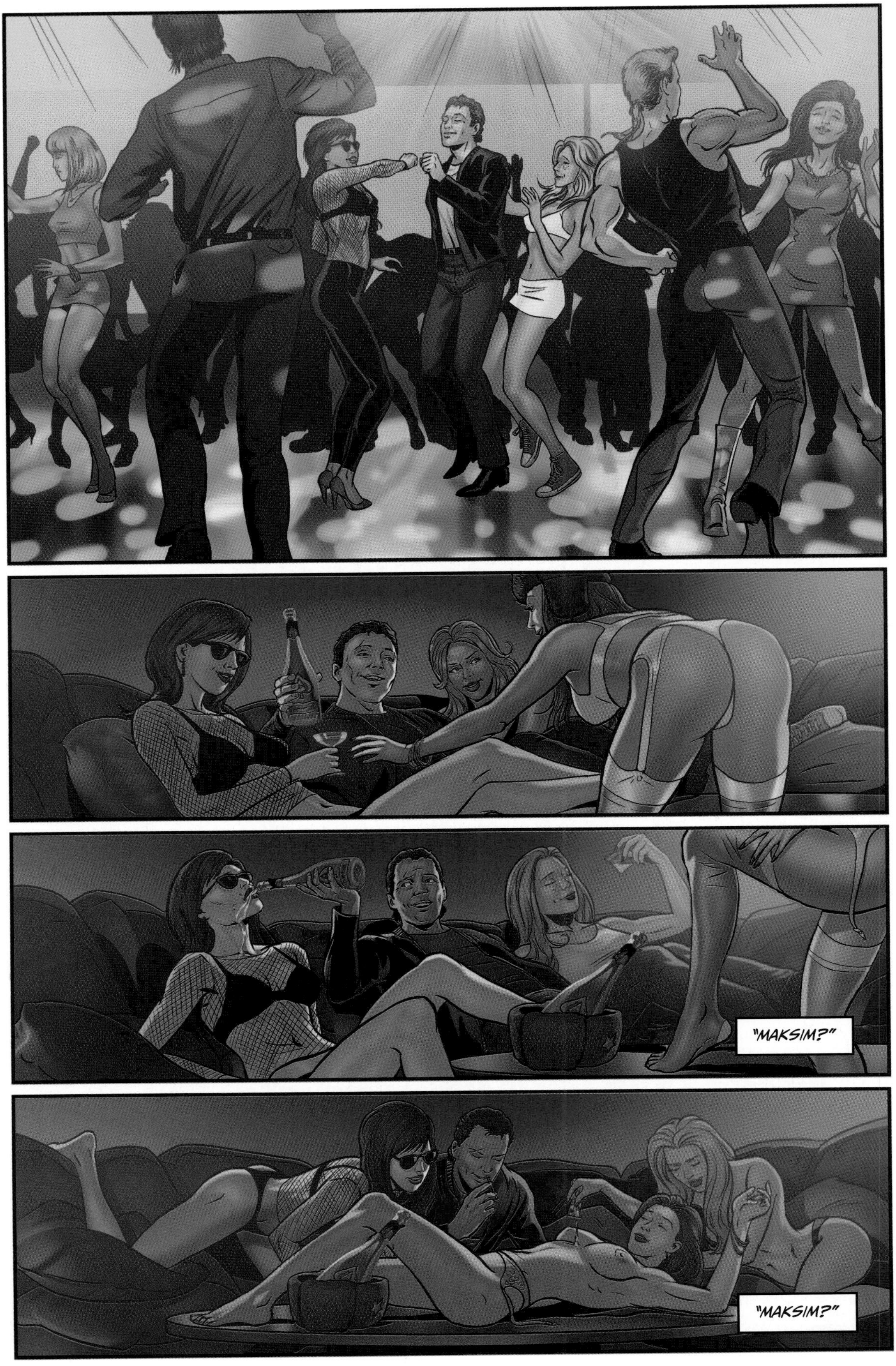
"MAKSIM?"
"MAKSIM?"

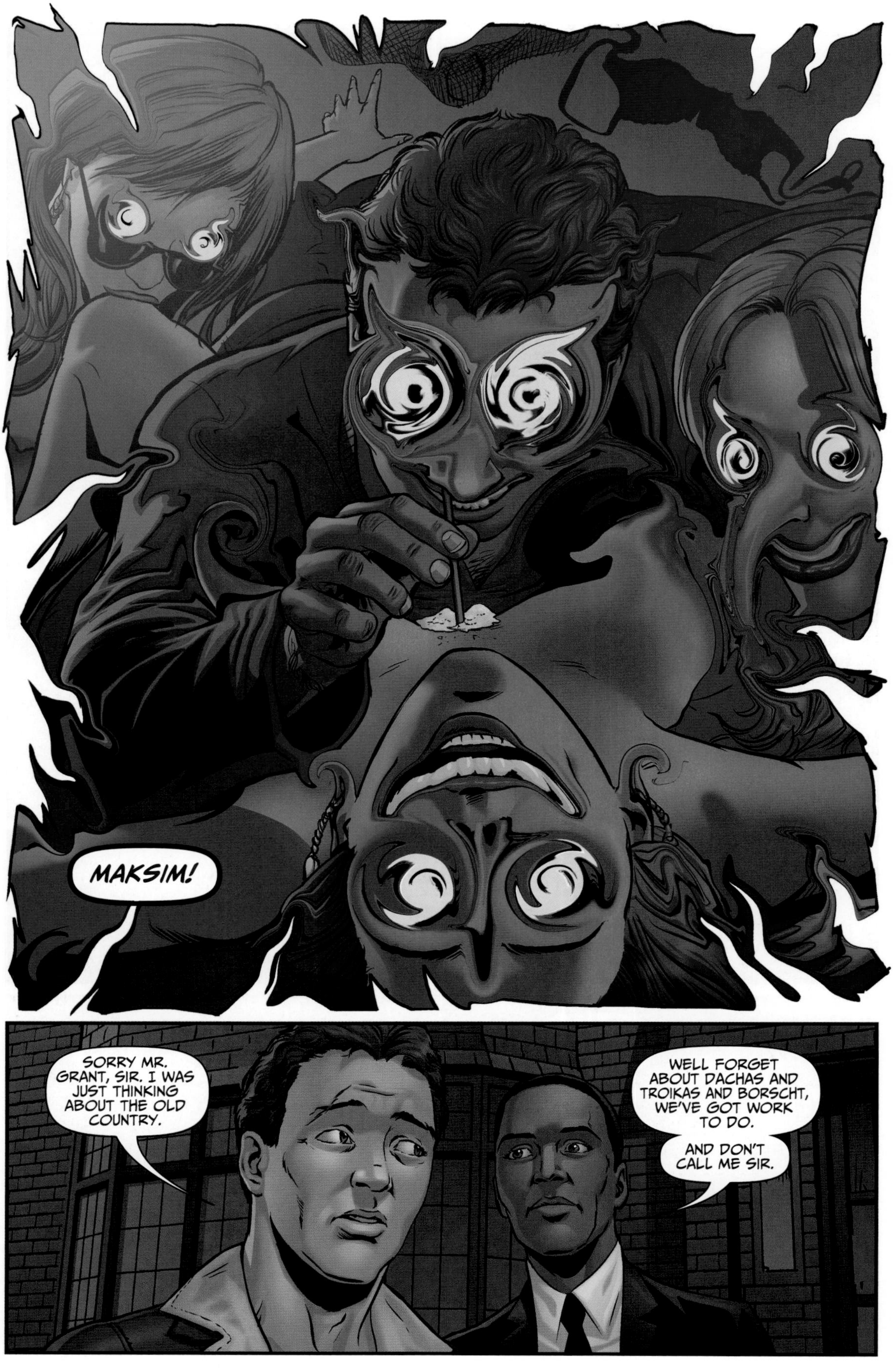
MAKSIM!
SORRY MR. GRANT, SIR. I WAS JUST THINKING ABOUT THE OLD COUNTRY.
WELL FORGET ABOUT DACHAS AND TROIKAS AND BORSCHT, WE'VE GOT WORK TO DO.
AND DON'T CALL ME SIR.

PUT THIS ON.

WE DON'T WANT THAT STUFF TO GET ON US.

GOOD, I HAVE SOME TOOLS THAT MIGHT BE HELPFUL.

MAKSIM, MATE, I THINK WE'RE A LITTLE BIT BEYOND HEDGE CLIPPERS HERE.

I WAS THINKING OF SOMETHING MORE SUITABLE.

JESUS.

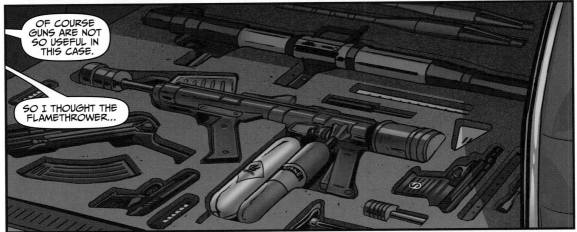

OF COURSE GUNS ARE NOT SO USEFUL IN THIS CASE.

SO I THOUGHT THE FLAMETHROWER...

NO, MAKSIM. NOT THE FLAMETHROWER.

PERHAPS THE RPG-7?

NO. SCIENCE WILL BE OUR WEAPON.

WE USE THESE.

IT'S A PITY TO WASTE SUCH EXCELLENT VINEGAR.

WE COULD USE IT TO PICKLE MUSHROOMS.

STRANGELY – THAT'S JUST WHAT WE'RE PLANNING TO DO.

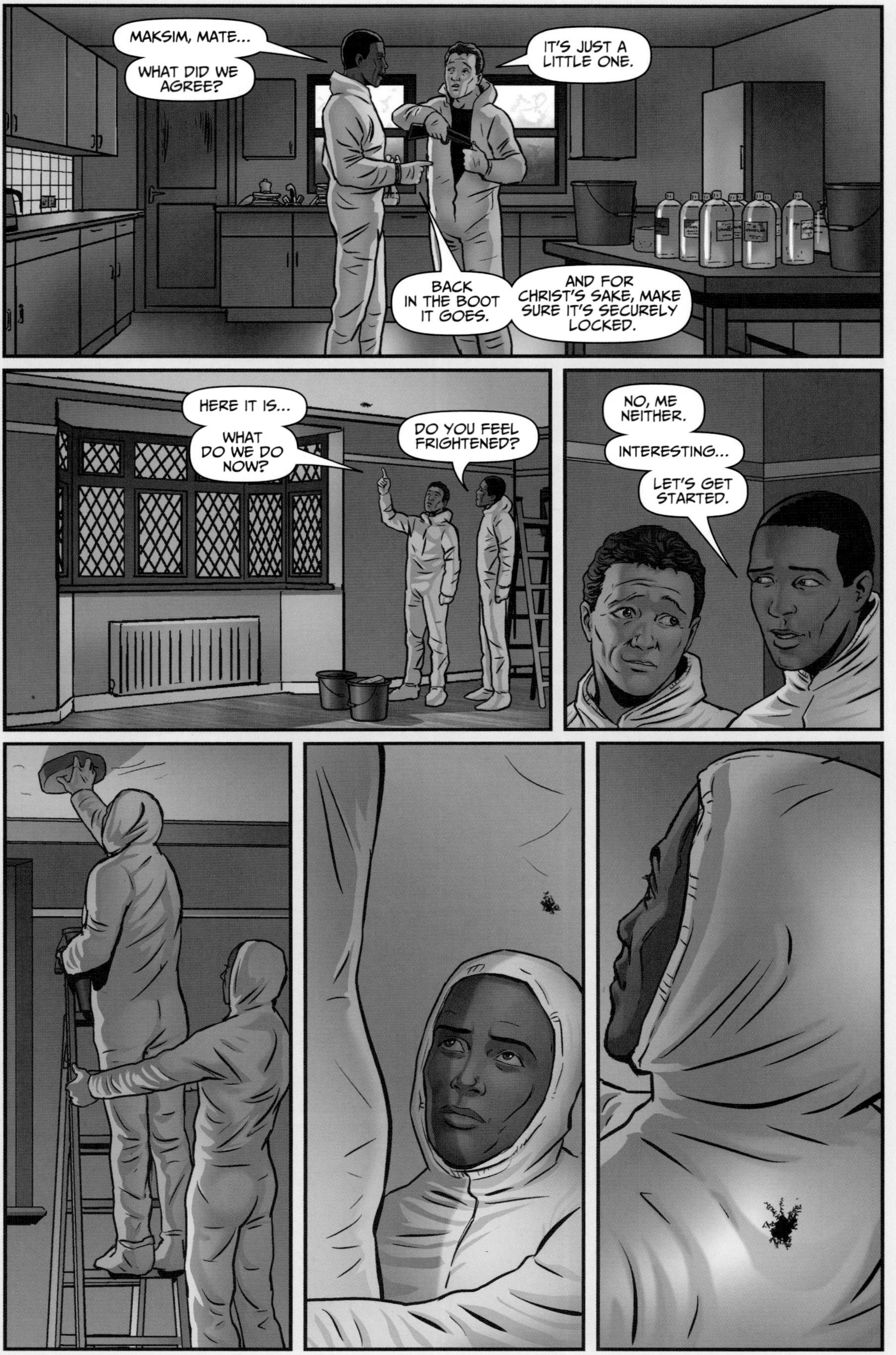
MAKSIM, MATE...
WHAT DID WE AGREE?
IT'S JUST A LITTLE ONE.
BACK IN THE BOOT IT GOES.
AND FOR CHRIST'S SAKE, MAKE SURE IT'S SECURELY LOCKED.
HERE IT IS...
WHAT DO WE DO NOW?
DO YOU FEEL FRIGHTENED?
NO, ME NEITHER.
INTERESTING...
LET'S GET STARTED.

THIS IS EXCELLENT VINEGAR.

CAN I USE THE REST OF IT FOR PICKLING?

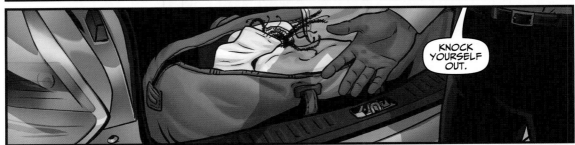

KNOCK YOURSELF OUT.

YOU GET PICKLED.

KLUNKKK

ASB 02

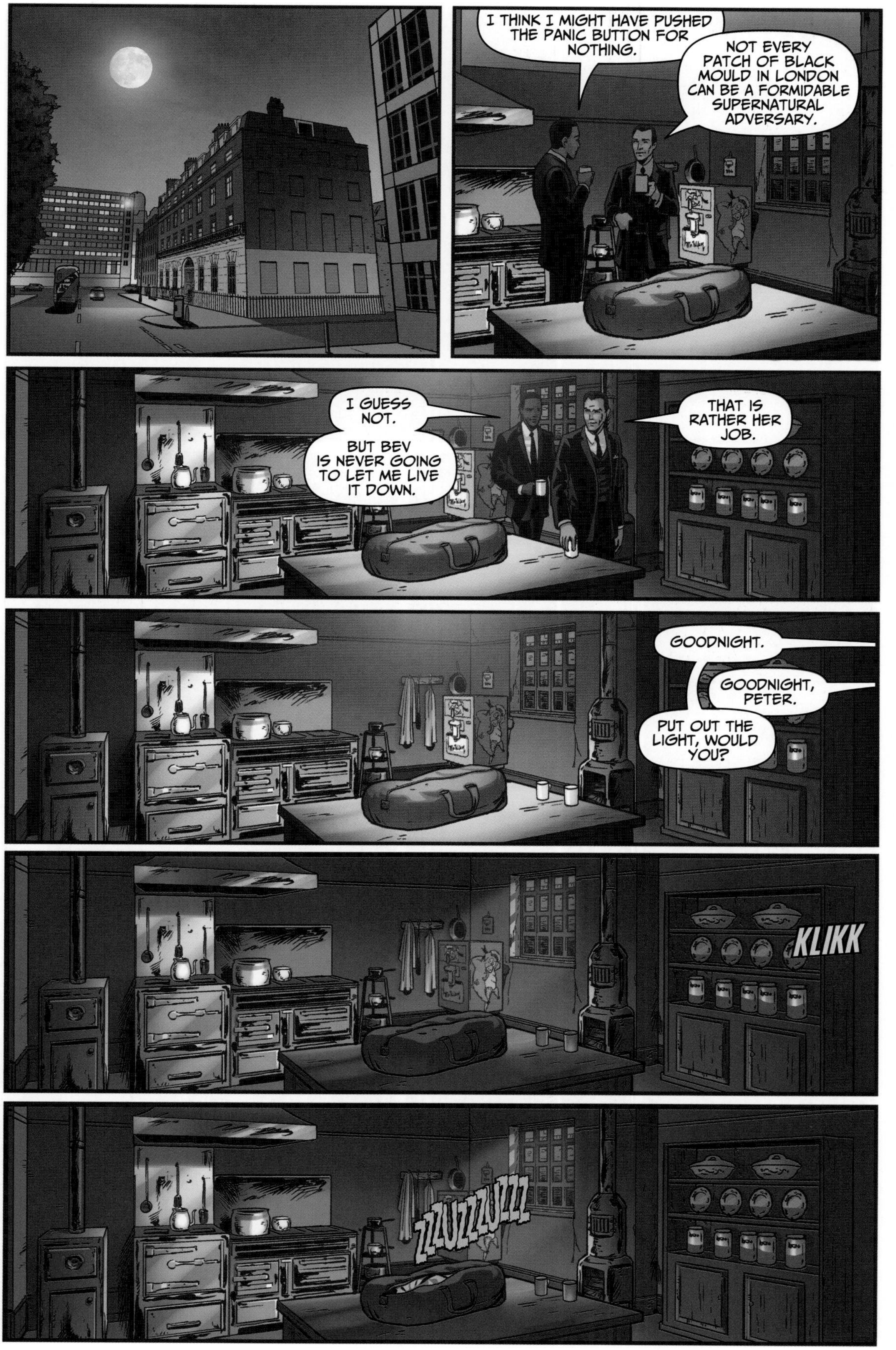
I THINK I MIGHT HAVE PUSHED THE PANIC BUTTON FOR NOTHING.
NOT EVERY PATCH OF BLACK MOULD IN LONDON CAN BE A FORMIDABLE SUPERNATURAL ADVERSARY.
I GUESS NOT.
BUT BEV IS NEVER GOING TO LET ME LIVE IT DOWN.
THAT IS RATHER HER JOB.
GOODNIGHT.
GOODNIGHT, PETER.
PUT OUT THE LIGHT, WOULD YOU?
KLIKK
ZZZUZZZUZZZ

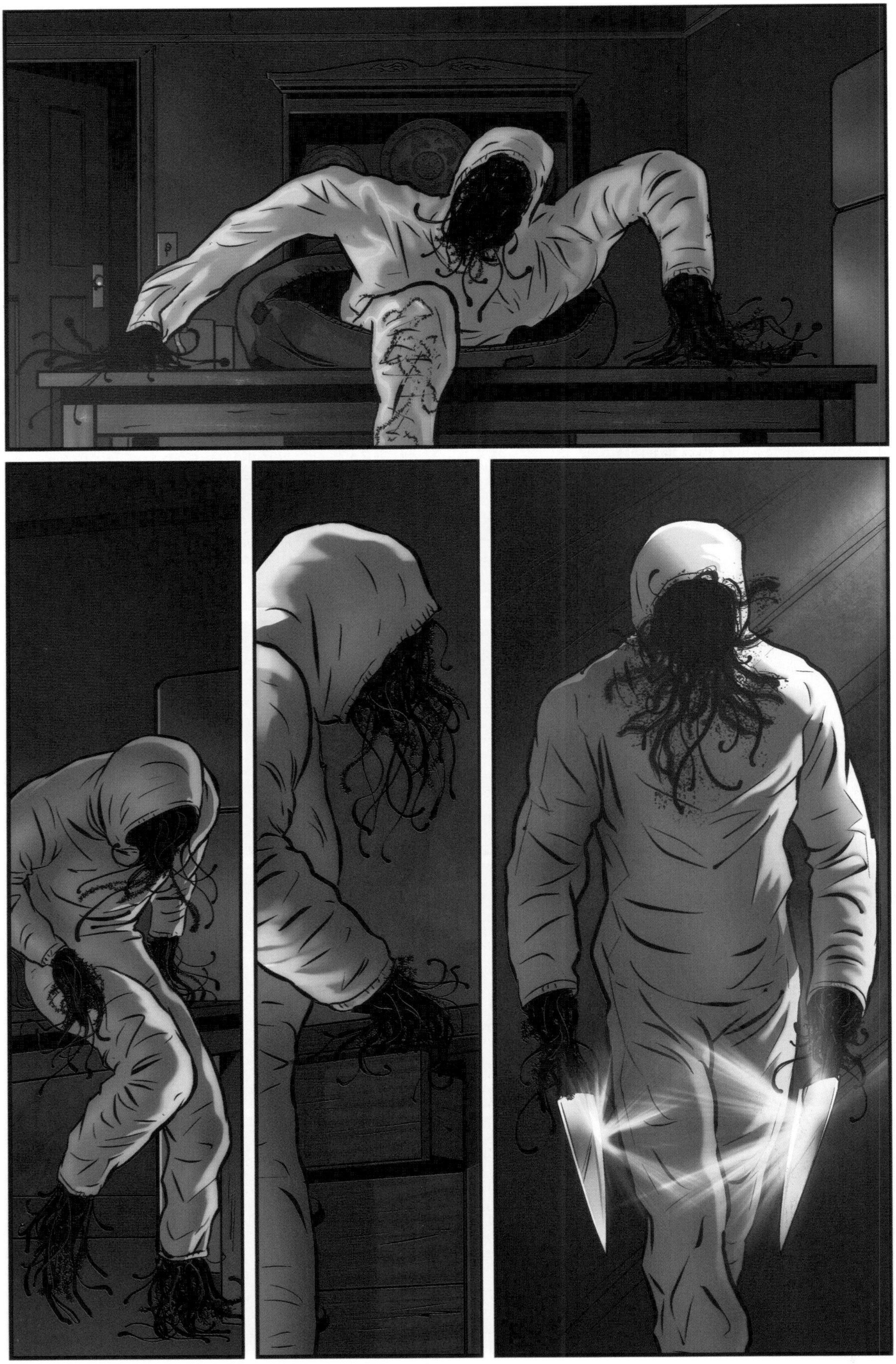

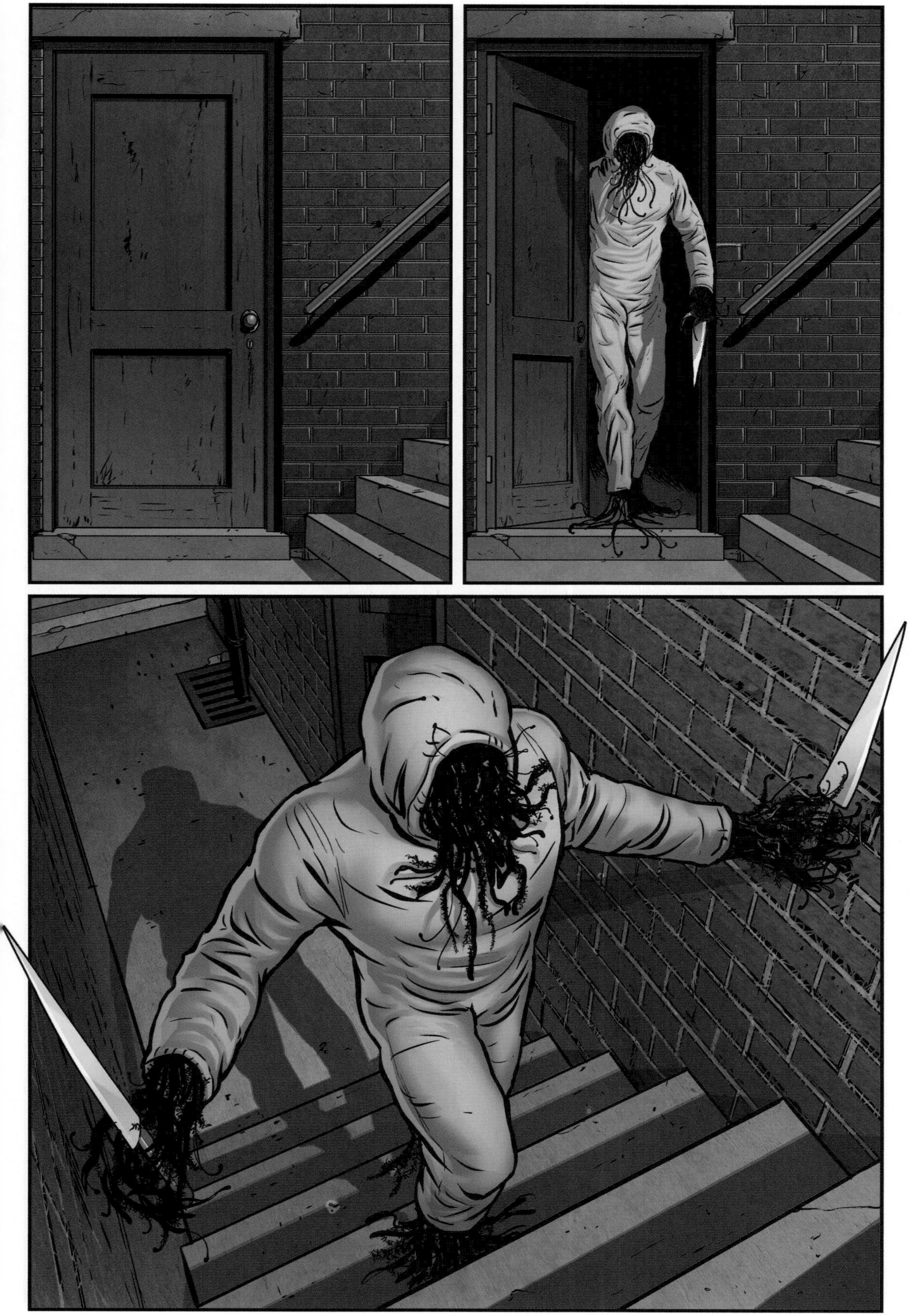

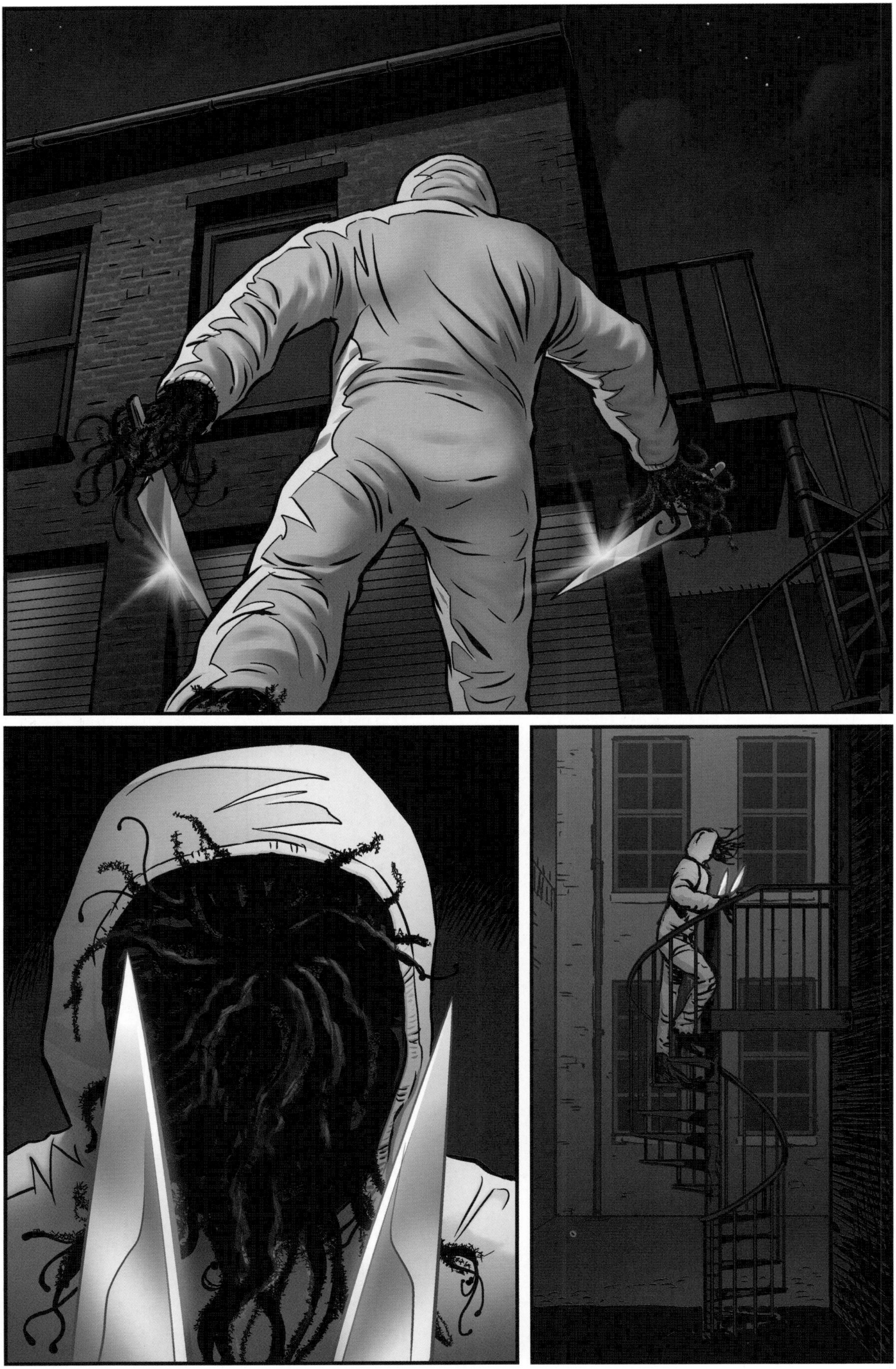

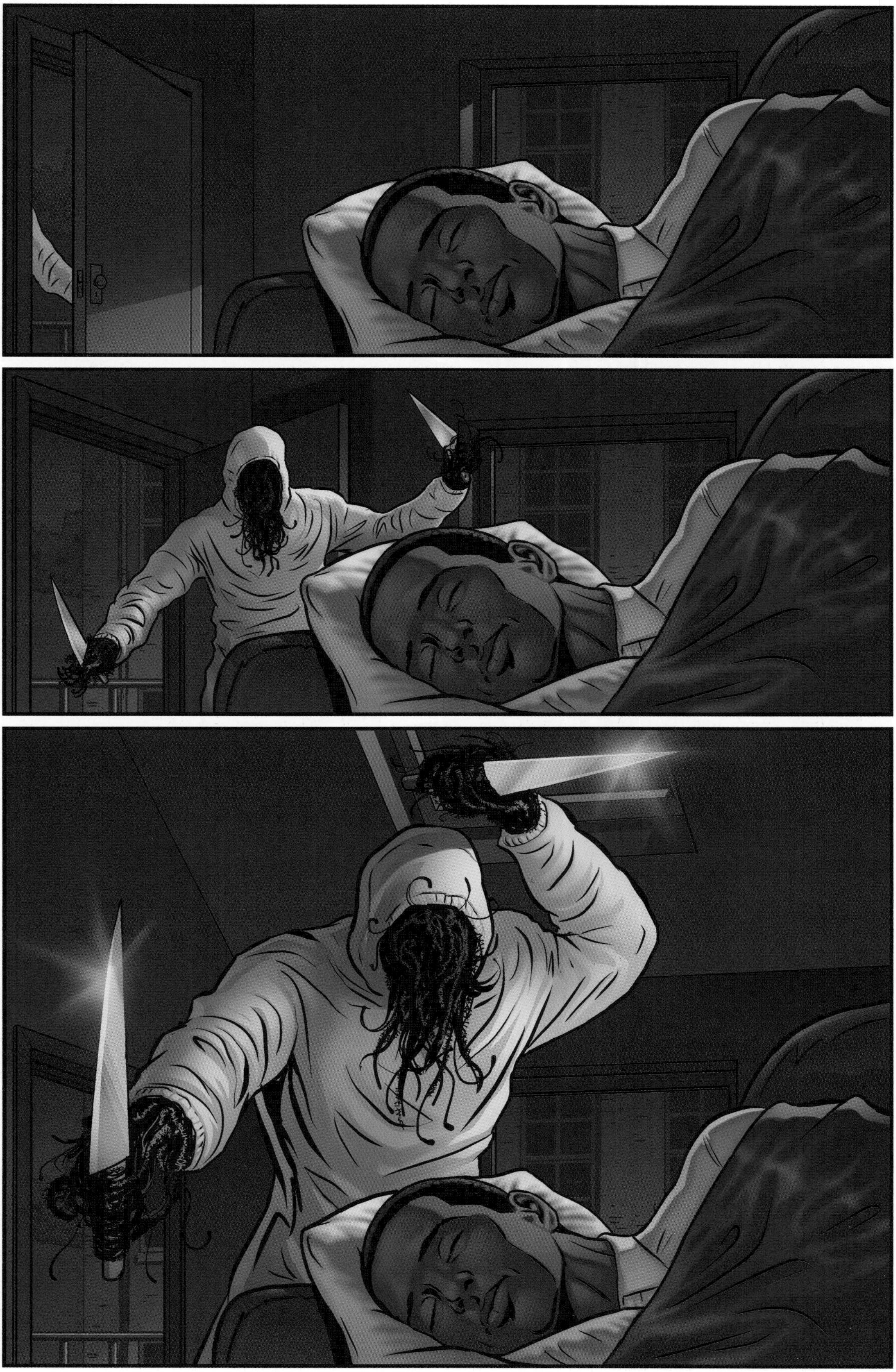

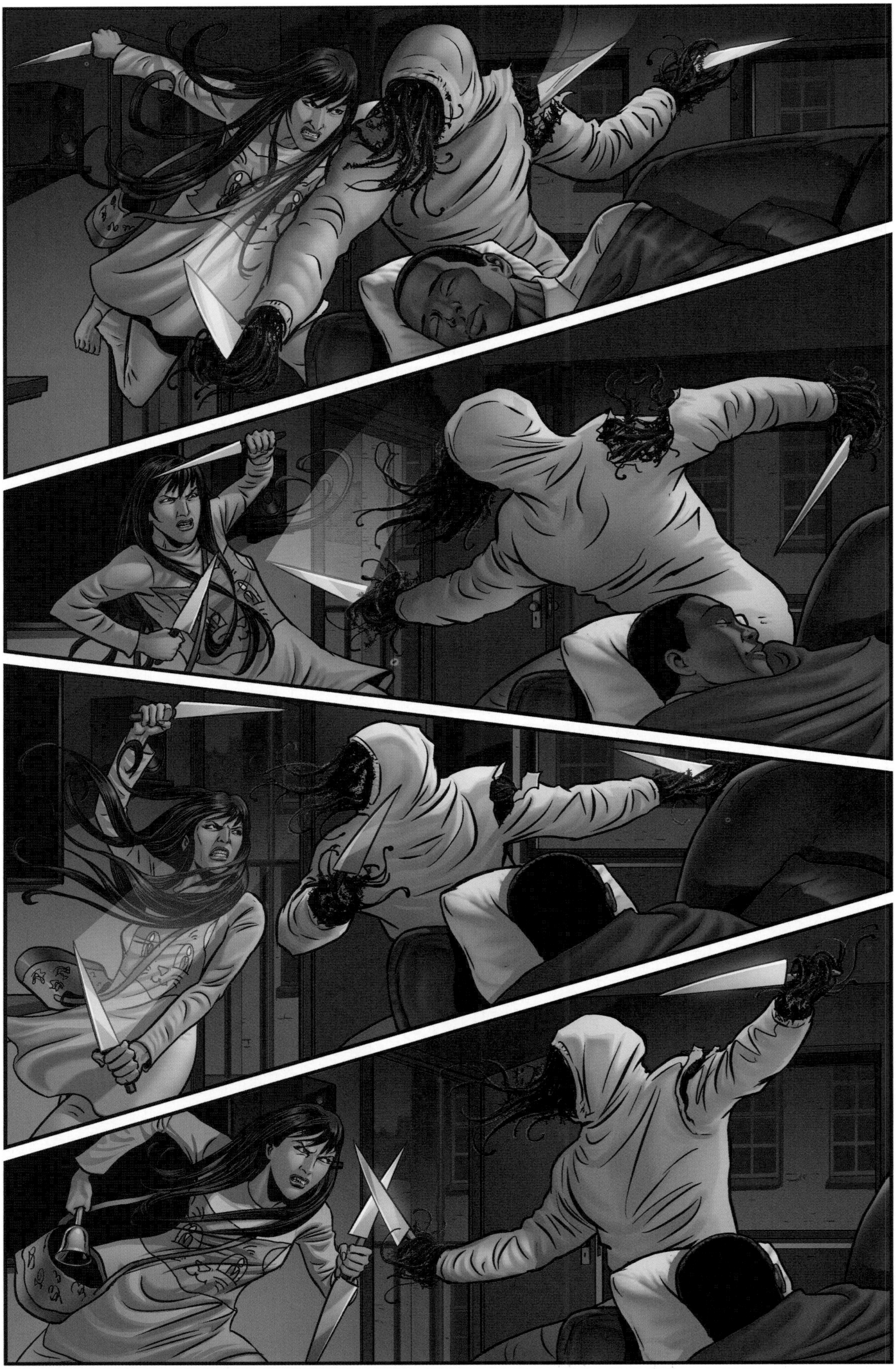

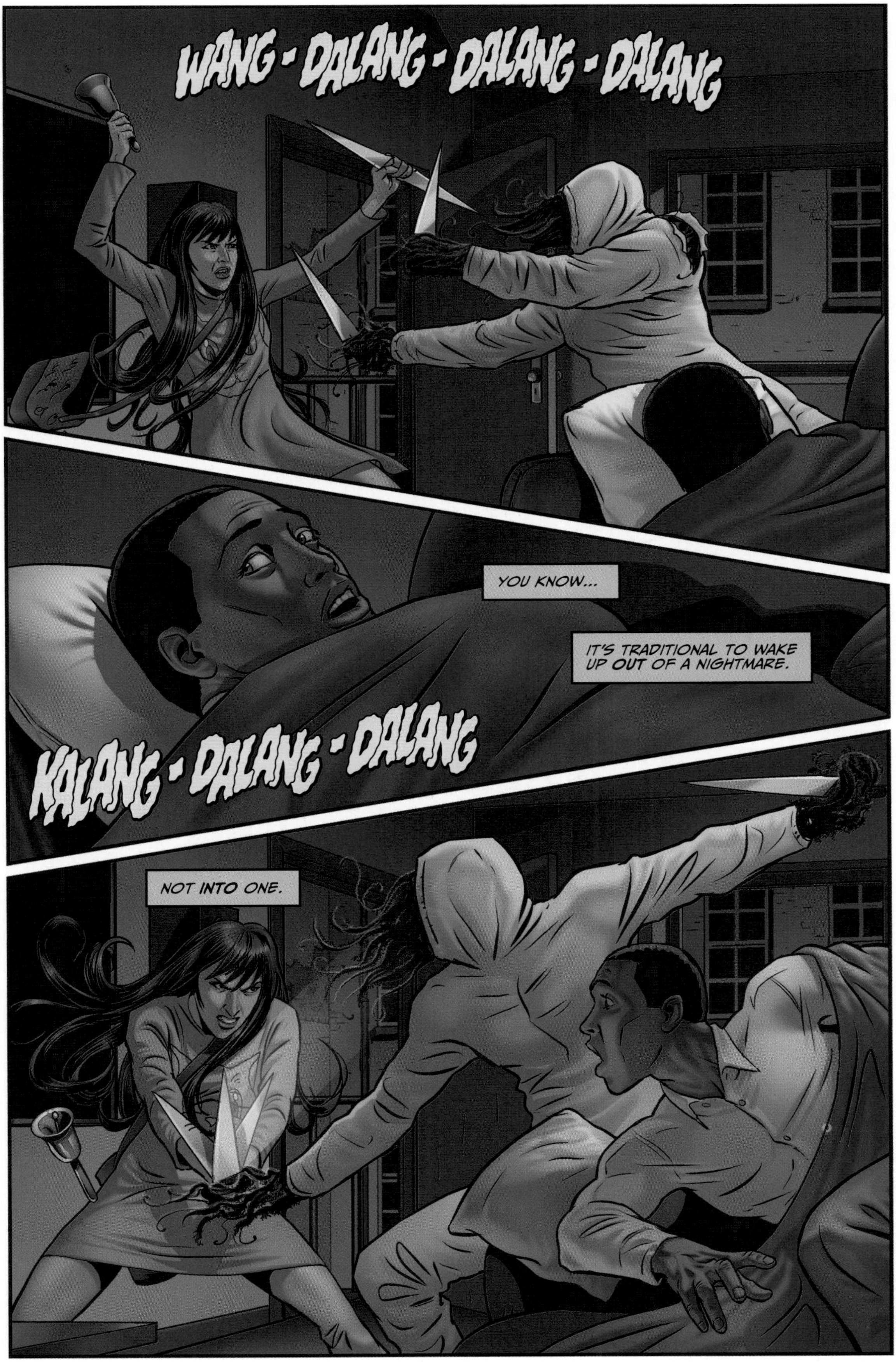
WANG - DALANG - DALANG - DALANG
YOU KNOW...
IT'S TRADITIONAL TO WAKE UP OUT OF A NIGHTMARE.
KALANG - DALANG - DALANG
NOT INTO ONE.

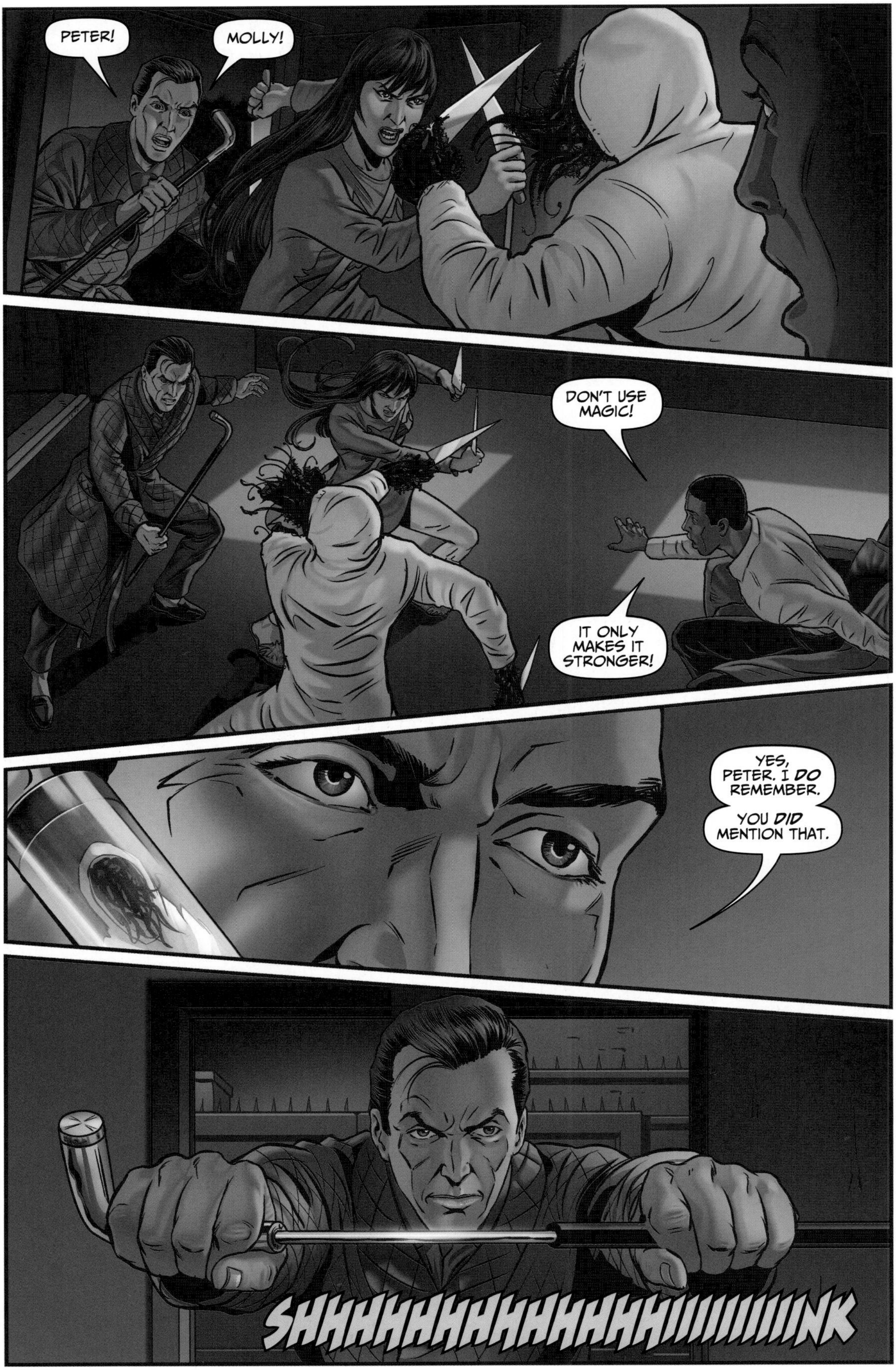
PETER!
MOLLY!
DON'T USE MAGIC!
IT ONLY MAKES IT STRONGER!
YES, PETER. I *DO* REMEMBER.
YOU *DID* MENTION THAT.
SHHHHHHHHHHHHHHHIIIIIIIIINK

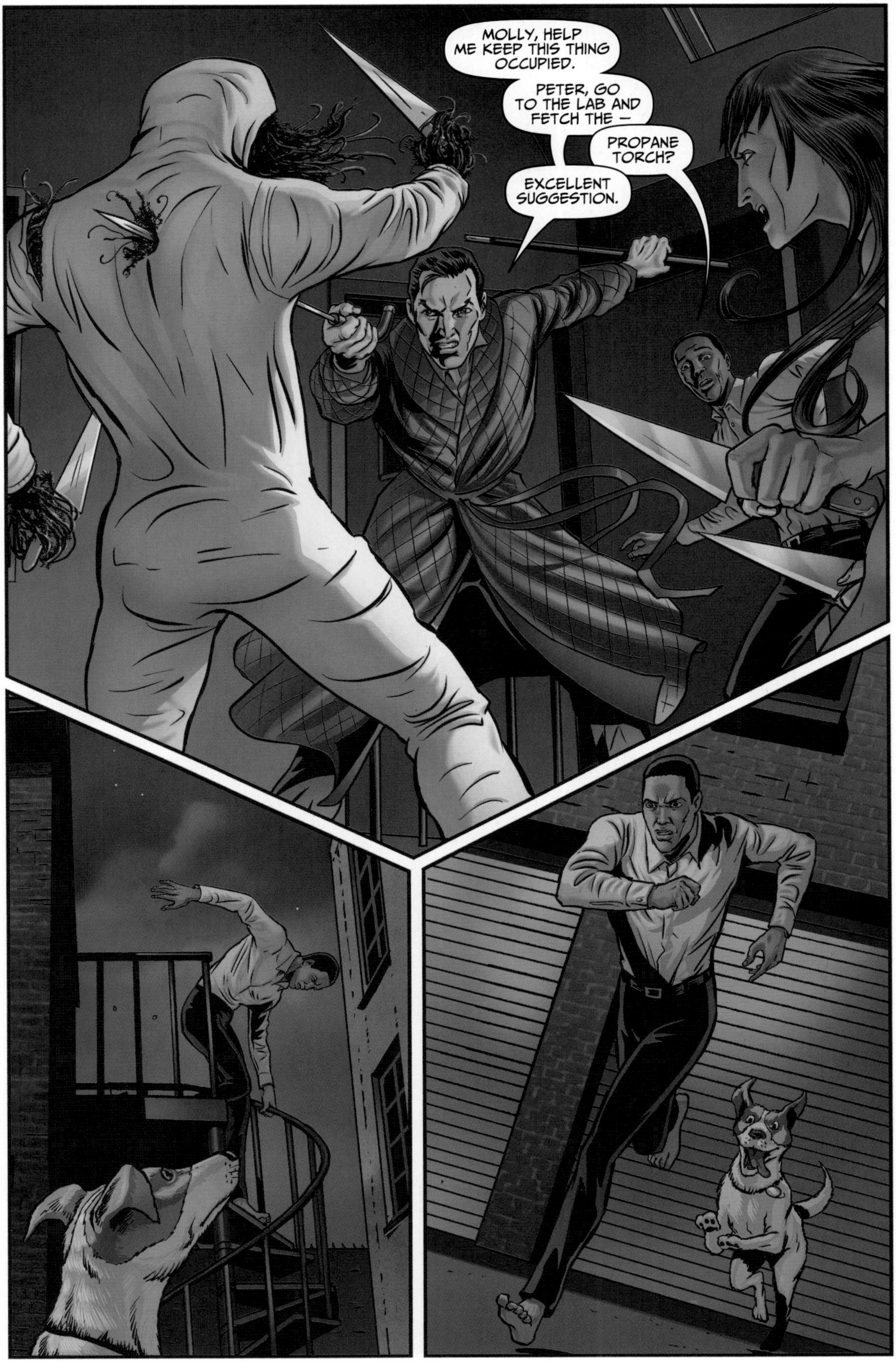
MOLLY, HELP ME KEEP THIS THING OCCUPIED.
PETER, GO TO THE LAB AND FETCH THE —
PROPANE TORCH?
EXCELLENT SUGGESTION.

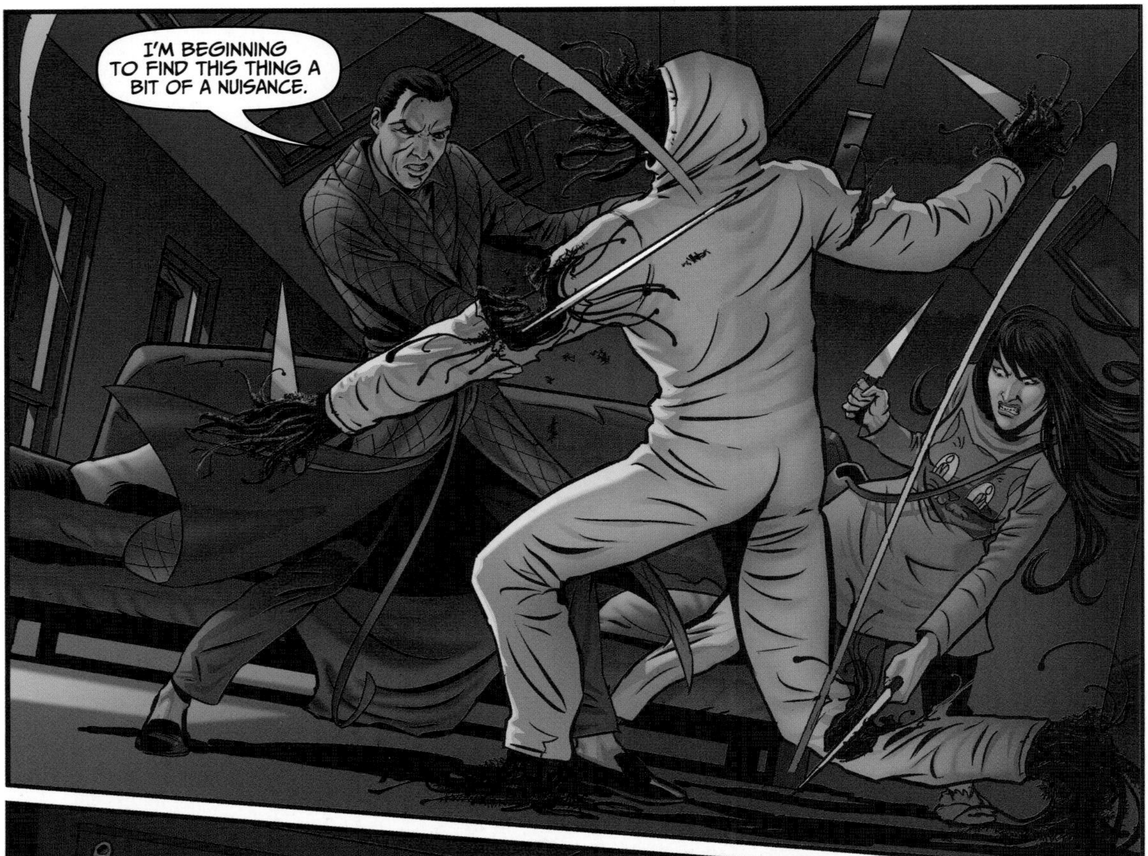
I'M BEGINNING TO FIND THIS THING A BIT OF A NUISANCE.

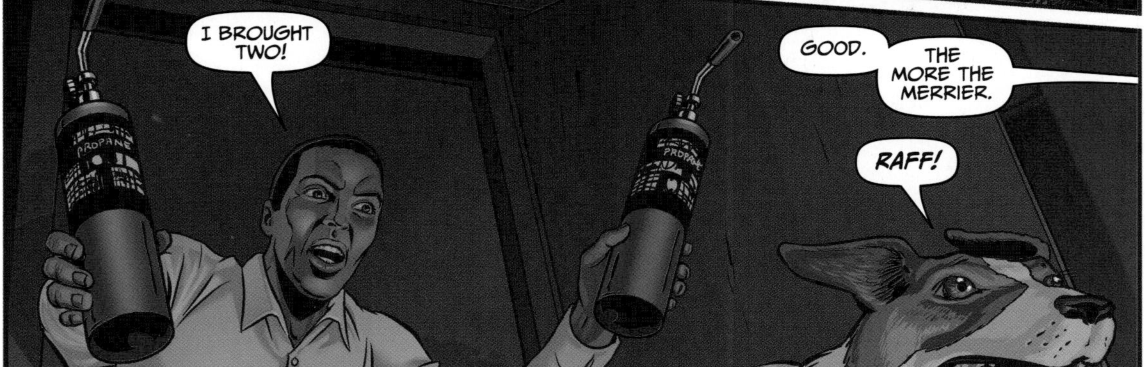
I BROUGHT TWO!
GOOD.
THE MORE THE MERRIER.
RAFF!
PROPANE
PROPANE

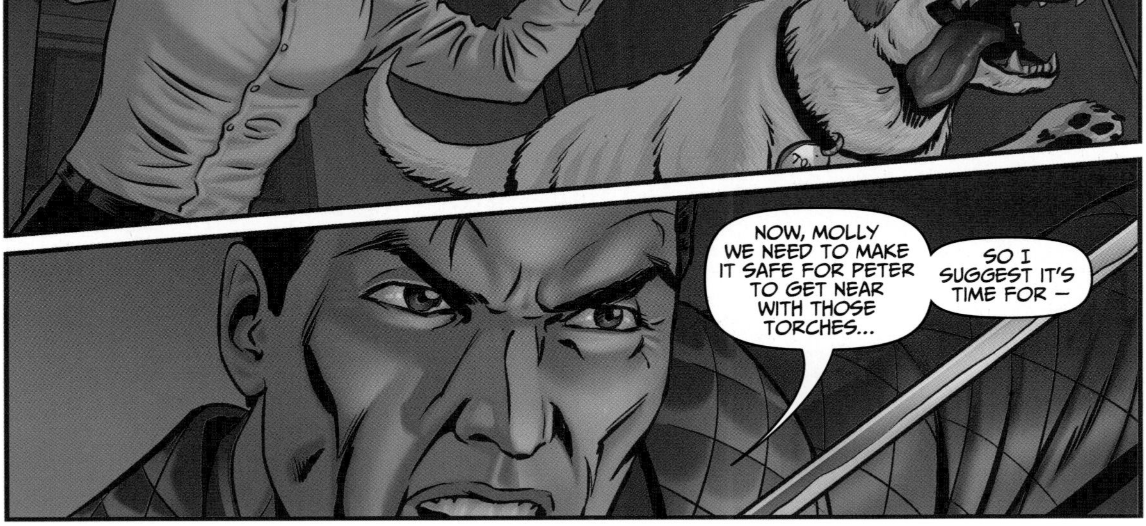
NOW, MOLLY WE NEED TO MAKE IT SAFE FOR PETER TO GET NEAR WITH THOSE TORCHES...
SO I SUGGEST IT'S TIME FOR —

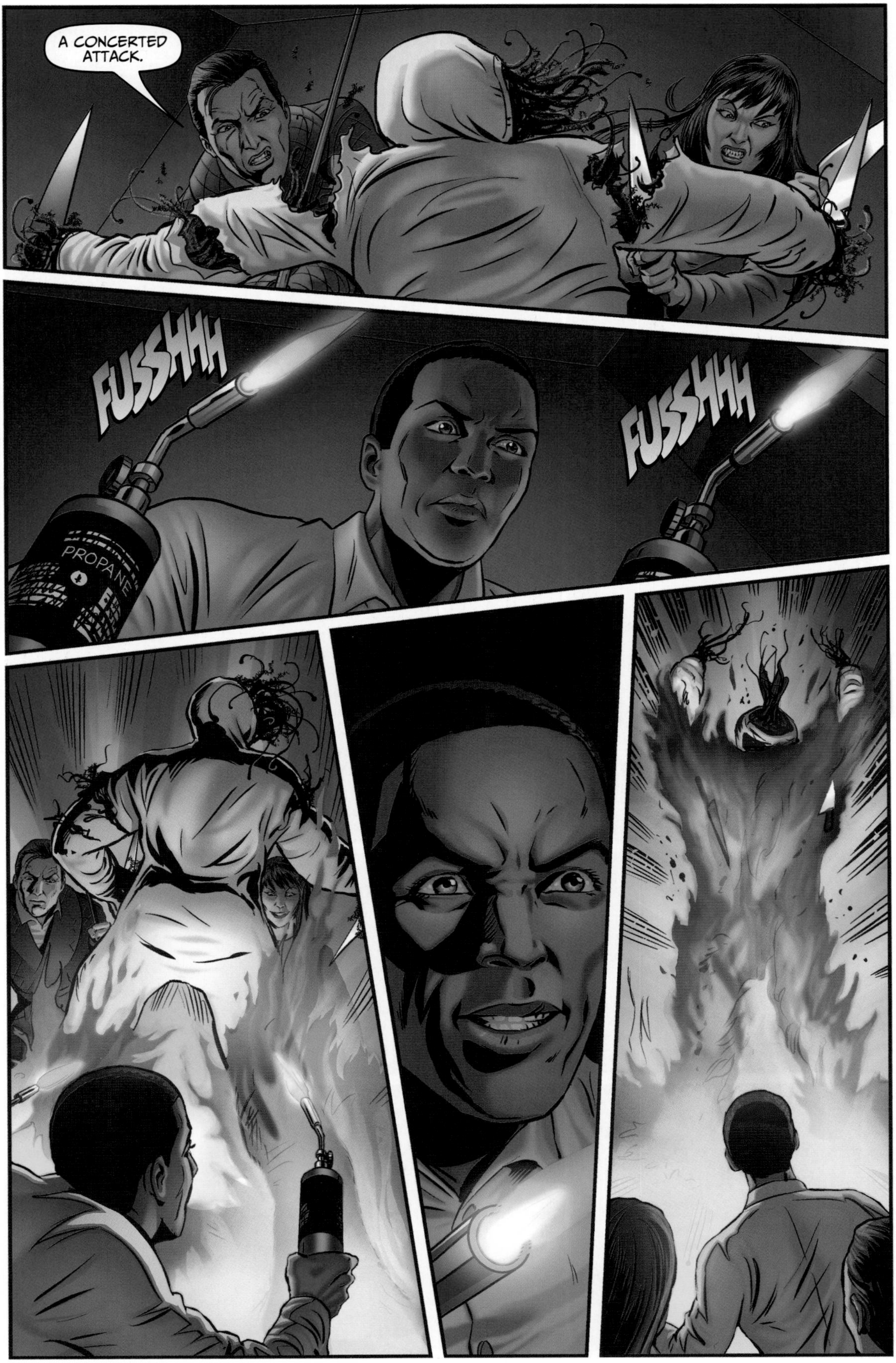
A CONCERTED ATTACK.
FUSSHHH
FUSSHHH
PROPANE

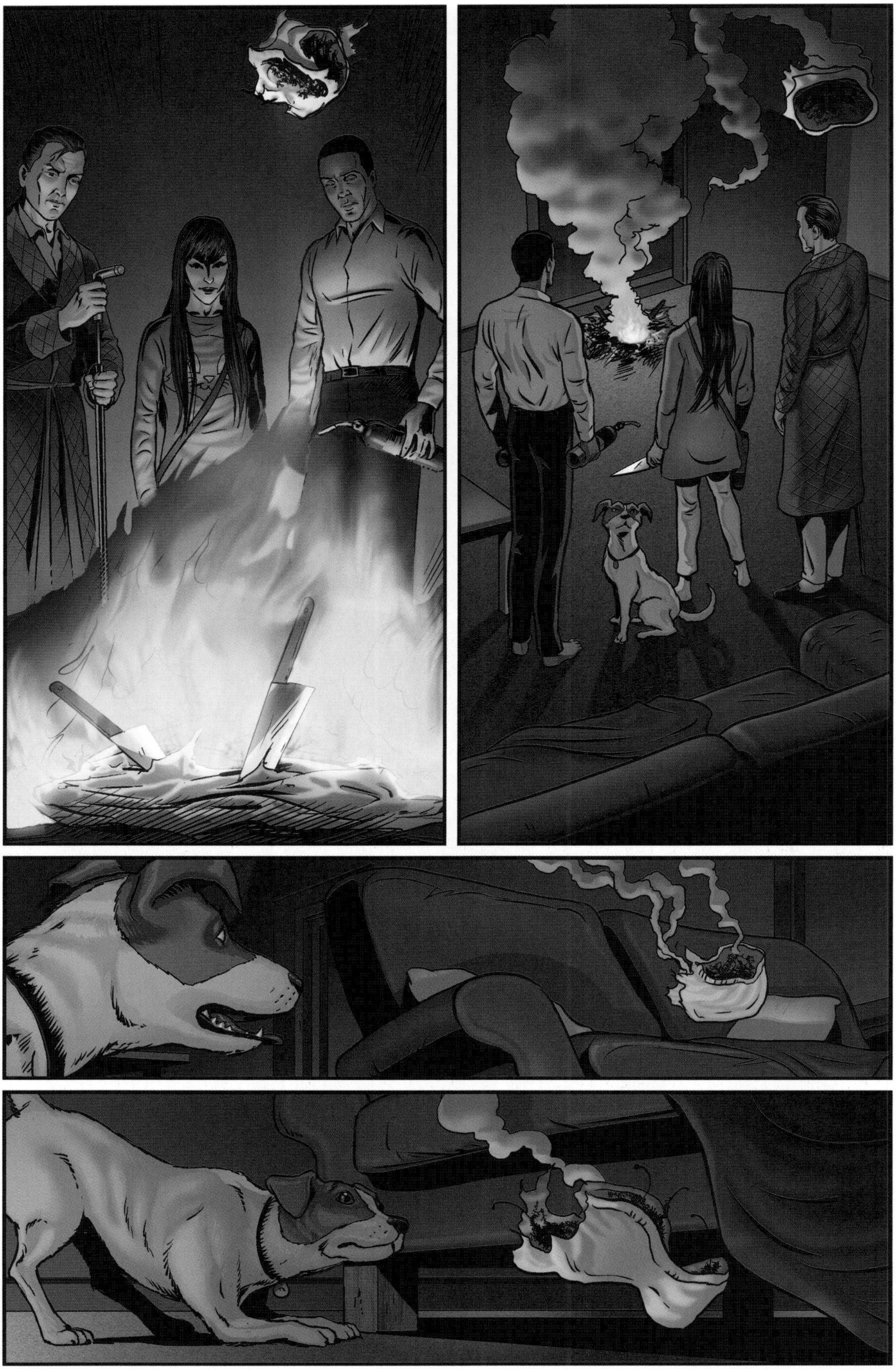

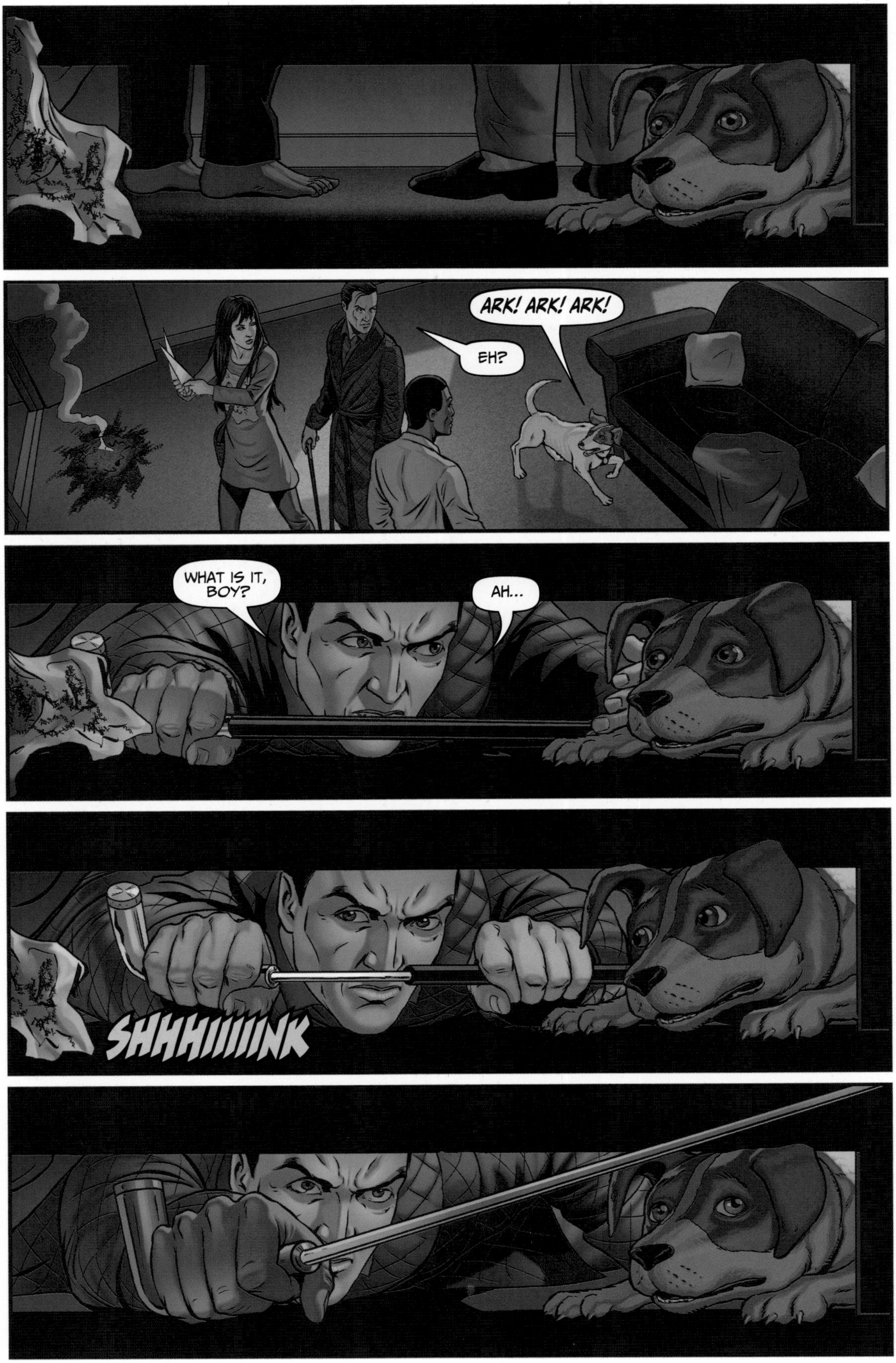

ARK! ARK! ARK!
EH?
WHAT IS IT, BOY?
AH...
SHHHIIIIINK

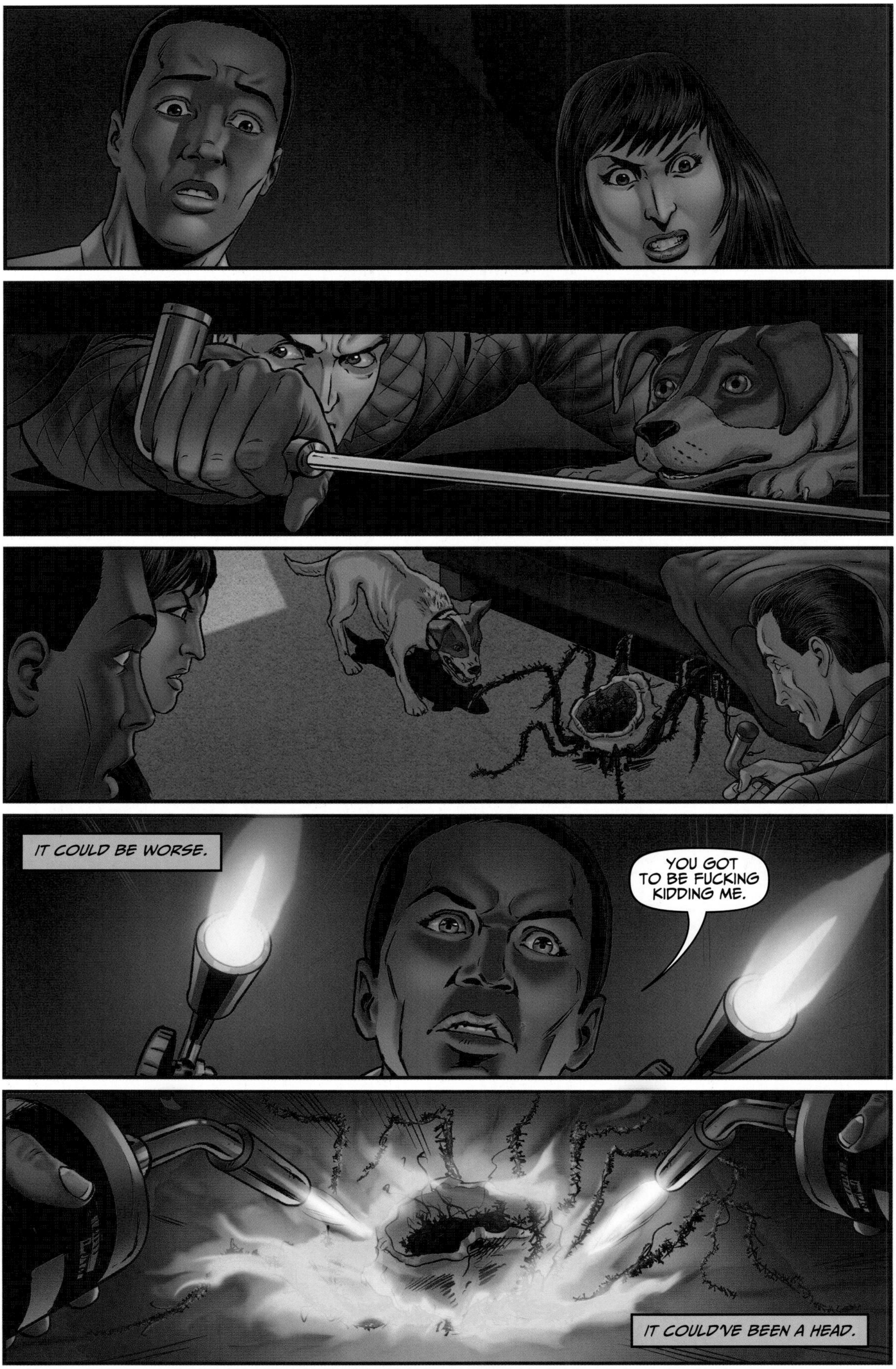
IT COULD BE WORSE.
YOU GOT TO BE FUCKING KIDDING ME.
IT COULD'VE BEEN A HEAD.

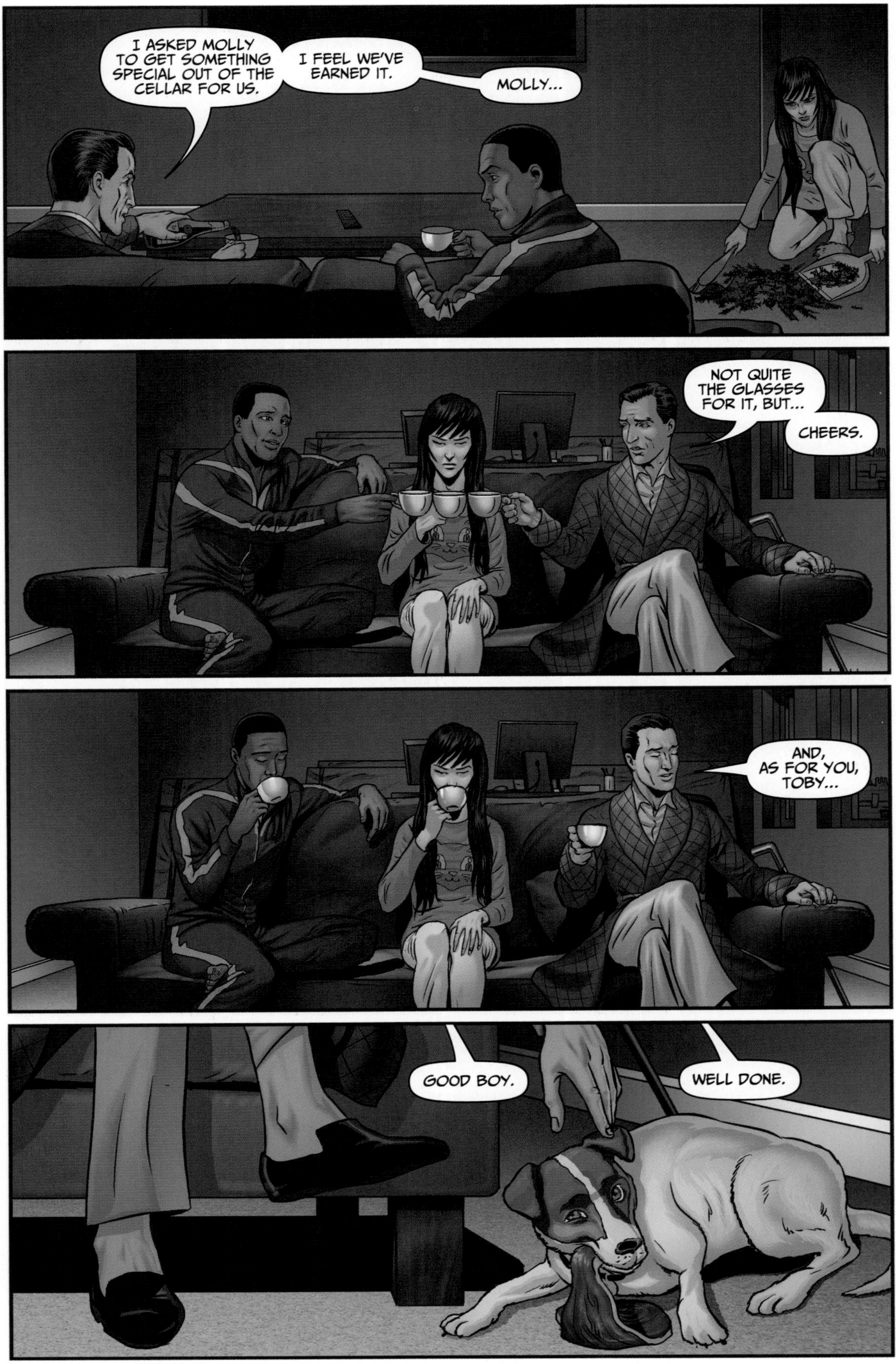
I ASKED MOLLY TO GET SOMETHING SPECIAL OUT OF THE CELLAR FOR US.
I FEEL WE'VE EARNED IT.
MOLLY...
NOT QUITE THE GLASSES FOR IT, BUT...
CHEERS.
AND, AS FOR YOU, TOBY...
GOOD BOY.
WELL DONE.

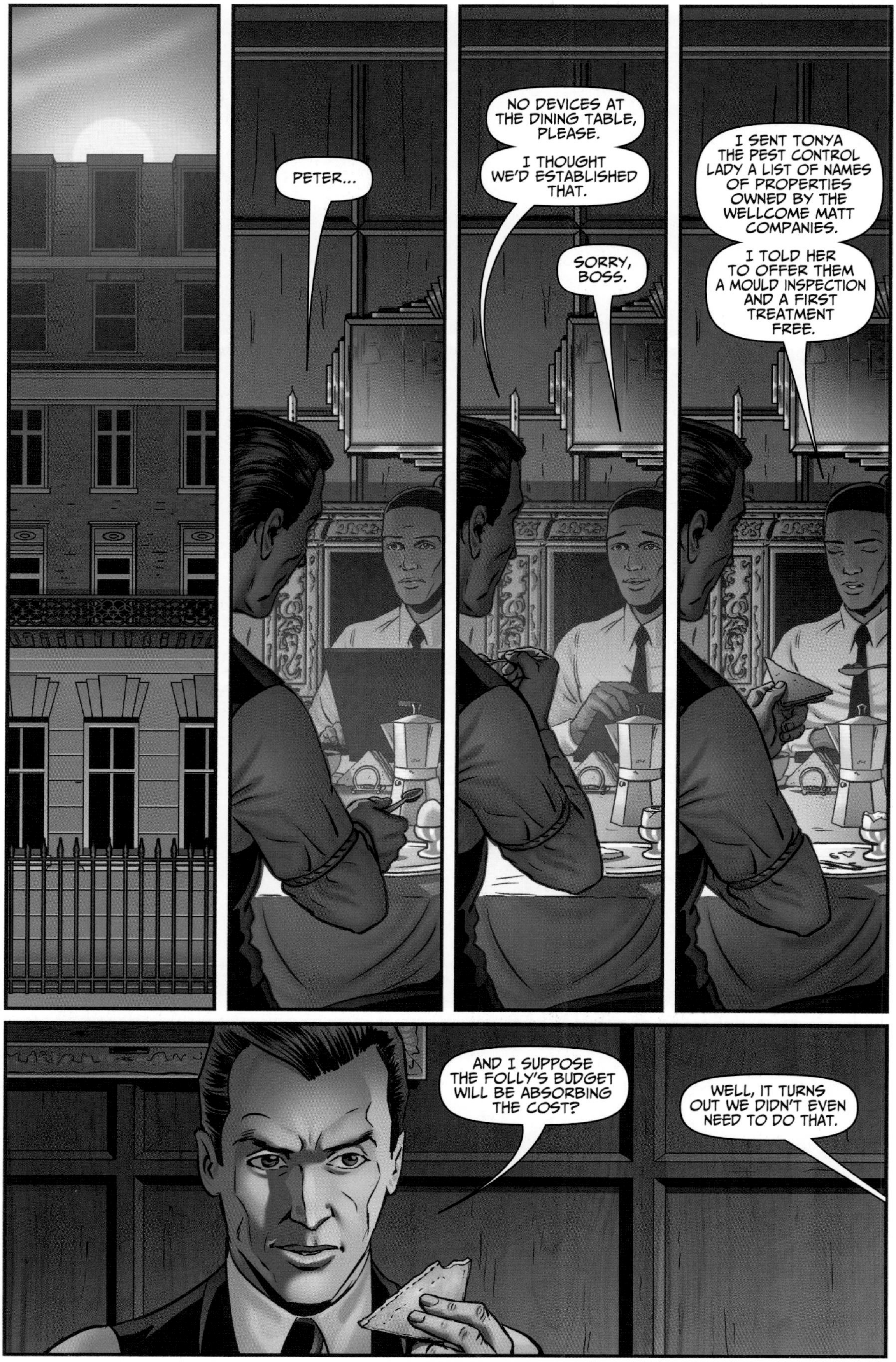
PETER...
NO DEVICES AT THE DINING TABLE, PLEASE.
I THOUGHT WE'D ESTABLISHED THAT.
SORRY, BOSS.
I SENT TONYA THE PEST CONTROL LADY A LIST OF NAMES OF PROPERTIES OWNED BY THE WELLCOME MATT COMPANIES.
I TOLD HER TO OFFER THEM A MOULD INSPECTION AND A FIRST TREATMENT FREE.
AND I SUPPOSE THE FOLLY'S BUDGET WILL BE ABSORBING THE COST?
WELL, IT TURNS OUT WE DIDN'T EVEN NEED TO DO THAT.

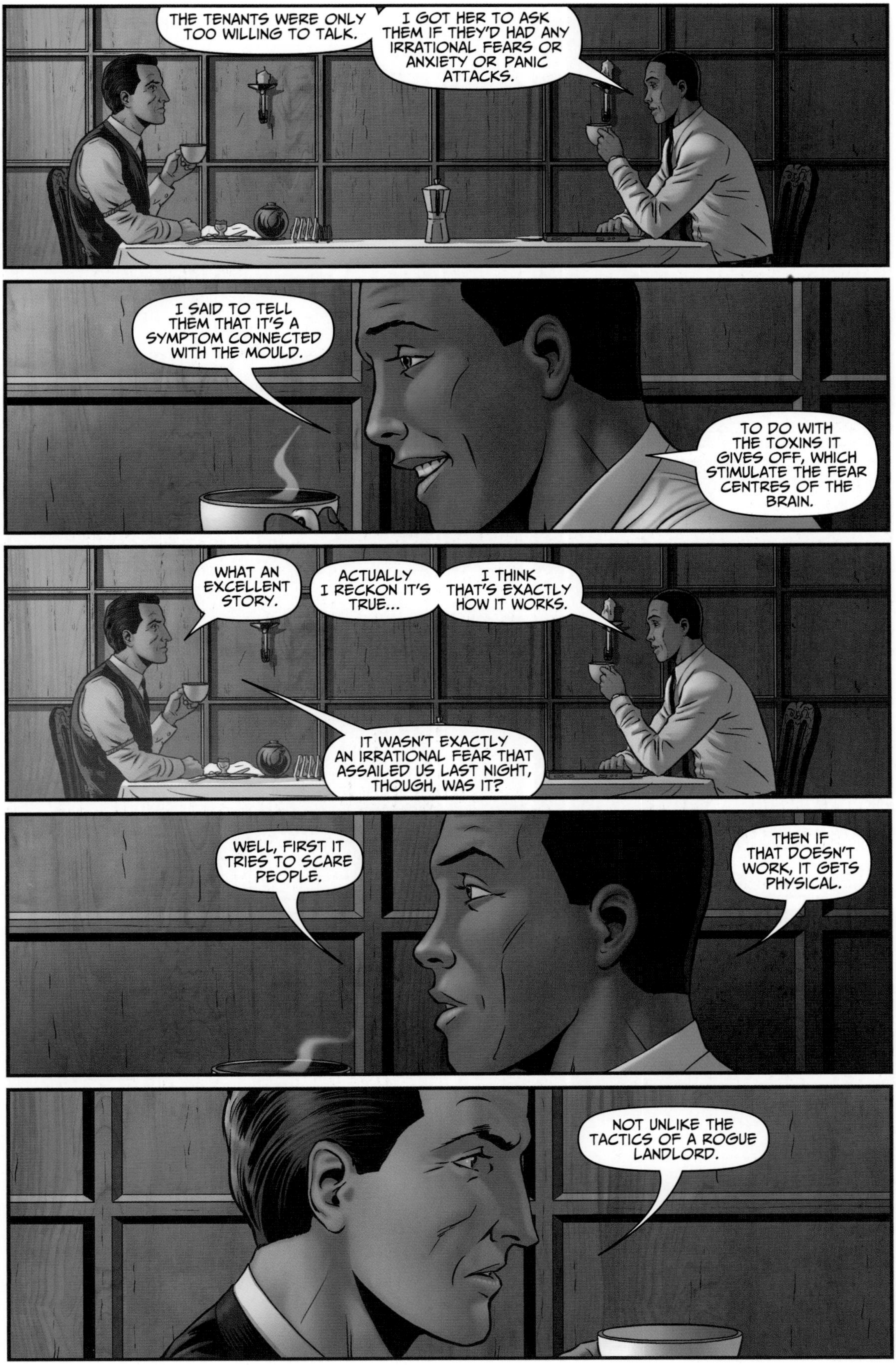
THE TENANTS WERE ONLY TOO WILLING TO TALK.
I GOT HER TO ASK THEM IF THEY'D HAD ANY IRRATIONAL FEARS OR ANXIETY OR PANIC ATTACKS.
I SAID TO TELL THEM THAT IT'S A SYMPTOM CONNECTED WITH THE MOULD.
TO DO WITH THE TOXINS IT GIVES OFF, WHICH STIMULATE THE FEAR CENTRES OF THE BRAIN.
WHAT AN EXCELLENT STORY.
ACTUALLY I RECKON IT'S TRUE...
I THINK THAT'S EXACTLY HOW IT WORKS.
IT WASN'T EXACTLY AN IRRATIONAL FEAR THAT ASSAILED US LAST NIGHT, THOUGH, WAS IT?
WELL, FIRST IT TRIES TO SCARE PEOPLE.
THEN IF THAT DOESN'T WORK, IT GETS PHYSICAL.
NOT UNLIKE THE TACTICS OF A ROGUE LANDLORD.

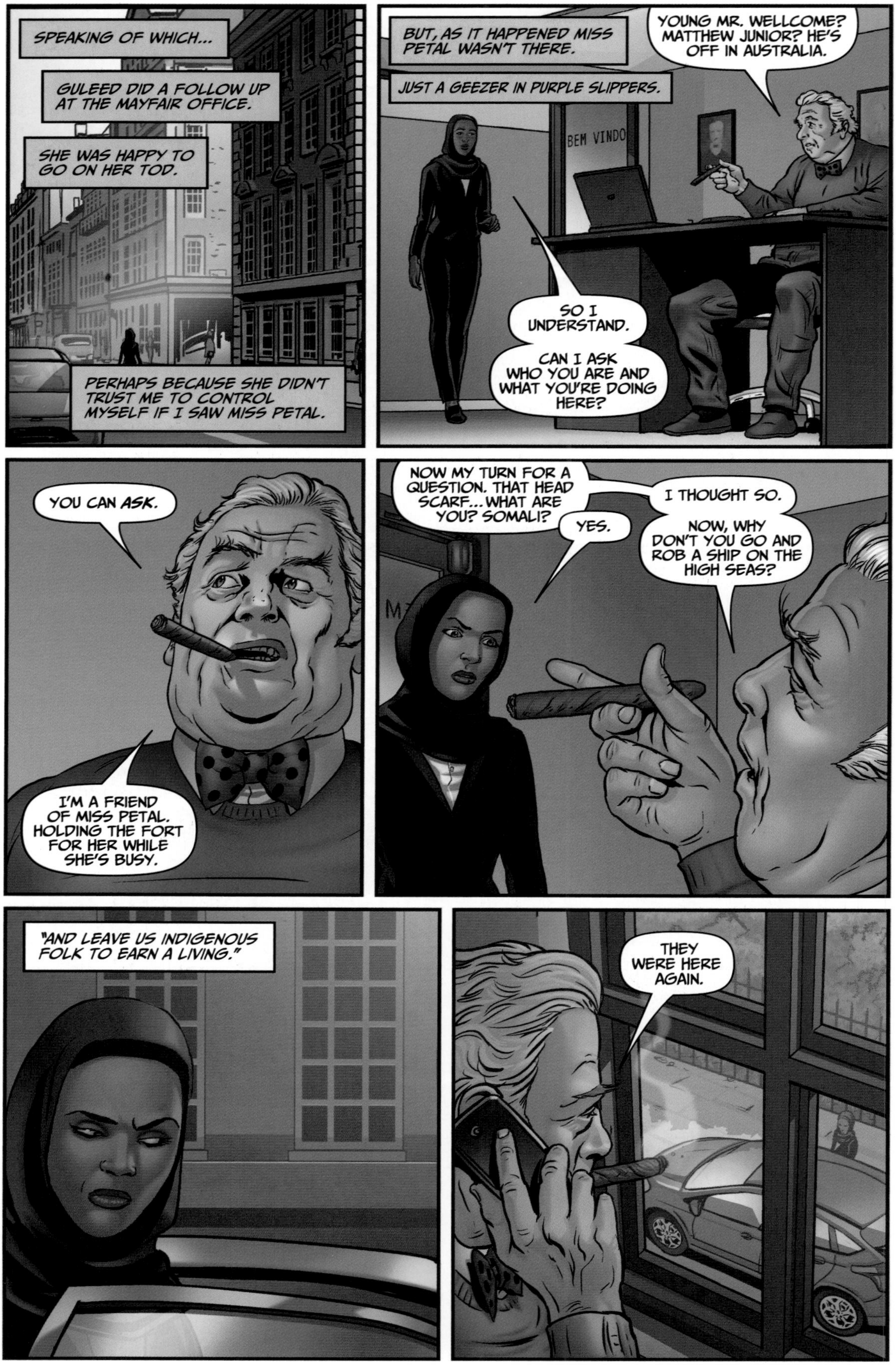
SPEAKING OF WHICH...
GULEED DID A FOLLOW UP AT THE MAYFAIR OFFICE.
SHE WAS HAPPY TO GO ON HER TOD.
PERHAPS BECAUSE SHE DIDN'T TRUST ME TO CONTROL MYSELF IF I SAW MISS PETAL.
BUT, AS IT HAPPENED MISS PETAL WASN'T THERE.
JUST A GEEZER IN PURPLE SLIPPERS.
BEM VINDO
YOUNG MR. WELLCOME? MATTHEW JUNIOR? HE'S OFF IN AUSTRALIA.
SO I UNDERSTAND.
CAN I ASK WHO YOU ARE AND WHAT YOU'RE DOING HERE?
YOU CAN ASK.
I'M A FRIEND OF MISS PETAL. HOLDING THE FORT FOR HER WHILE SHE'S BUSY.
NOW MY TURN FOR A QUESTION. THAT HEAD SCARF... WHAT ARE YOU? SOMALI?
YES.
I THOUGHT SO.
NOW, WHY DON'T YOU GO AND ROB A SHIP ON THE HIGH SEAS?
"AND LEAVE US INDIGENOUS FOLK TO EARN A LIVING."
THEY WERE HERE AGAIN.

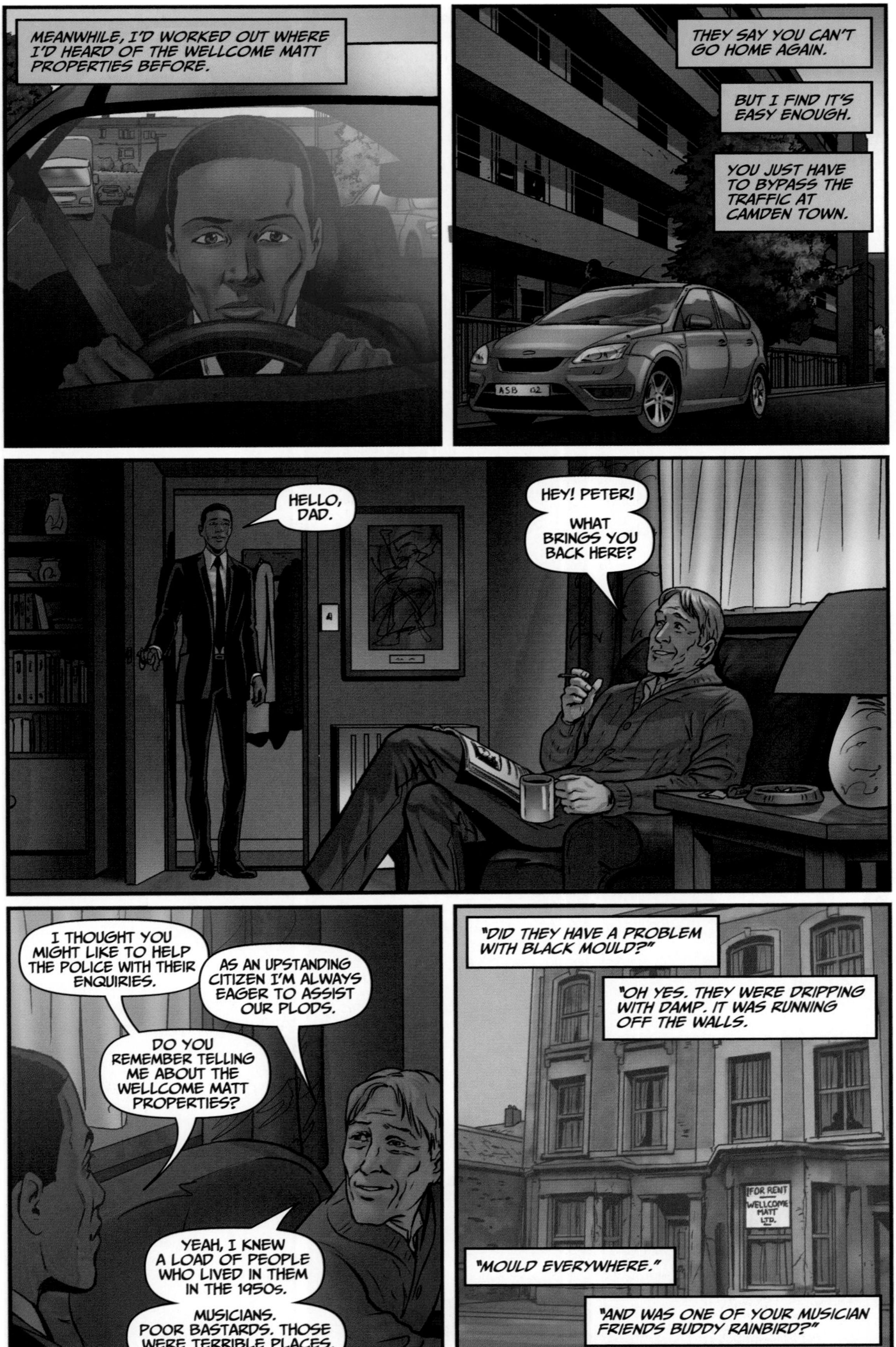

MEANWHILE, I'D WORKED OUT WHERE I'D HEARD OF THE WELLCOME MATT PROPERTIES BEFORE.
THEY SAY YOU CAN'T GO HOME AGAIN.
BUT I FIND IT'S EASY ENOUGH.
YOU JUST HAVE TO BYPASS THE TRAFFIC AT CAMDEN TOWN.
ASB 02
HELLO, DAD.
HEY! PETER!
WHAT BRINGS YOU BACK HERE?
I THOUGHT YOU MIGHT LIKE TO HELP THE POLICE WITH THEIR ENQUIRIES.
AS AN UPSTANDING CITIZEN I'M ALWAYS EAGER TO ASSIST OUR PLODS.
DO YOU REMEMBER TELLING ME ABOUT THE WELLCOME MATT PROPERTIES?
YEAH, I KNEW A LOAD OF PEOPLE WHO LIVED IN THEM IN THE 1950s.
MUSICIANS. POOR BASTARDS. THOSE WERE TERRIBLE PLACES.
"DID THEY HAVE A PROBLEM WITH BLACK MOULD?"
"OH YES. THEY WERE DRIPPING WITH DAMP. IT WAS RUNNING OFF THE WALLS.
FOR RENT
WELLCOME MATT LTD.
"MOULD EVERYWHERE."
"AND WAS ONE OF YOUR MUSICIAN FRIENDS BUDDY RAINBIRD?"

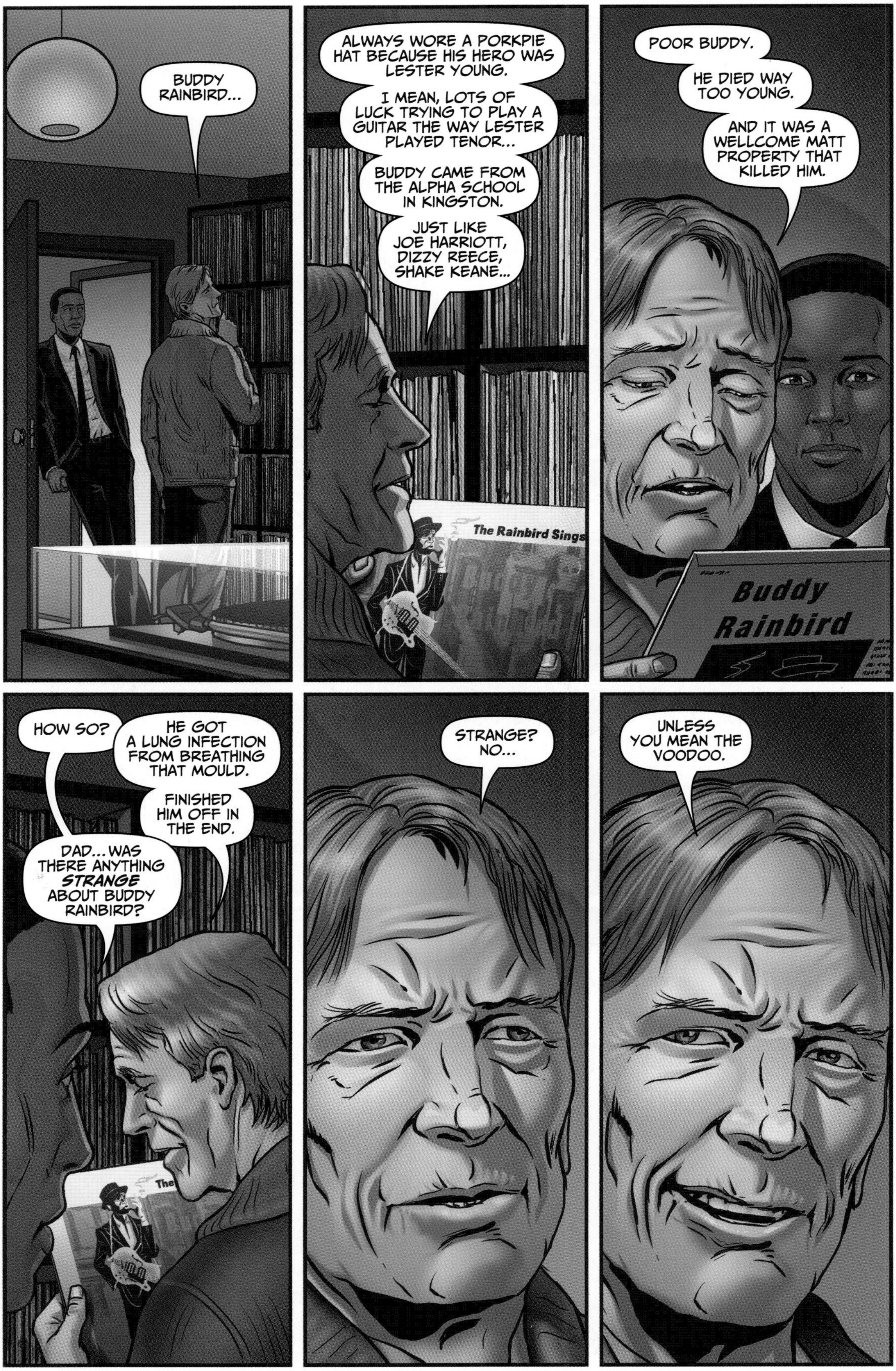
BUDDY RAINBIRD...
ALWAYS WORE A PORKPIE HAT BECAUSE HIS HERO WAS LESTER YOUNG.
I MEAN, LOTS OF LUCK TRYING TO PLAY A GUITAR THE WAY LESTER PLAYED TENOR...
BUDDY CAME FROM THE ALPHA SCHOOL IN KINGSTON.
JUST LIKE JOE HARRIOTT, DIZZY REECE, SHAKE KEANE...
The Rainbird Sings
POOR BUDDY.
HE DIED WAY TOO YOUNG.
AND IT WAS A WELLCOME MATT PROPERTY THAT KILLED HIM.
Buddy Rainbird
HOW SO?
HE GOT A LUNG INFECTION FROM BREATHING THAT MOULD.
FINISHED HIM OFF IN THE END.
DAD...WAS THERE ANYTHING *STRANGE* ABOUT BUDDY RAINBIRD?
STRANGE? NO...
UNLESS YOU MEAN THE VOODOO.

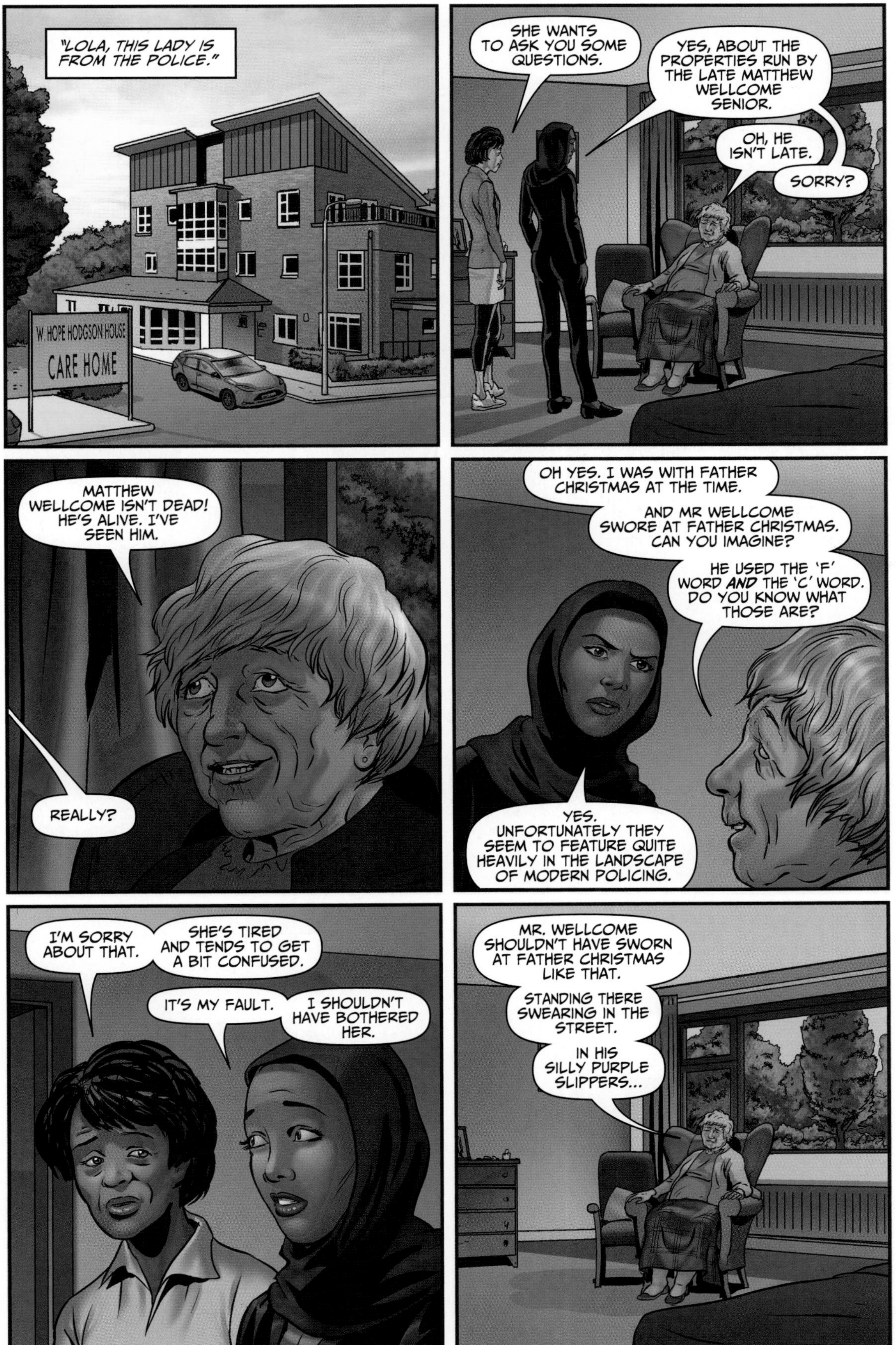
"LOLA, THIS LADY IS FROM THE POLICE."
W. HOPE HODGSON HOUSE
CARE HOME
SHE WANTS TO ASK YOU SOME QUESTIONS.
YES, ABOUT THE PROPERTIES RUN BY THE LATE MATTHEW WELLCOME SENIOR.
OH, HE ISN'T LATE.
SORRY?
MATTHEW WELLCOME ISN'T DEAD! HE'S ALIVE. I'VE SEEN HIM.
REALLY?
OH YES. I WAS WITH FATHER CHRISTMAS AT THE TIME.
AND MR WELLCOME SWORE AT FATHER CHRISTMAS. CAN YOU IMAGINE?
HE USED THE 'F' WORD AND THE 'C' WORD. DO YOU KNOW WHAT THOSE ARE?
YES. UNFORTUNATELY THEY SEEM TO FEATURE QUITE HEAVILY IN THE LANDSCAPE OF MODERN POLICING.
I'M SORRY ABOUT THAT.
SHE'S TIRED AND TENDS TO GET A BIT CONFUSED.
IT'S MY FAULT.
I SHOULDN'T HAVE BOTHERED HER.
MR. WELLCOME SHOULDN'T HAVE SWORN AT FATHER CHRISTMAS LIKE THAT.
STANDING THERE SWEARING IN THE STREET.
IN HIS SILLY PURPLE SLIPPERS...

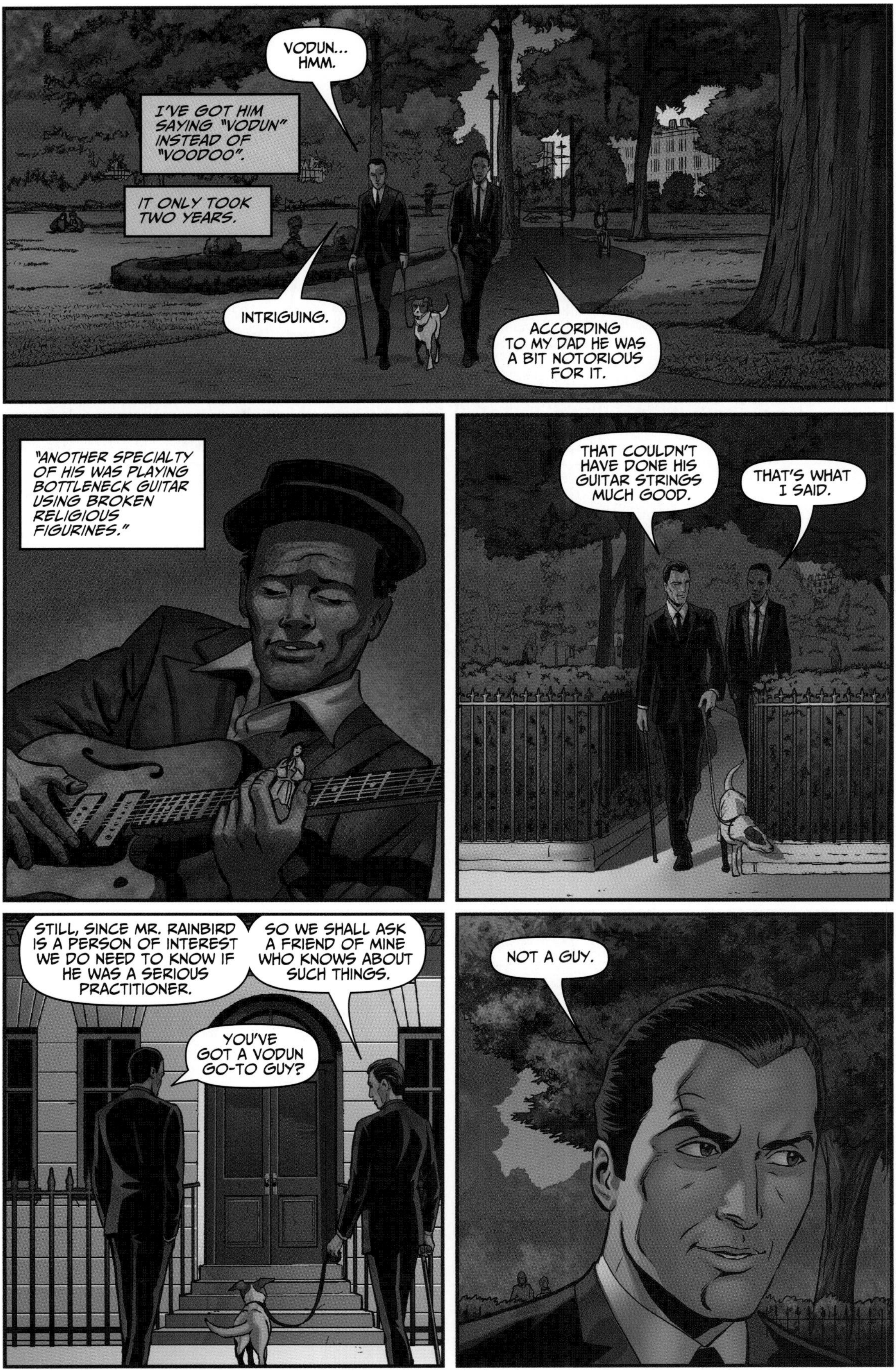
VODUN... HMM.
I'VE GOT HIM SAYING "VODUN" INSTEAD OF "VOODOO".
IT ONLY TOOK TWO YEARS.
INTRIGUING.
ACCORDING TO MY DAD HE WAS A BIT NOTORIOUS FOR IT.
"ANOTHER SPECIALTY OF HIS WAS PLAYING BOTTLENECK GUITAR USING BROKEN RELIGIOUS FIGURINES."
THAT COULDN'T HAVE DONE HIS GUITAR STRINGS MUCH GOOD.
THAT'S WHAT I SAID.
STILL, SINCE MR. RAINBIRD IS A PERSON OF INTEREST WE DO NEED TO KNOW IF HE WAS A SERIOUS PRACTITIONER.
SO WE SHALL ASK A FRIEND OF MINE WHO KNOWS ABOUT SUCH THINGS.
YOU'VE GOT A VODUN GO-TO GUY?
NOT A GUY.

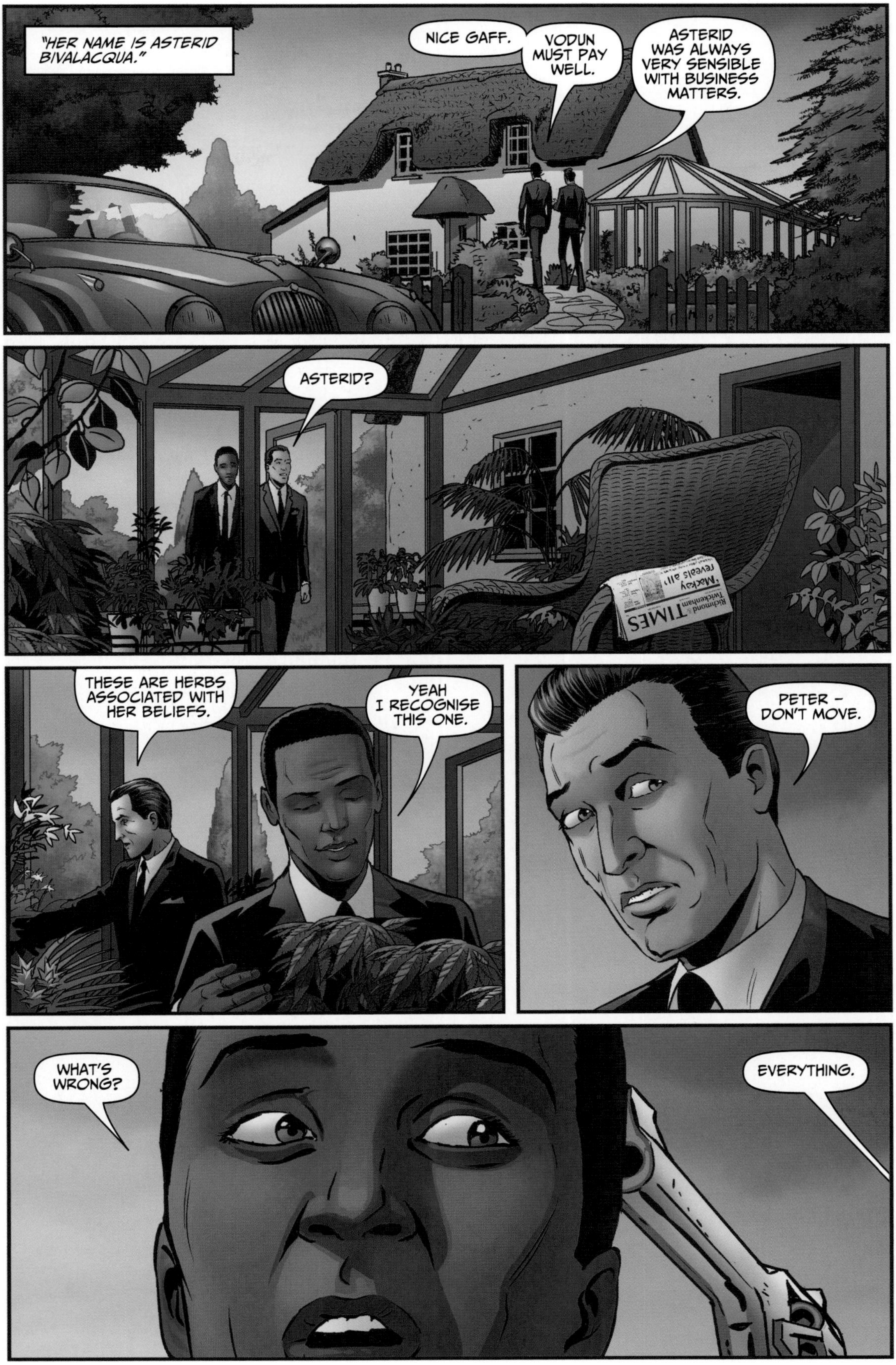
"HER NAME IS ASTERID BIVALACQUA."
NICE GAFF.
VODUN MUST PAY WELL.
ASTERID WAS ALWAYS VERY SENSIBLE WITH BUSINESS MATTERS.
ASTERID?
THESE ARE HERBS ASSOCIATED WITH HER BELIEFS.
YEAH I RECOGNISE THIS ONE.
PETER – DON'T MOVE.
WHAT'S WRONG?
EVERYTHING.

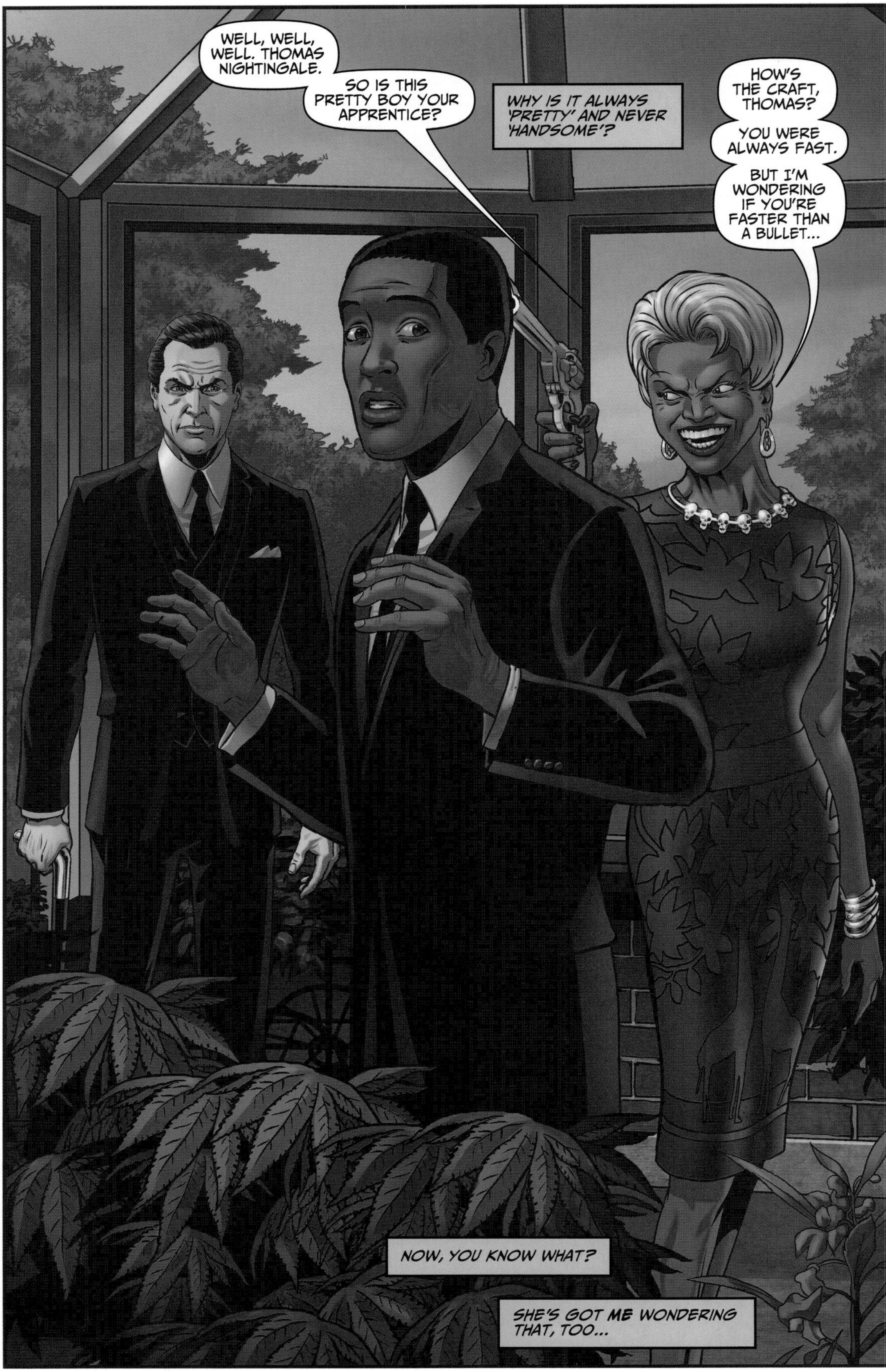
WELL, WELL, WELL. THOMAS NIGHTINGALE.
SO IS THIS PRETTY BOY YOUR APPRENTICE?
WHY IS IT ALWAYS 'PRETTY' AND NEVER 'HANDSOME'?
HOW'S THE CRAFT, THOMAS?
YOU WERE ALWAYS FAST.
BUT I'M WONDERING IF YOU'RE FASTER THAN A BULLET...
NOW, YOU KNOW WHAT?
SHE'S GOT ME WONDERING THAT, TOO...

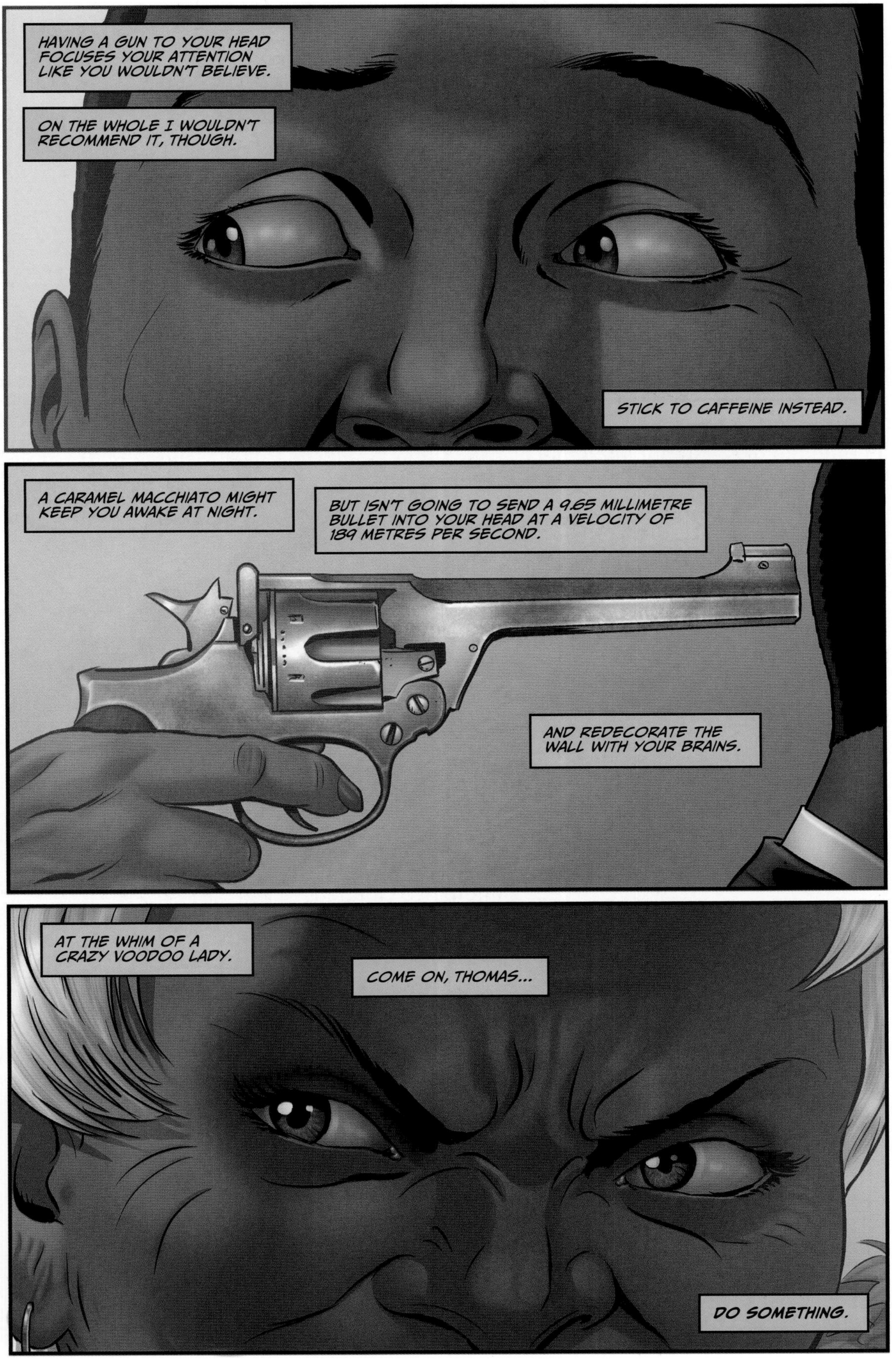
HAVING A GUN TO YOUR HEAD FOCUSES YOUR ATTENTION LIKE YOU WOULDN'T BELIEVE.
ON THE WHOLE I WOULDN'T RECOMMEND IT, THOUGH.
STICK TO CAFFEINE INSTEAD.
A CARAMEL MACCHIATO MIGHT KEEP YOU AWAKE AT NIGHT.
BUT ISN'T GOING TO SEND A 9.65 MILLIMETRE BULLET INTO YOUR HEAD AT A VELOCITY OF 189 METRES PER SECOND.
AND REDECORATE THE WALL WITH YOUR BRAINS.
AT THE WHIM OF A CRAZY VOODOO LADY.
COME ON, THOMAS...
DO SOMETHING.

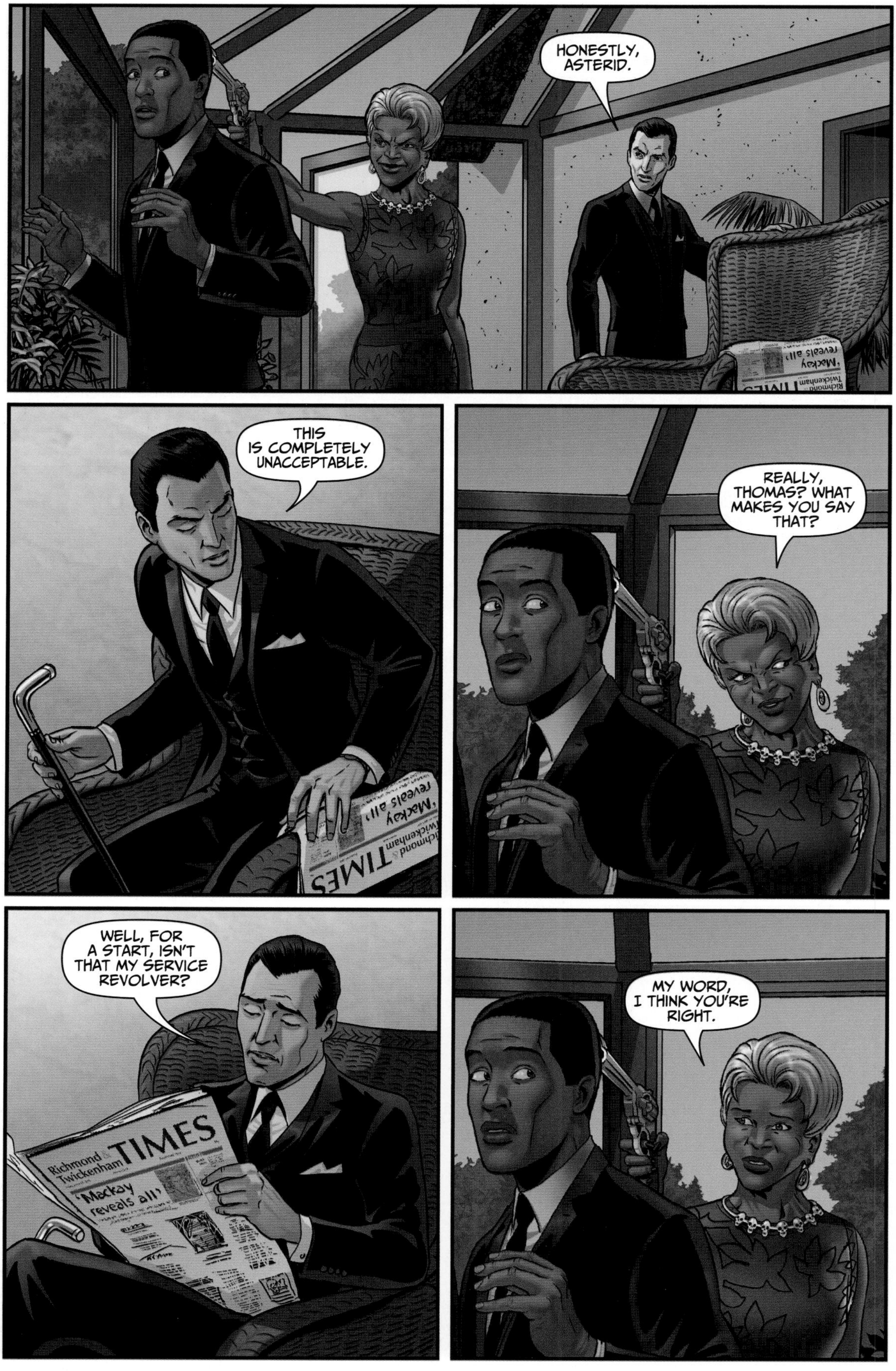
HONESTLY, ASTERID.
THIS IS COMPLETELY UNACCEPTABLE.
REALLY, THOMAS? WHAT MAKES YOU SAY THAT?
WELL, FOR A START, ISN'T THAT MY SERVICE REVOLVER?
Richmond & Twickenham TIMES
'Mackay reveals all'
MY WORD, I THINK YOU'RE RIGHT.

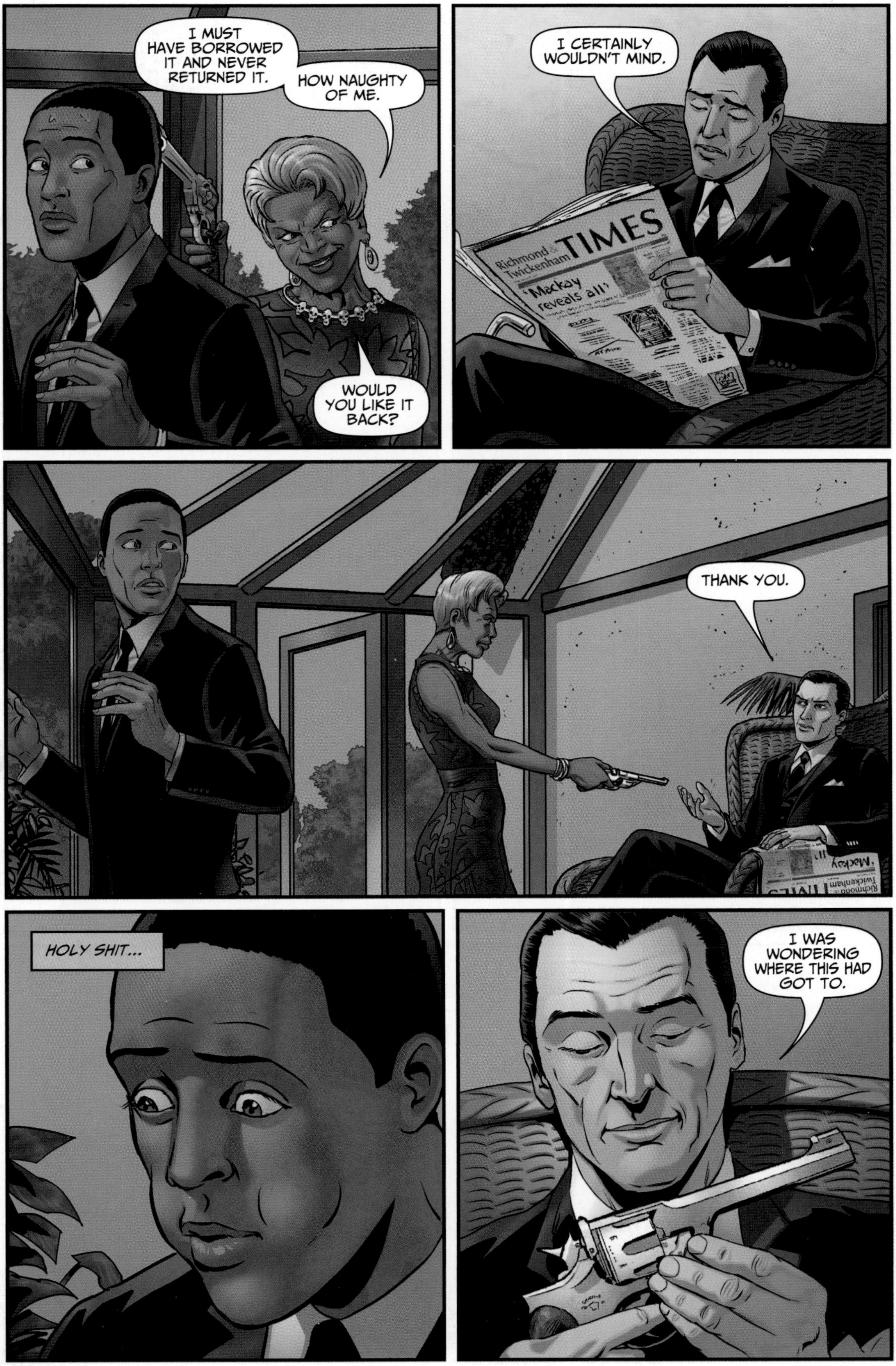
I MUST HAVE BORROWED IT AND NEVER RETURNED IT.
HOW NAUGHTY OF ME.
WOULD YOU LIKE IT BACK?
I CERTAINLY WOULDN'T MIND.
Richmond & Twickenham TIMES
'Mackay reveals all'
THANK YOU.
HOLY SHIT...
I WAS WONDERING WHERE THIS HAD GOT TO.

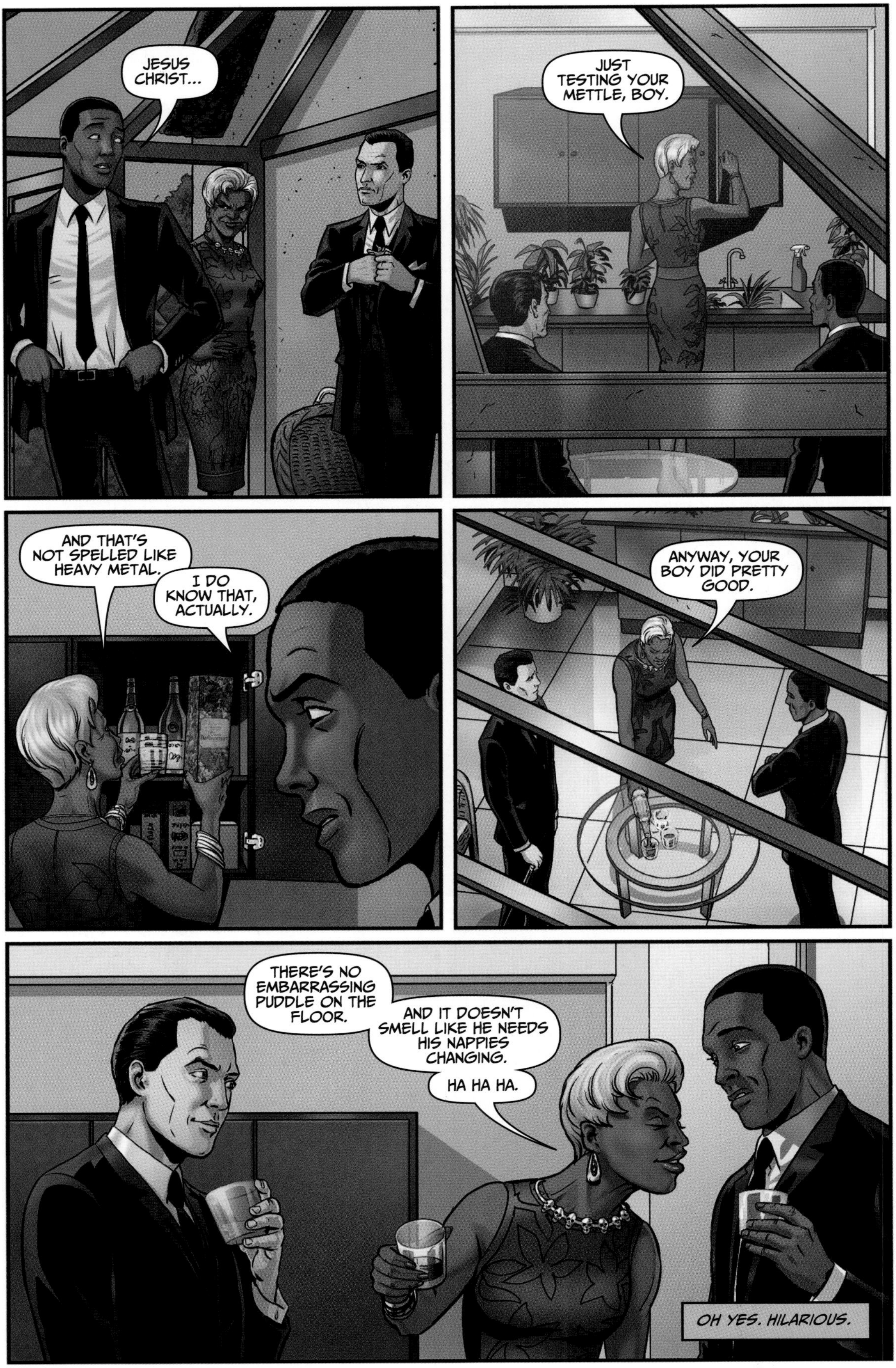
JESUS CHRIST...
JUST TESTING YOUR METTLE, BOY.
AND THAT'S NOT SPELLED LIKE HEAVY METAL.
I DO KNOW THAT, ACTUALLY.
ANYWAY, YOUR BOY DID PRETTY GOOD.
THERE'S NO EMBARRASSING PUDDLE ON THE FLOOR.
AND IT DOESN'T SMELL LIKE HE NEEDS HIS NAPPIES CHANGING.
HA HA HA.
OH YES. HILARIOUS.

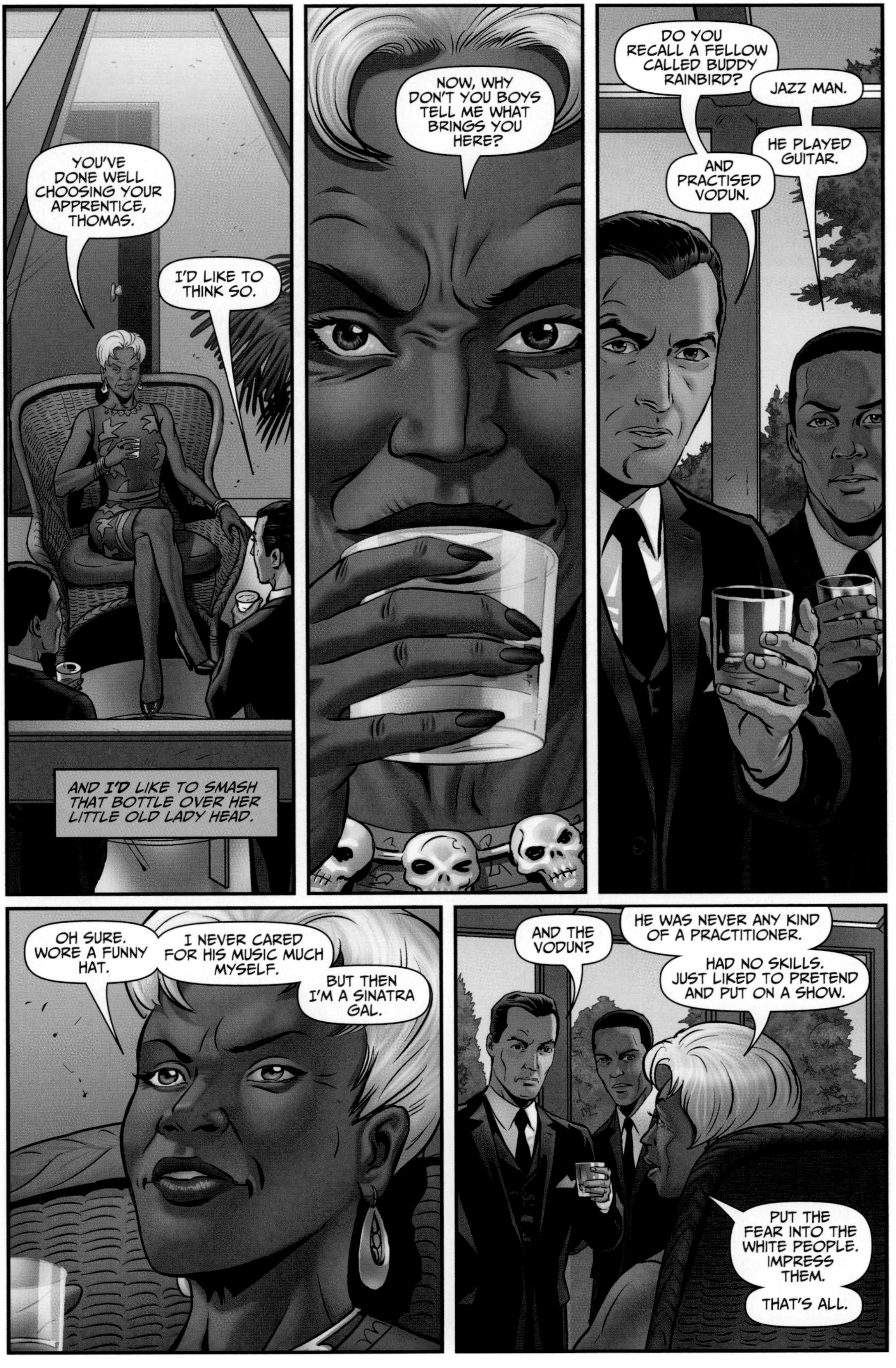
YOU'VE DONE WELL CHOOSING YOUR APPRENTICE, THOMAS.
I'D LIKE TO THINK SO.
AND I'D LIKE TO SMASH THAT BOTTLE OVER HER LITTLE OLD LADY HEAD.
NOW, WHY DON'T YOU BOYS TELL ME WHAT BRINGS YOU HERE?
DO YOU RECALL A FELLOW CALLED BUDDY RAINBIRD?
JAZZ MAN.
HE PLAYED GUITAR.
AND PRACTISED VODUN.
OH SURE. WORE A FUNNY HAT.
I NEVER CARED FOR HIS MUSIC MUCH MYSELF.
BUT THEN I'M A SINATRA GAL.
AND THE VODUN?
HE WAS NEVER ANY KIND OF A PRACTITIONER.
HAD NO SKILLS. JUST LIKED TO PRETEND AND PUT ON A SHOW.
PUT THE FEAR INTO THE WHITE PEOPLE. IMPRESS THEM.
THAT'S ALL.

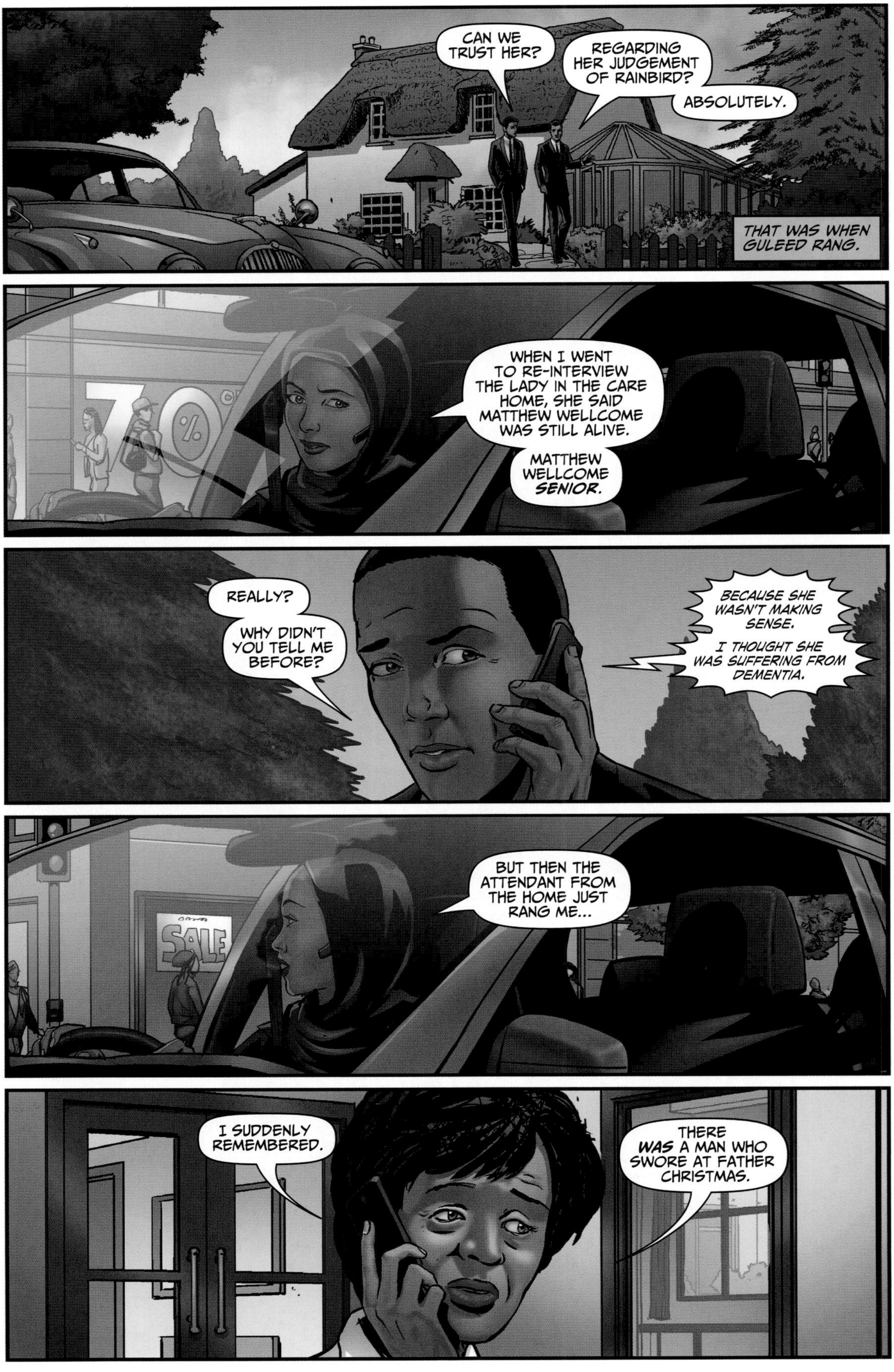
CAN WE TRUST HER?
REGARDING HER JUDGEMENT OF RAINBIRD?
ABSOLUTELY.
THAT WAS WHEN GULEED RANG.
WHEN I WENT TO RE-INTERVIEW THE LADY IN THE CARE HOME, SHE SAID MATTHEW WELLCOME WAS STILL ALIVE.
MATTHEW WELLCOME *SENIOR*.
REALLY?
WHY DIDN'T YOU TELL ME BEFORE?
BECAUSE SHE WASN'T MAKING SENSE.
I THOUGHT SHE WAS SUFFERING FROM DEMENTIA.
BUT THEN THE ATTENDANT FROM THE HOME JUST RANG ME...
SALE
I SUDDENLY REMEMBERED.
THERE *WAS* A MAN WHO SWORE AT FATHER CHRISTMAS.

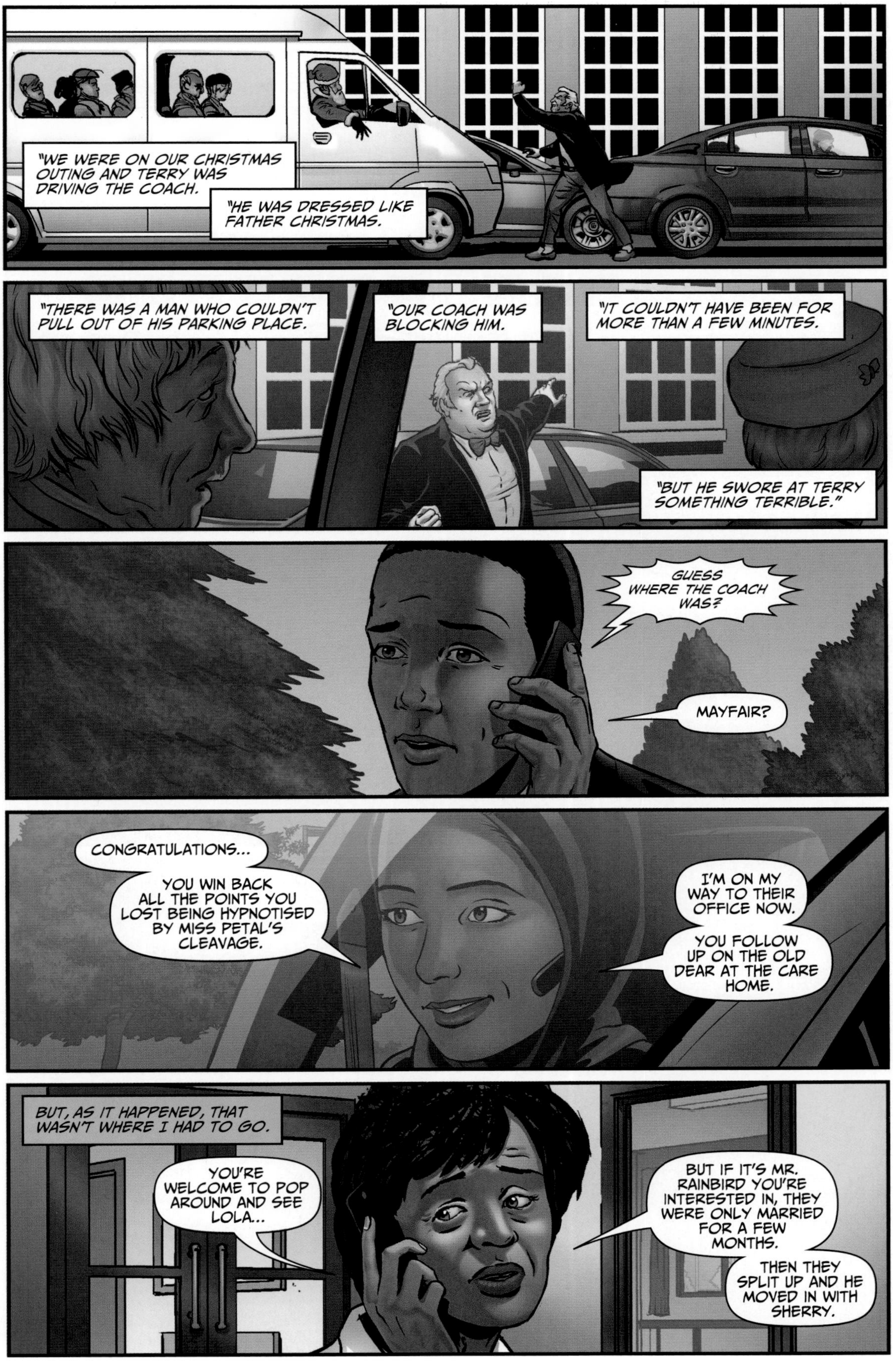
"WE WERE ON OUR CHRISTMAS OUTING AND TERRY WAS DRIVING THE COACH.
"HE WAS DRESSED LIKE FATHER CHRISTMAS.
"THERE WAS A MAN WHO COULDN'T PULL OUT OF HIS PARKING PLACE.
"OUR COACH WAS BLOCKING HIM.
"IT COULDN'T HAVE BEEN FOR MORE THAN A FEW MINUTES.
"BUT HE SWORE AT TERRY SOMETHING TERRIBLE."
GUESS WHERE THE COACH WAS?
MAYFAIR?
CONGRATULATIONS...
YOU WIN BACK ALL THE POINTS YOU LOST BEING HYPNOTISED BY MISS PETAL'S CLEAVAGE.
I'M ON MY WAY TO THEIR OFFICE NOW.
YOU FOLLOW UP ON THE OLD DEAR AT THE CARE HOME.
BUT, AS IT HAPPENED, THAT WASN'T WHERE I HAD TO GO.
YOU'RE WELCOME TO POP AROUND AND SEE LOLA...
BUT IF IT'S MR. RAINBIRD YOU'RE INTERESTED IN, THEY WERE ONLY MARRIED FOR A FEW MONTHS.
THEN THEY SPLIT UP AND HE MOVED IN WITH SHERRY.

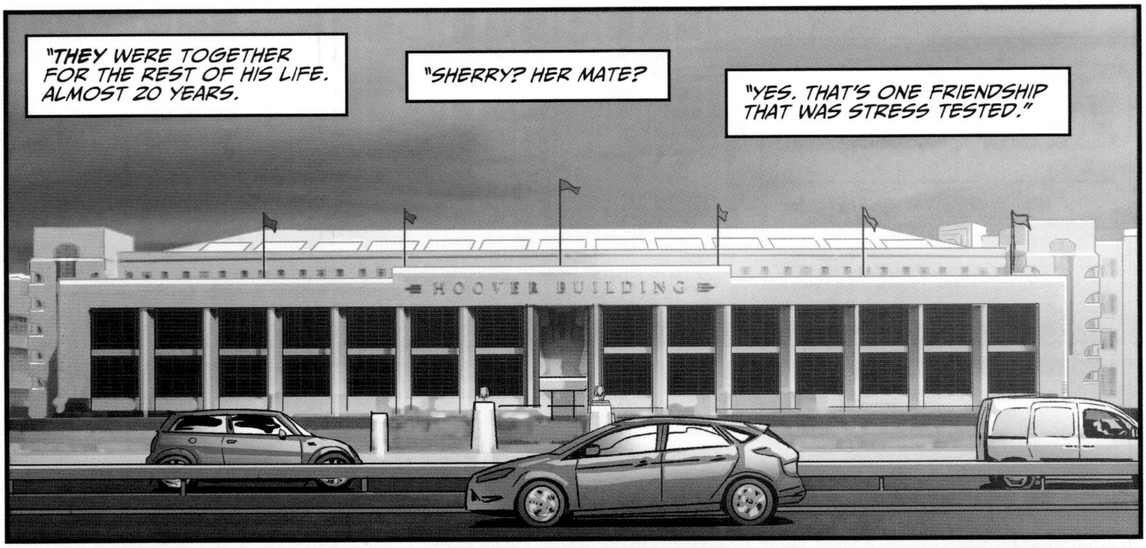
"THEY WERE TOGETHER FOR THE REST OF HIS LIFE. ALMOST 20 YEARS.
"SHERRY? HER MATE?
"YES. THAT'S ONE FRIENDSHIP THAT WAS STRESS TESTED."
HOOVER BUILDING

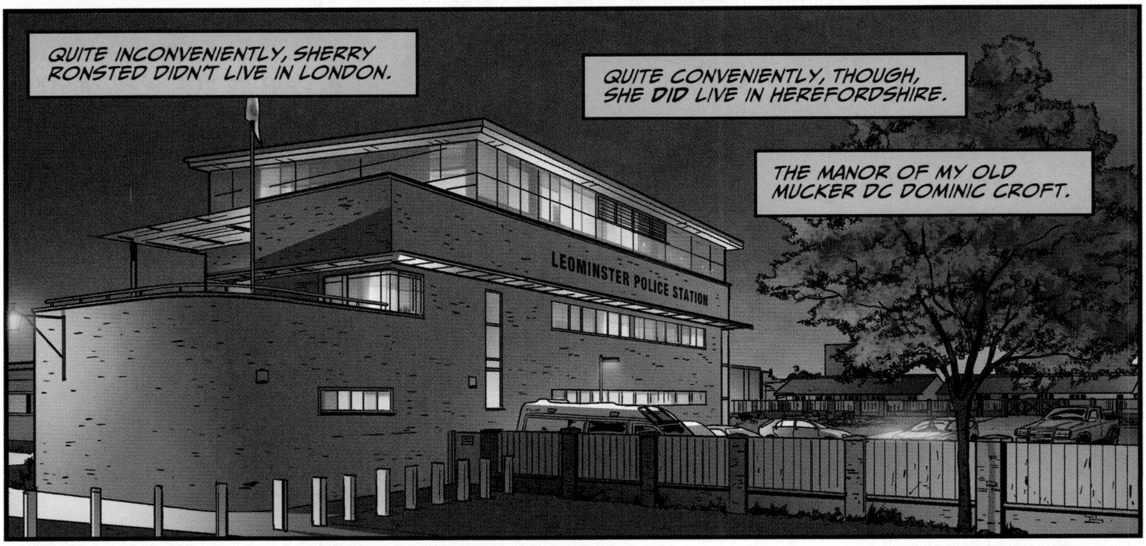
QUITE INCONVENIENTLY, SHERRY RONSTED DIDN'T LIVE IN LONDON.
QUITE CONVENIENTLY, THOUGH, SHE DID LIVE IN HEREFORDSHIRE.
THE MANOR OF MY OLD MUCKER DC DOMINIC CROFT.
LEOMINSTER POLICE STATION

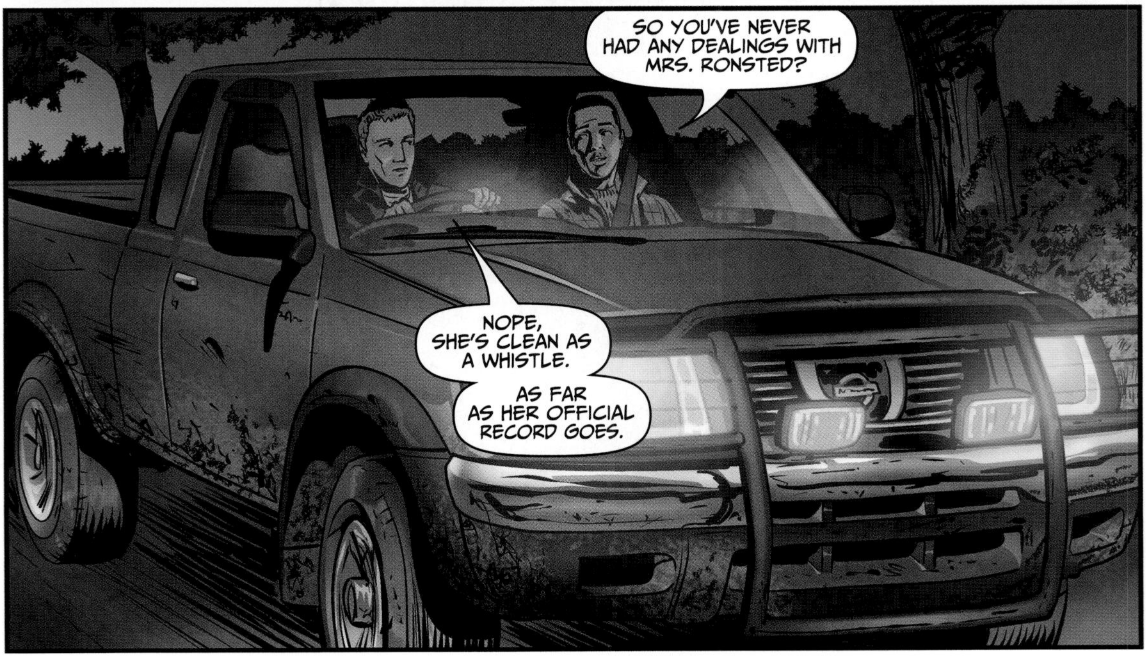
SO YOU'VE NEVER HAD ANY DEALINGS WITH MRS. RONSTED?
NOPE, SHE'S CLEAN AS A WHISTLE.
AS FAR AS HER OFFICIAL RECORD GOES.

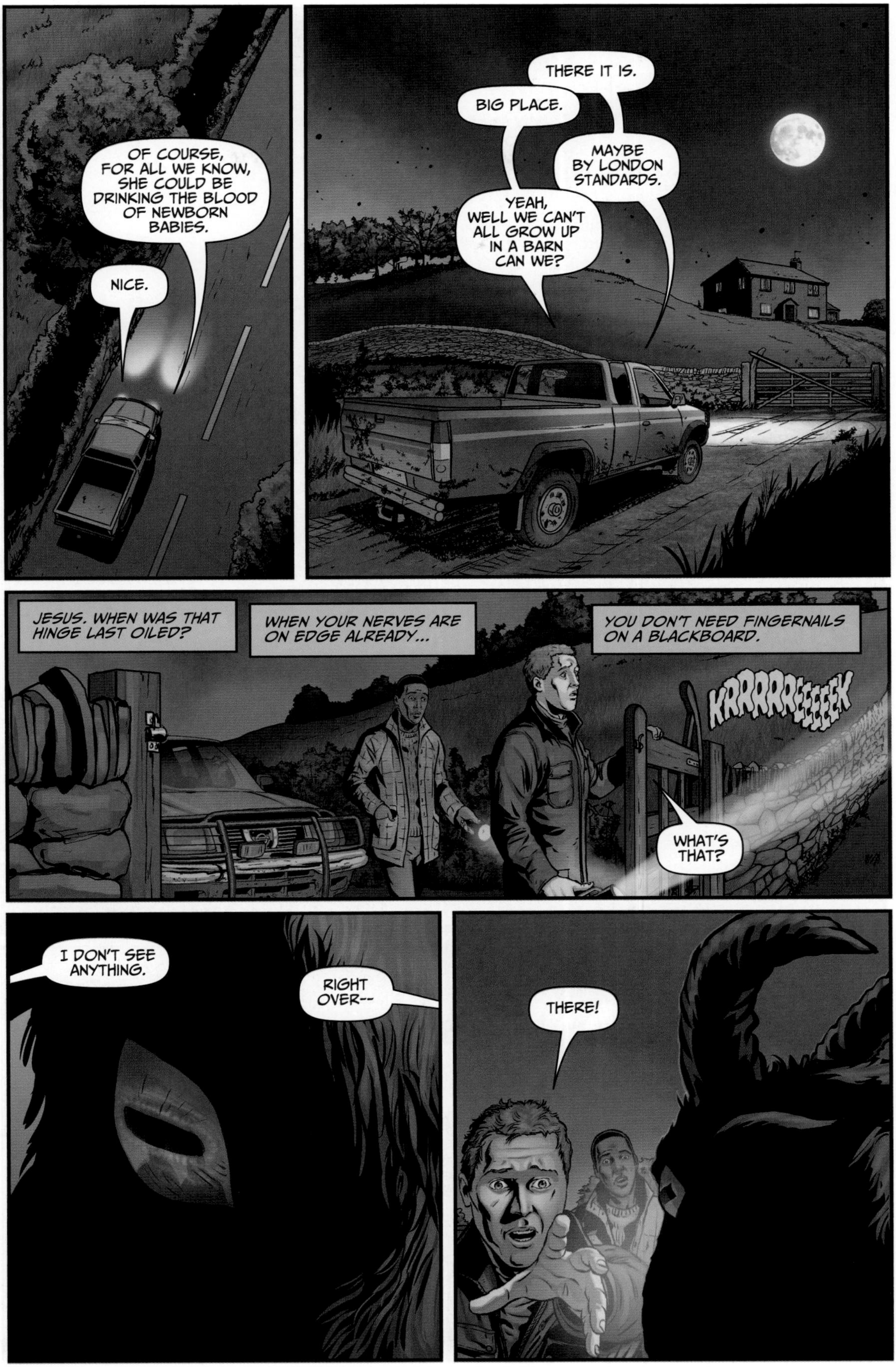
OF COURSE, FOR ALL WE KNOW, SHE COULD BE DRINKING THE BLOOD OF NEWBORN BABIES.
NICE.
THERE IT IS.
BIG PLACE.
MAYBE BY LONDON STANDARDS.
YEAH, WELL WE CAN'T ALL GROW UP IN A BARN CAN WE?
JESUS. WHEN WAS THAT HINGE LAST OILED?
WHEN YOUR NERVES ARE ON EDGE ALREADY...
YOU DON'T NEED FINGERNAILS ON A BLACKBOARD.
KRRRRREEEEEK
WHAT'S THAT?
I DON'T SEE ANYTHING.
RIGHT OVER--
THERE!

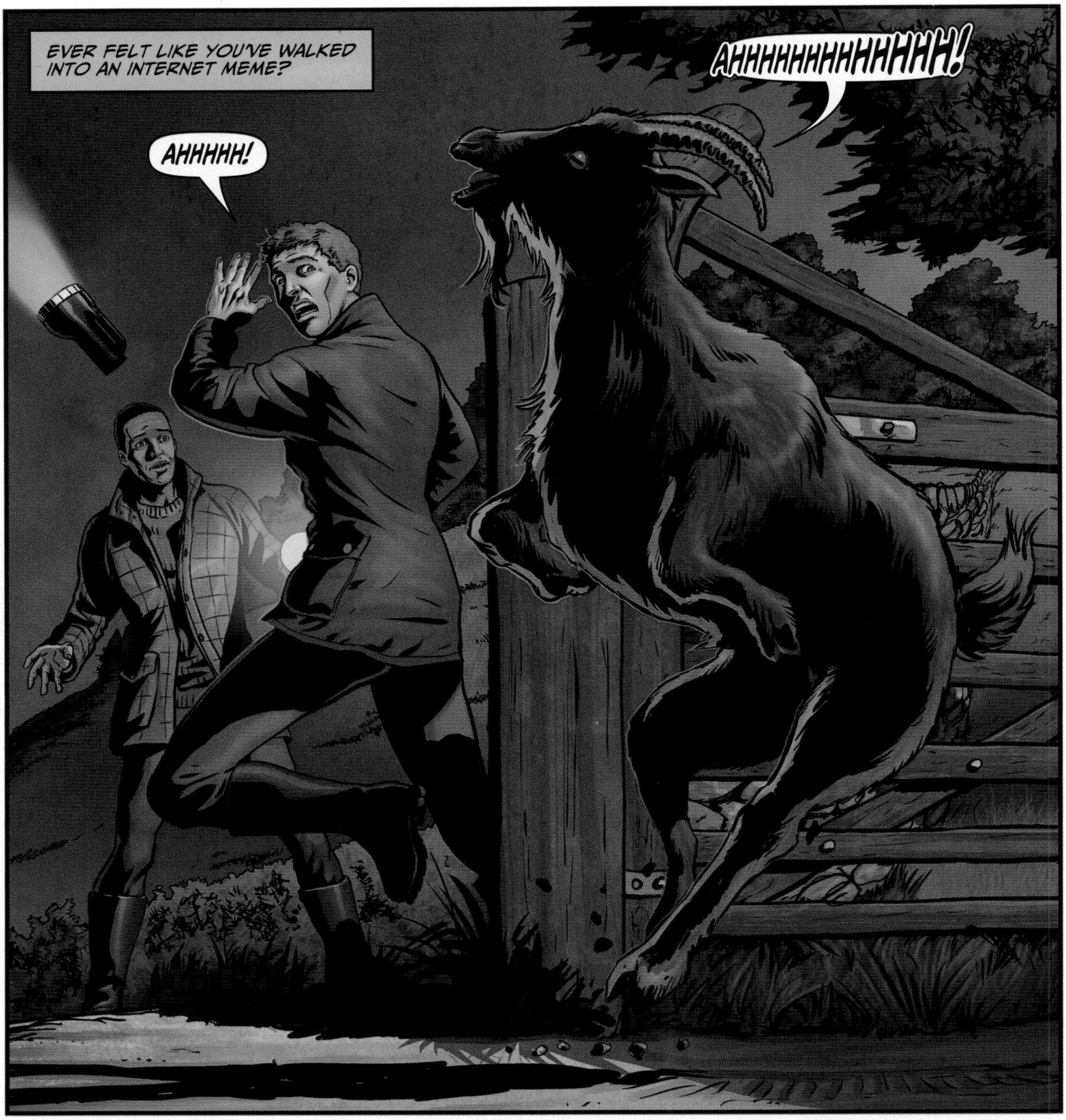
EVER FELT LIKE YOU'VE WALKED INTO AN INTERNET MEME?
AHHHHH!
AHHHHHHHHHHHHH!

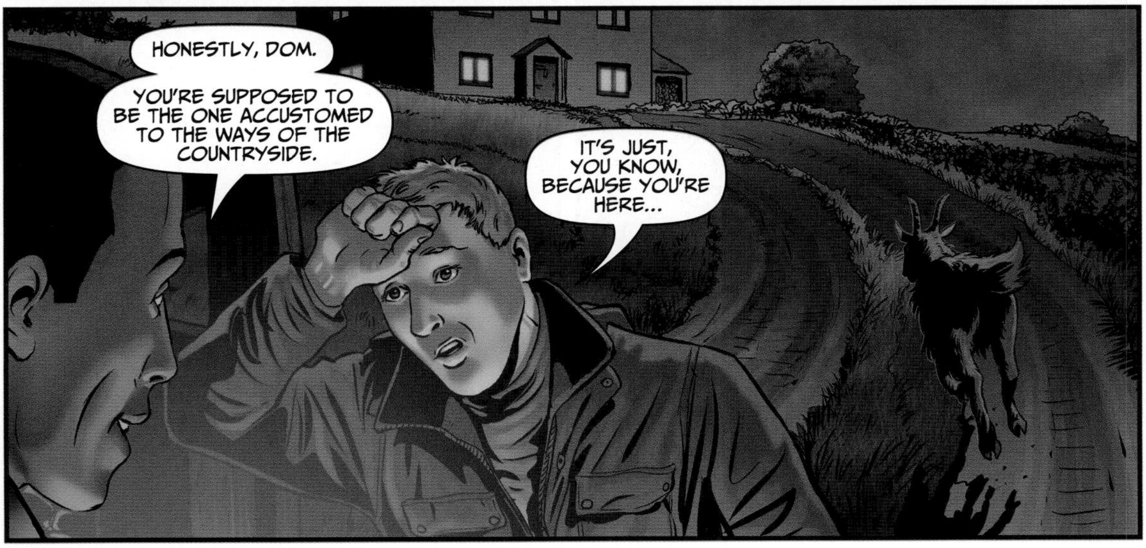
HONESTLY, DOM.
YOU'RE SUPPOSED TO BE THE ONE ACCUSTOMED TO THE WAYS OF THE COUNTRYSIDE.
IT'S JUST, YOU KNOW, BECAUSE YOU'RE HERE...

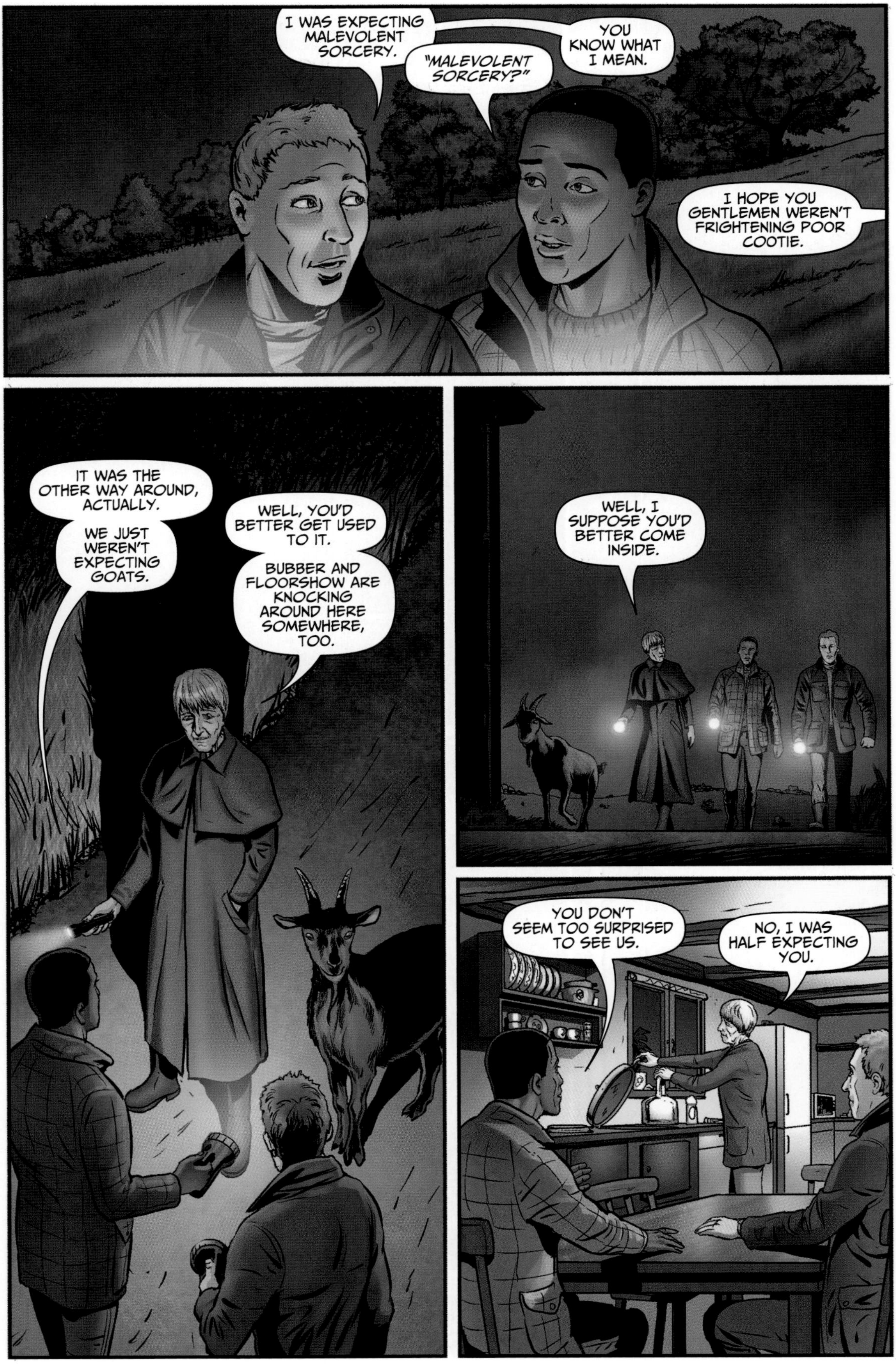
I WAS EXPECTING MALEVOLENT SORCERY.
"MALEVOLENT SORCERY?"
YOU KNOW WHAT I MEAN.
I HOPE YOU GENTLEMEN WEREN'T FRIGHTENING POOR COOTIE.
IT WAS THE OTHER WAY AROUND, ACTUALLY.
WE JUST WEREN'T EXPECTING GOATS.
WELL, YOU'D BETTER GET USED TO IT.
BUBBER AND FLOORSHOW ARE KNOCKING AROUND HERE SOMEWHERE, TOO.
WELL, I SUPPOSE YOU'D BETTER COME INSIDE.
YOU DON'T SEEM TOO SURPRISED TO SEE US.
NO, I WAS HALF EXPECTING YOU.

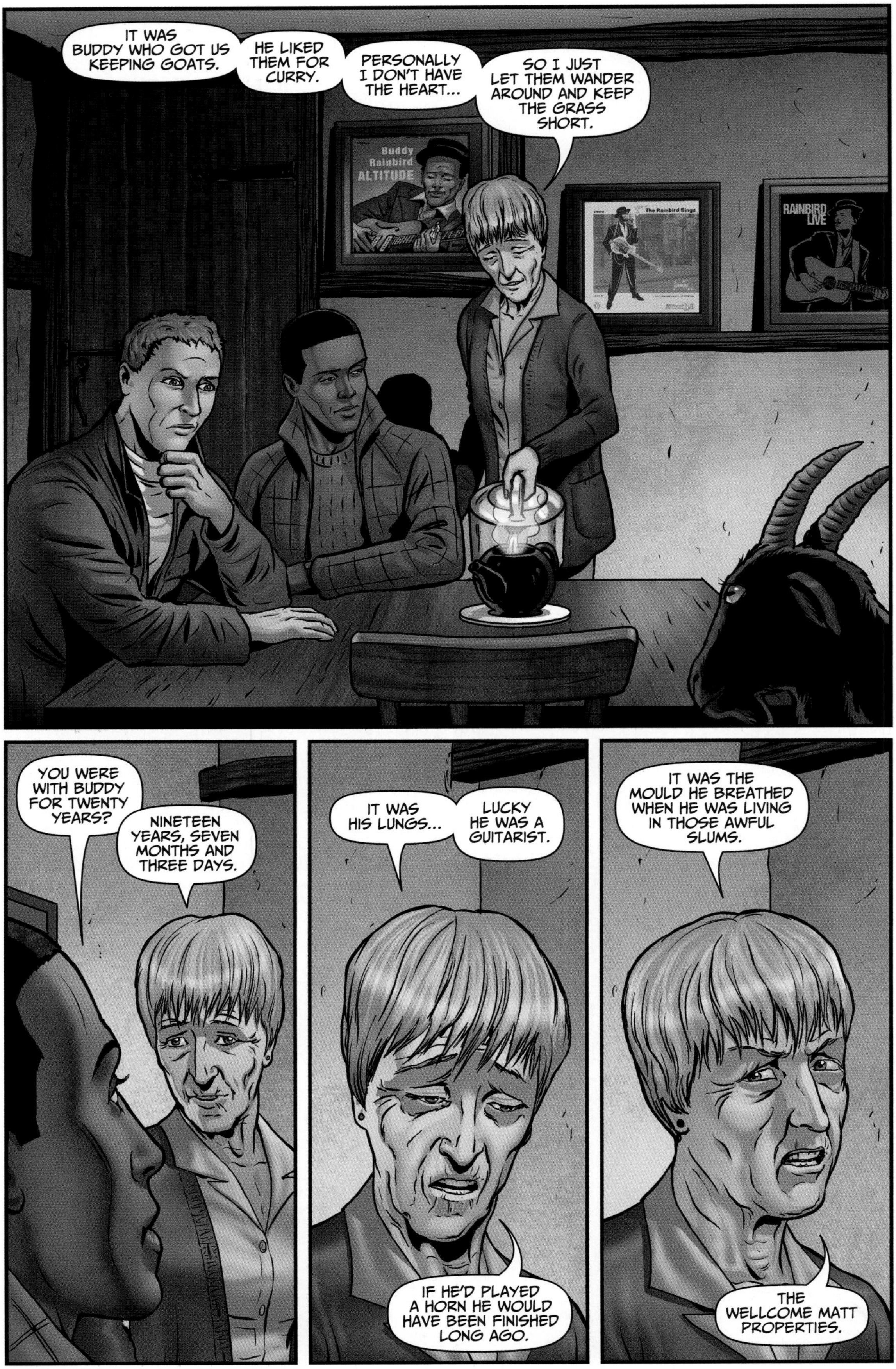
IT WAS BUDDY WHO GOT US KEEPING GOATS.
HE LIKED THEM FOR CURRY.
PERSONALLY I DON'T HAVE THE HEART...
SO I JUST LET THEM WANDER AROUND AND KEEP THE GRASS SHORT.
Buddy Rainbird ALTITUDE
The Rainbird Sings
RAINBIRD LIVE
YOU WERE WITH BUDDY FOR TWENTY YEARS?
NINETEEN YEARS, SEVEN MONTHS AND THREE DAYS.
IT WAS HIS LUNGS...
LUCKY HE WAS A GUITARIST.
IF HE'D PLAYED A HORN HE WOULD HAVE BEEN FINISHED LONG AGO.
IT WAS THE MOULD HE BREATHED WHEN HE WAS LIVING IN THOSE AWFUL SLUMS.
THE WELLCOME MATT PROPERTIES.

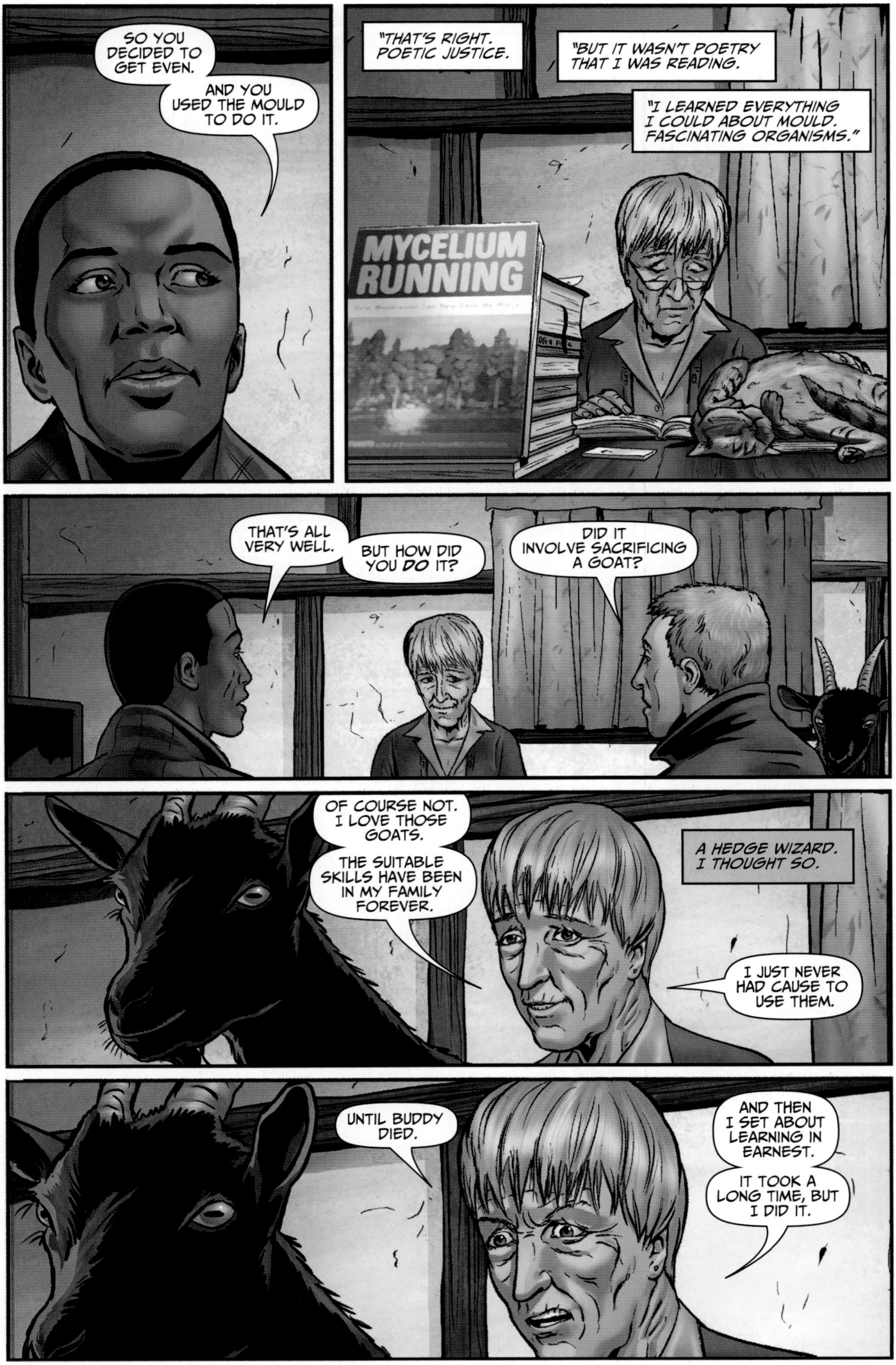
SO YOU DECIDED TO GET EVEN.
AND YOU USED THE MOULD TO DO IT.
"THAT'S RIGHT. POETIC JUSTICE.
"BUT IT WASN'T POETRY THAT I WAS READING.
"I LEARNED EVERYTHING I COULD ABOUT MOULD. FASCINATING ORGANISMS."
MYCELIUM RUNNING
THAT'S ALL VERY WELL.
BUT HOW DID YOU DO IT?
DID IT INVOLVE SACRIFICING A GOAT?
OF COURSE NOT. I LOVE THOSE GOATS.
THE SUITABLE SKILLS HAVE BEEN IN MY FAMILY FOREVER.
A HEDGE WIZARD. I THOUGHT SO.
I JUST NEVER HAD CAUSE TO USE THEM.
UNTIL BUDDY DIED.
AND THEN I SET ABOUT LEARNING IN EARNEST.
IT TOOK A LONG TIME, BUT I DID IT.

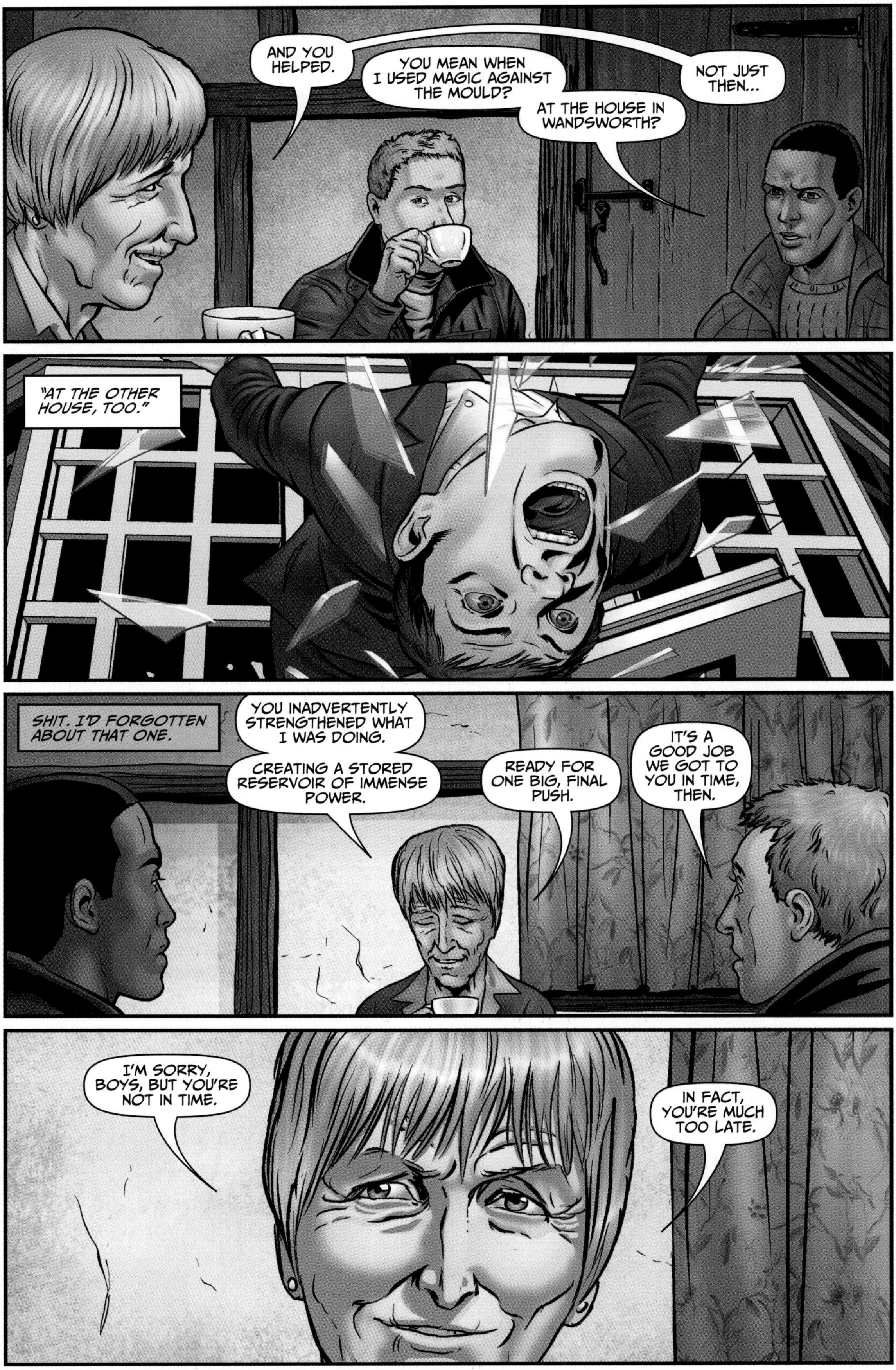
AND YOU HELPED.
YOU MEAN WHEN I USED MAGIC AGAINST THE MOULD?
AT THE HOUSE IN WANDSWORTH?
NOT JUST THEN...
"AT THE OTHER HOUSE, TOO."
SHIT. I'D FORGOTTEN ABOUT THAT ONE.
YOU INADVERTENTLY STRENGTHENED WHAT I WAS DOING.
CREATING A STORED RESERVOIR OF IMMENSE POWER.
READY FOR ONE BIG, FINAL PUSH.
IT'S A GOOD JOB WE GOT TO YOU IN TIME, THEN.
I'M SORRY, BOYS, BUT YOU'RE NOT IN TIME.
IN FACT, YOU'RE MUCH TOO LATE.

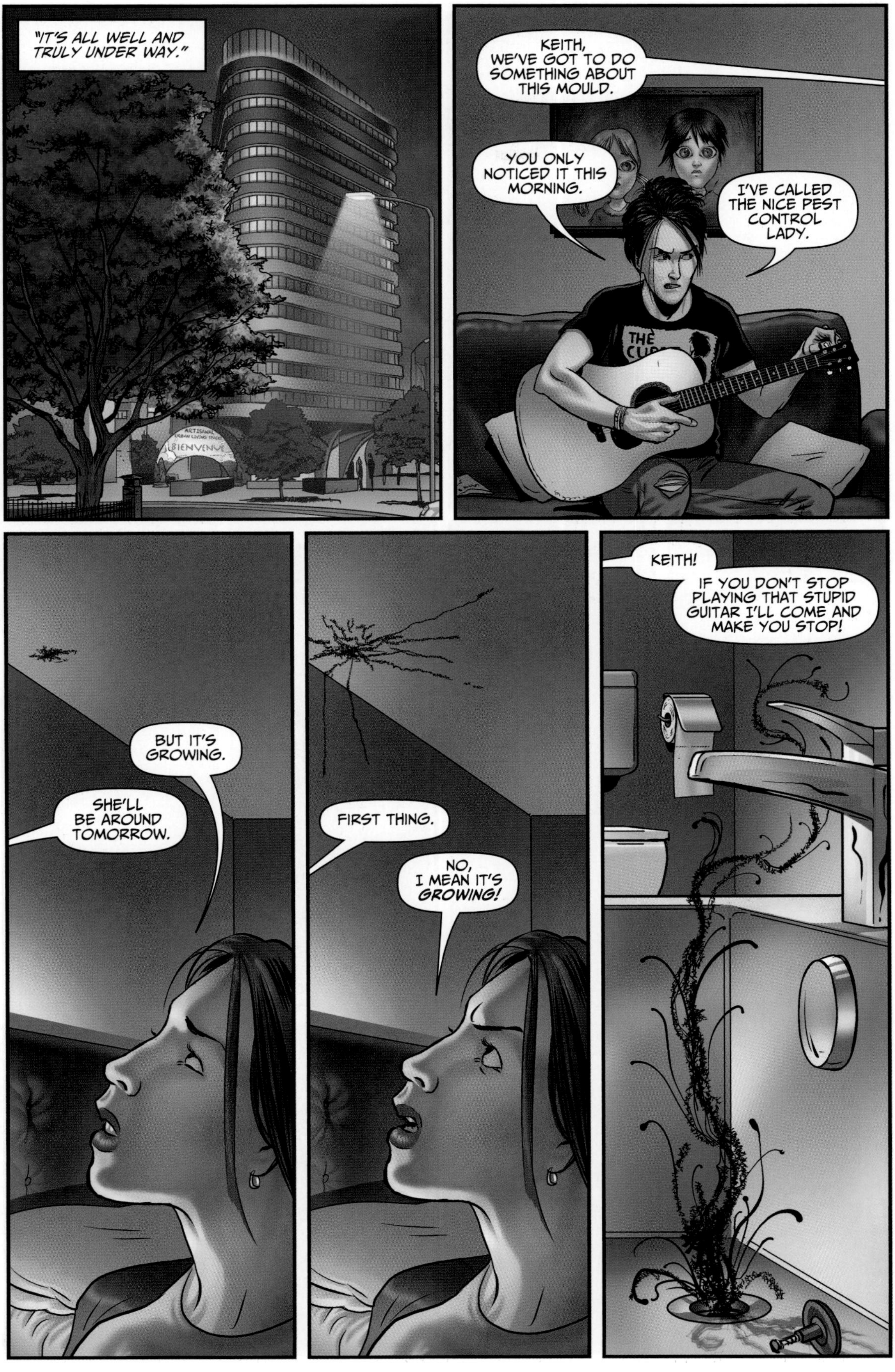
"IT'S ALL WELL AND TRULY UNDER WAY."
BIENVENUE
KEITH, WE'VE GOT TO DO SOMETHING ABOUT THIS MOULD.
YOU ONLY NOTICED IT THIS MORNING.
I'VE CALLED THE NICE PEST CONTROL LADY.
BUT IT'S GROWING.
SHE'LL BE AROUND TOMORROW.
FIRST THING.
NO, I MEAN IT'S *GROWING!*
KEITH!
IF YOU DON'T STOP PLAYING THAT STUPID GUITAR I'LL COME AND MAKE YOU STOP!

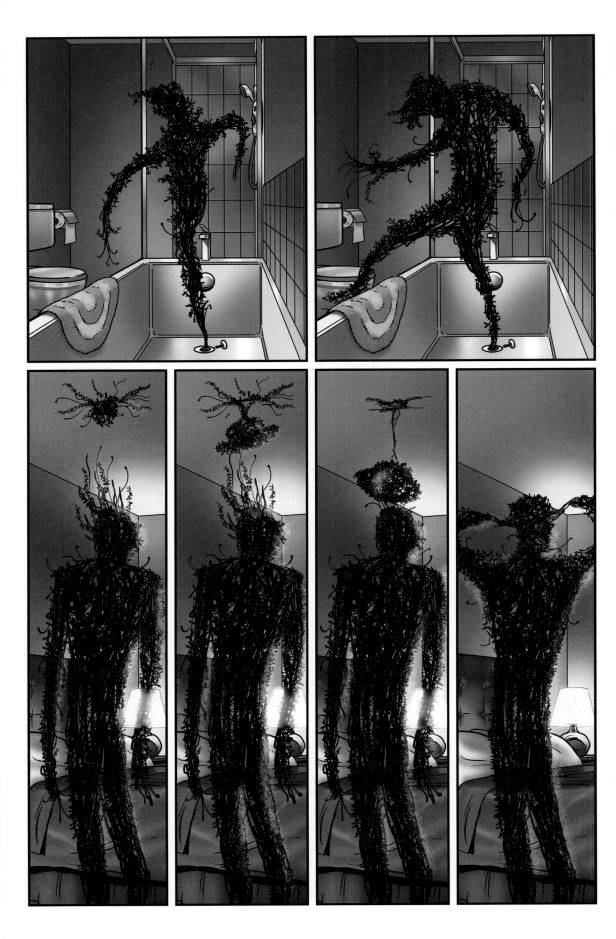

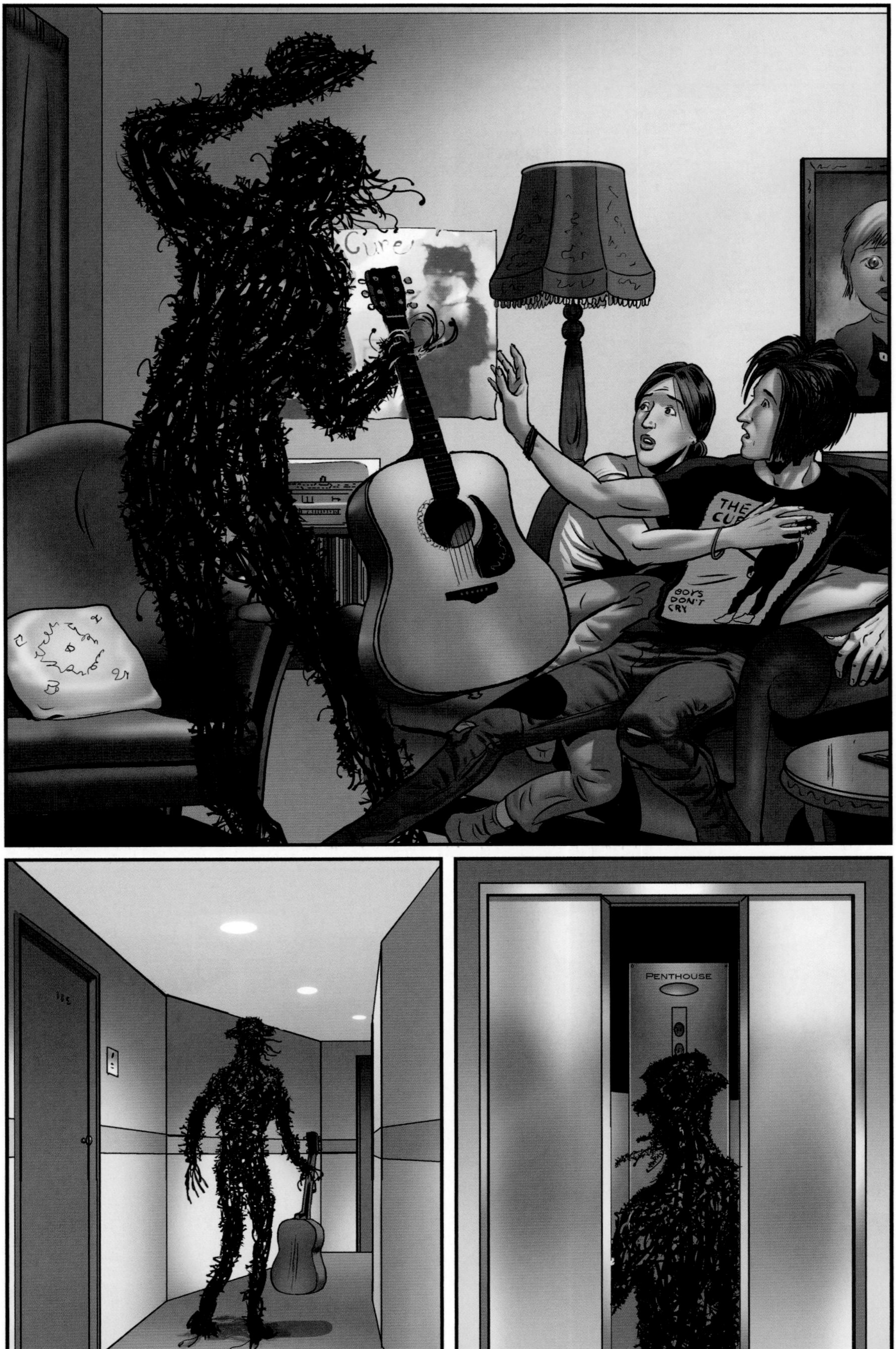
Cure
THE CU
BOYS DON'T CRY
PENTHOUSE

WE'D GIVEN OUR BUSINESS CARDS TO CISSIE AND KEITH...

TOLD THEM TO RING IF ANYTHING UNUSUAL HAPPENED...

AND THIS CERTAINLY SEEMED TO QUALIFY.

ARTISANAL
URBAN LIVING SPACES
BROUGHT TO YOU BY
ENVENUE
PROPERTY DEVELOPMENT

SAHRA. ANY DEVELOPMENTS?

YES...

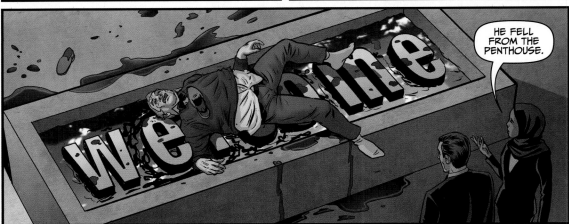

HE FELL FROM THE PENTHOUSE.

I'M PRETTY SURE IT'S MATTHEW WELLCOME.

THE SLUM LORD.

STAY DOWN HERE.

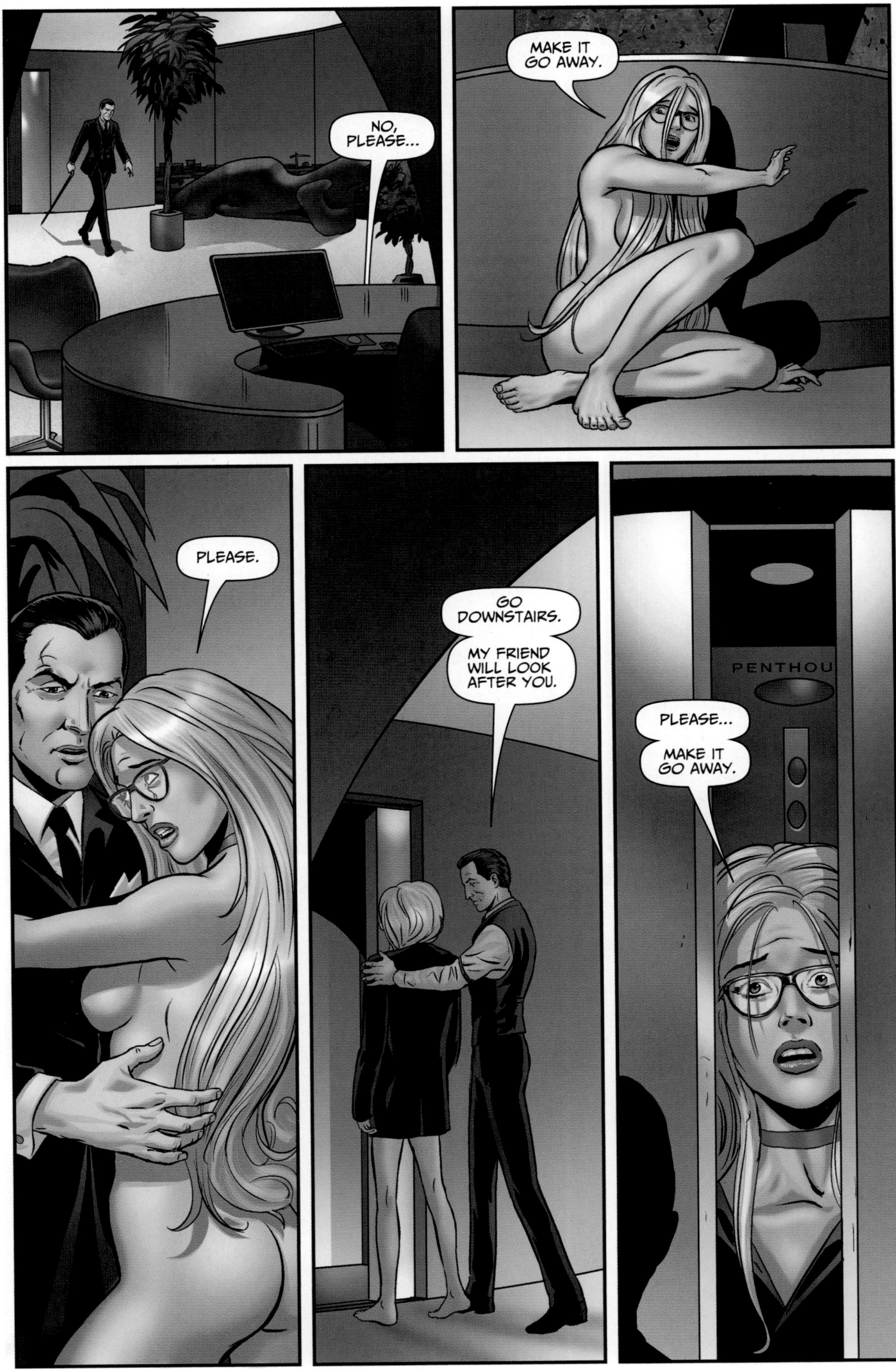
NO, PLEASE...
MAKE IT GO AWAY.
PLEASE.
GO DOWNSTAIRS.
MY FRIEND WILL LOOK AFTER YOU.
PENTHOU
PLEASE...
MAKE IT GO AWAY.

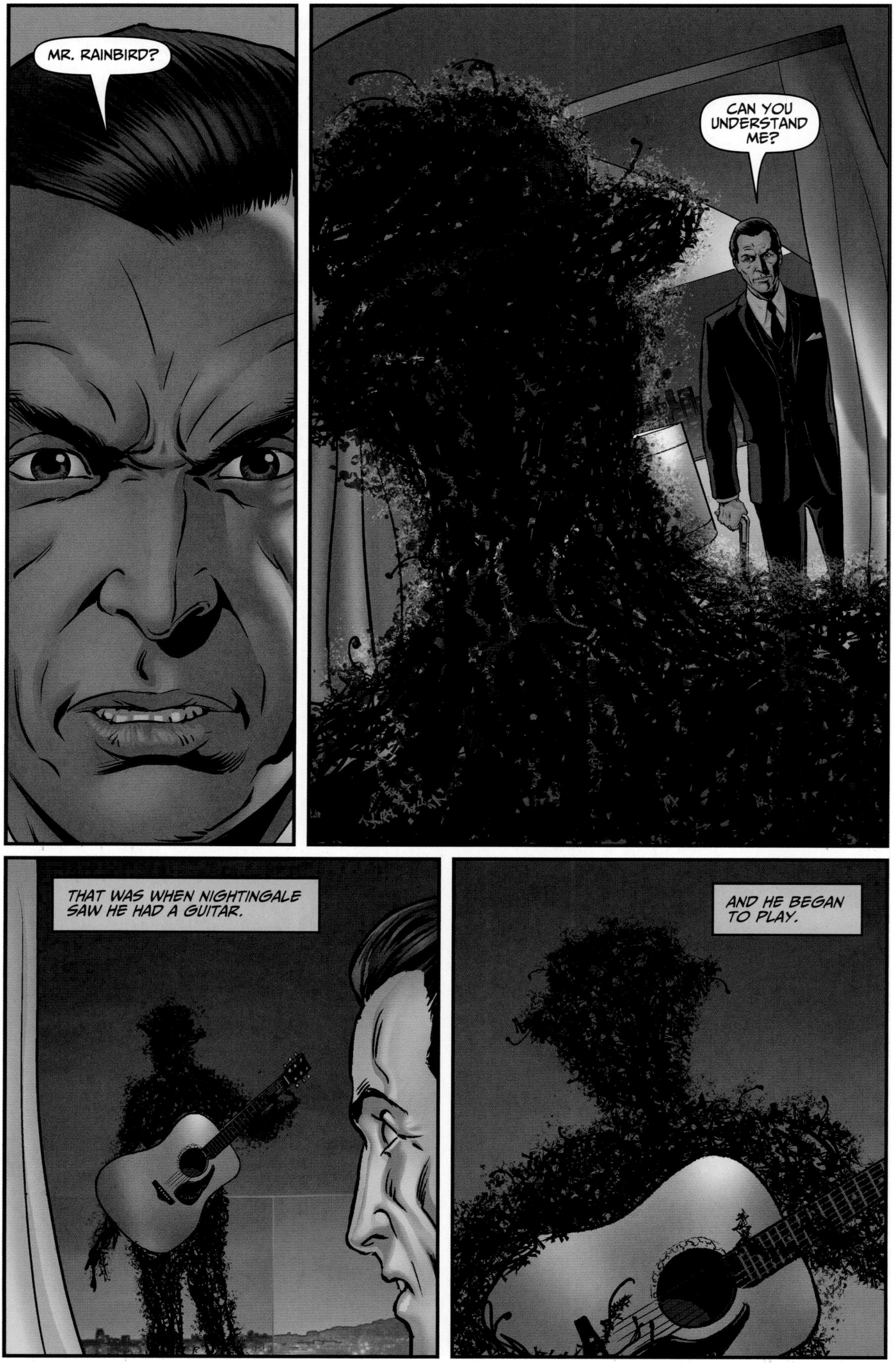
MR. RAINBIRD?
CAN YOU UNDERSTAND ME?
THAT WAS WHEN NIGHTINGALE SAW HE HAD A GUITAR.
AND HE BEGAN TO PLAY.

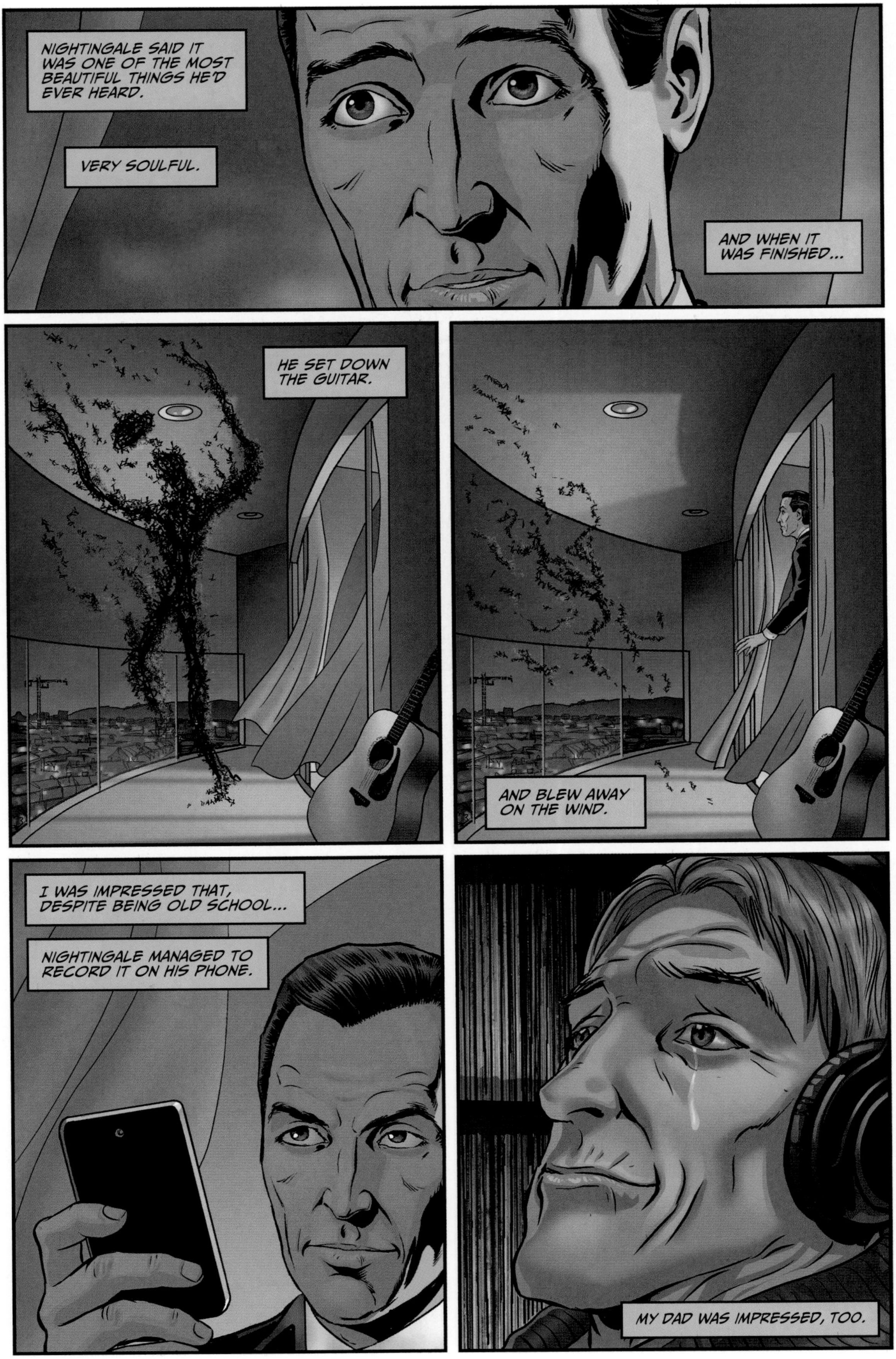
NIGHTINGALE SAID IT WAS ONE OF THE MOST BEAUTIFUL THINGS HE'D EVER HEARD.
VERY SOULFUL.
AND WHEN IT WAS FINISHED...
HE SET DOWN THE GUITAR.
AND BLEW AWAY ON THE WIND.
I WAS IMPRESSED THAT, DESPITE BEING OLD SCHOOL...
NIGHTINGALE MANAGED TO RECORD IT ON HIS PHONE.
MY DAD WAS IMPRESSED, TOO.

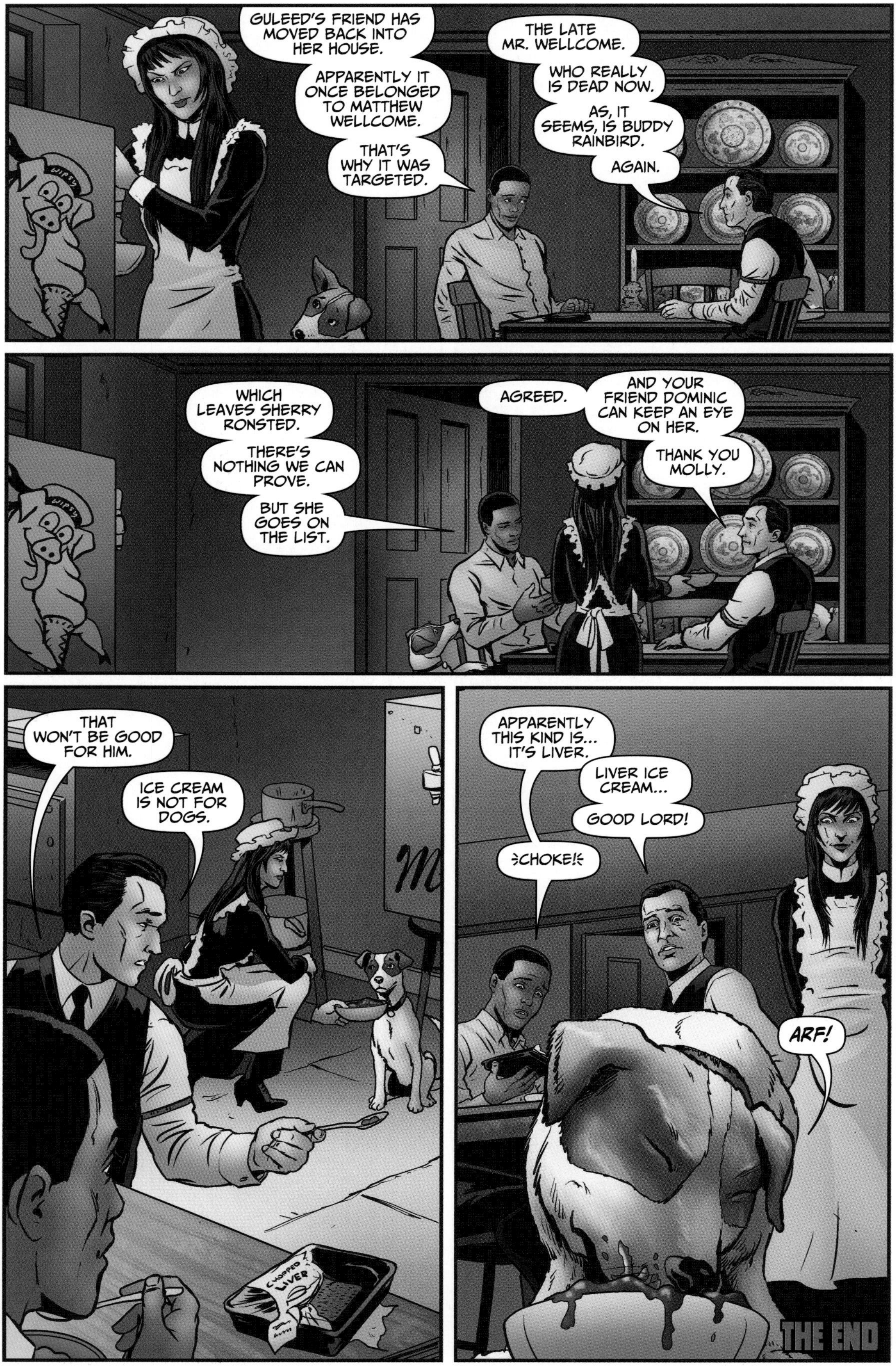
GULEED'S FRIEND HAS MOVED BACK INTO HER HOUSE.
APPARENTLY IT ONCE BELONGED TO MATTHEW WELLCOME.
THAT'S WHY IT WAS TARGETED.
THE LATE MR. WELLCOME.
WHO REALLY IS DEAD NOW.
AS, IT SEEMS, IS BUDDY RAINBIRD.
AGAIN.
WHICH LEAVES SHERRY RONSTED.
THERE'S NOTHING WE CAN PROVE.
BUT SHE GOES ON THE LIST.
AGREED.
AND YOUR FRIEND DOMINIC CAN KEEP AN EYE ON HER.
THANK YOU MOLLY.
THAT WON'T BE GOOD FOR HIM.
ICE CREAM IS NOT FOR DOGS.
CHOPPED LIVER
APPARENTLY THIS KIND IS... IT'S LIVER.
LIVER ICE CREAM...
GOOD LORD!
CHOKE!
ARF!
THE END

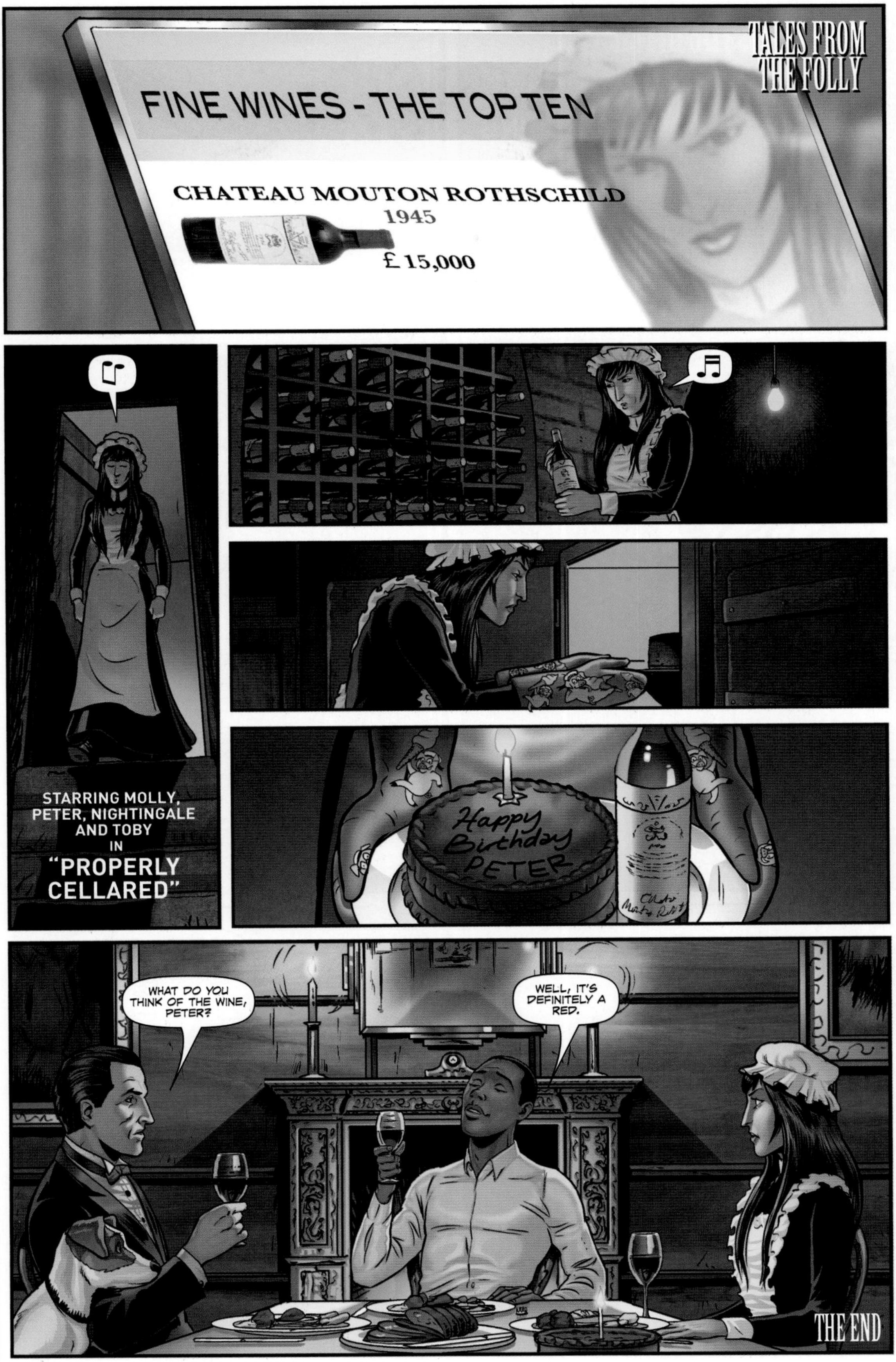
TALES FROM THE FOLLY
FINE WINES - THE TOP TEN
CHATEAU MOUTON ROTHSCHILD
1945
£15,000
STARRING MOLLY, PETER, NIGHTINGALE AND TOBY IN "PROPERLY CELLARED"
Happy Birthday PETER
WHAT DO YOU THINK OF THE WINE, PETER?
WELL, IT'S DEFINITELY A RED.
THE END

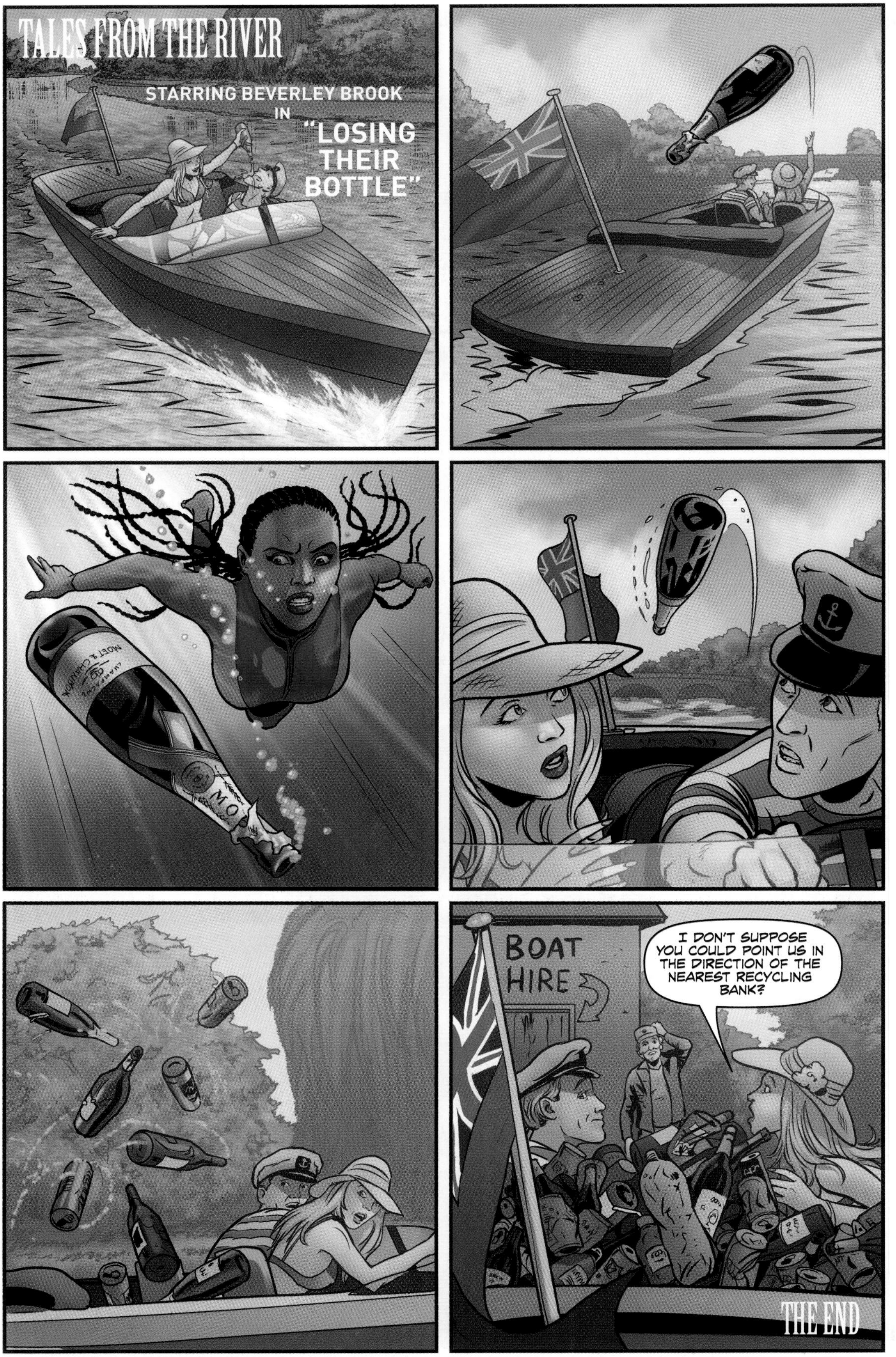
TALES FROM THE RIVER
STARRING BEVERLEY BROOK
IN
"LOSING THEIR BOTTLE"
MOET & CHANDON
CHAMPAGNE
BOAT HIRE
I DON'T SUPPOSE YOU COULD POINT US IN THE DIRECTION OF THE NEAREST RECYCLING BANK?
THE END

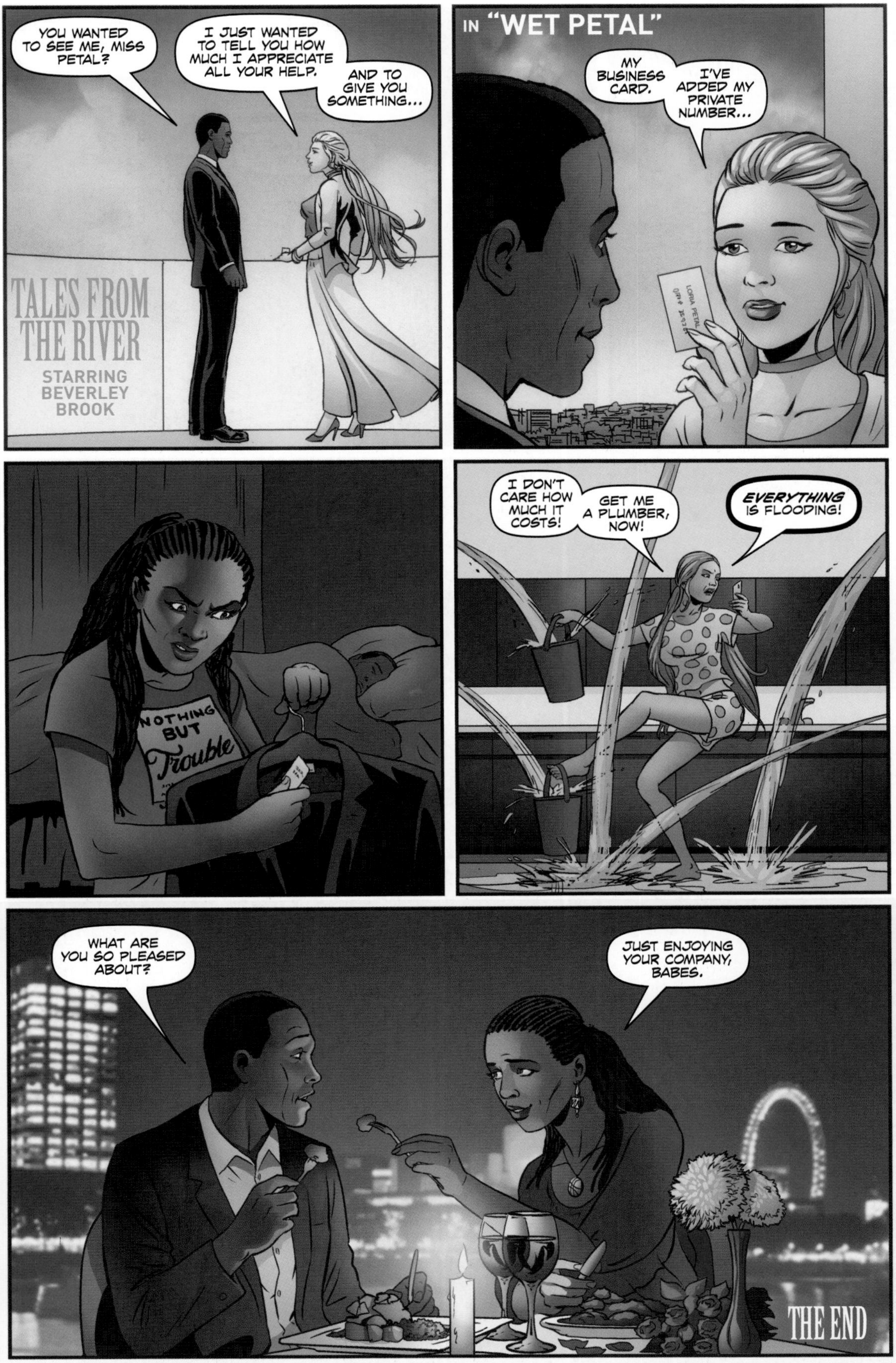
YOU WANTED TO SEE ME, MISS PETAL?
I JUST WANTED TO TELL YOU HOW MUCH I APPRECIATE ALL YOUR HELP.
AND TO GIVE YOU SOMETHING...
TALES FROM THE RIVER
STARRING BEVERLEY BROOK
IN "WET PETAL"
MY BUSINESS CARD.
I'VE ADDED MY PRIVATE NUMBER...
NOTHING BUT Trouble
I DON'T CARE HOW MUCH IT COSTS!
GET ME A PLUMBER, NOW!
EVERYTHING IS FLOODING!
WHAT ARE YOU SO PLEASED ABOUT?
JUST ENJOYING YOUR COMPANY, BABES.
THE END

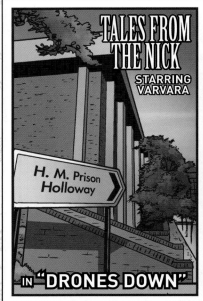

TALES FROM THE NICK

STARRING VARVARA

H. M. Prison Holloway

IN "DRONES DOWN"

IT SEEMS WE'RE FINALLY GETTING THE DRONE SITUATION UNDER CONTROL.

IN THE PAST WEEK WE'VE CONFISCATED TWELVE MOBILE PHONES, NINE WRAPS OF HEROIN, ELEVEN OF COCAINE, EIGHTEEN BAGS OF CANNABIS AND A BOXED SET OF *BREAKING BAD*.

ALL BEFORE THEY GOT ANYWHERE NEAR OUR GUESTS.

EXCELLENT WORK, HATWELL.

THANK YOU, MA'AM.

GOVERNOR

IT SEEMS THE DRONES CARRYING CONTRABAND JUST KEEP DROPPING FROM THE SKY.

HOW EXTRAORDINARY.

HERE'S THE SHOPPING YOU ASKED FOR.

AND TOMORROW YOU MOVE TO YOUR NEW CELL.

TOVARITCH

THE END

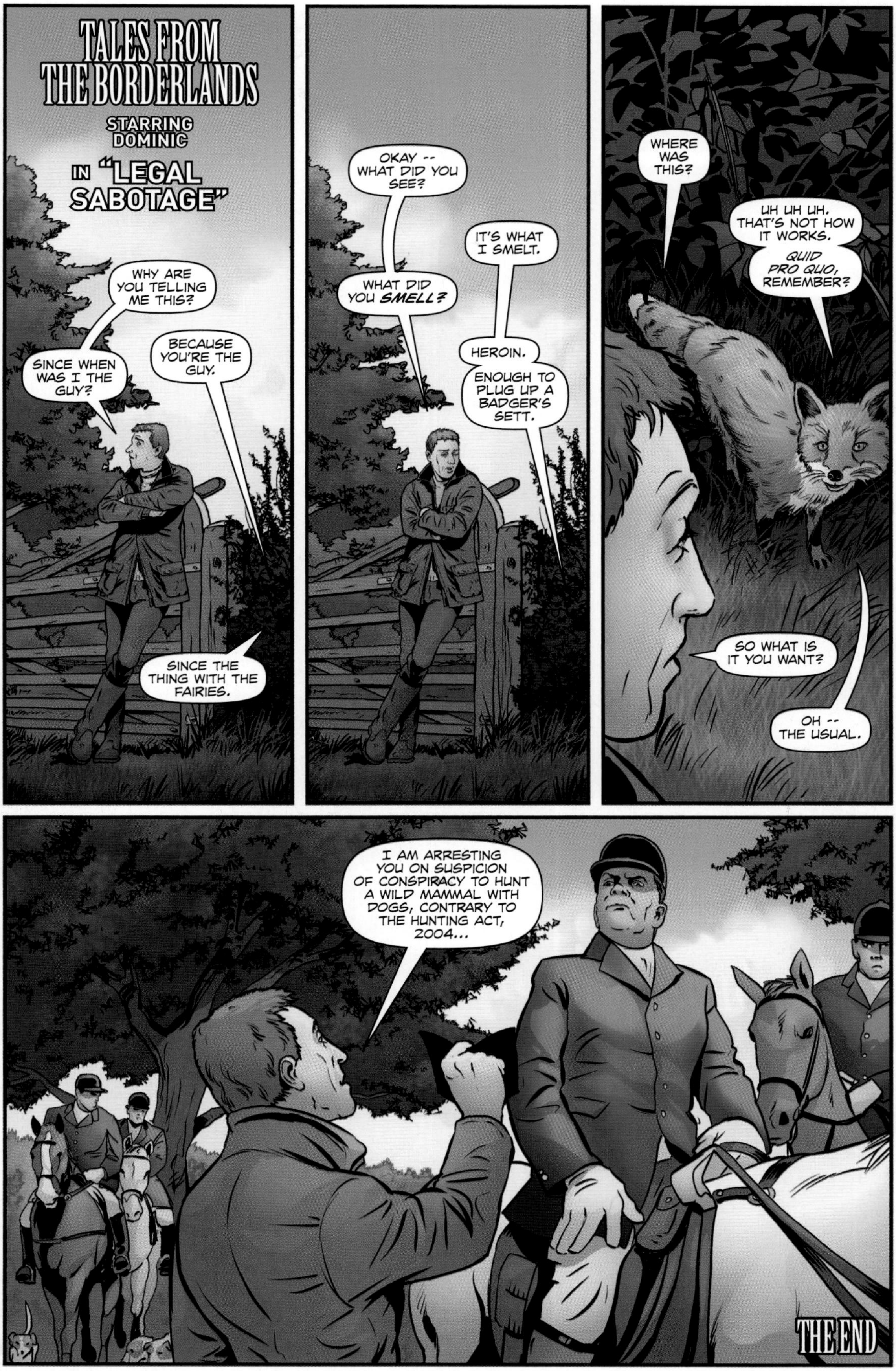
TALES FROM THE BORDERLANDS
STARRING DOMINIC
IN "LEGAL SABOTAGE"
WHY ARE YOU TELLING ME THIS?
BECAUSE YOU'RE THE GUY.
SINCE WHEN WAS I THE GUY?
SINCE THE THING WITH THE FAIRIES.
OKAY -- WHAT DID YOU SEE?
IT'S WHAT I SMELT.
WHAT DID YOU *SMELL?*
HEROIN.
ENOUGH TO PLUG UP A BADGER'S SETT.
WHERE WAS THIS?
UH UH UH. THAT'S NOT HOW IT WORKS.
QUID PRO QUO, REMEMBER?
SO WHAT IS IT YOU WANT?
OH -- THE USUAL.
I AM ARRESTING YOU ON SUSPICION OF CONSPIRACY TO HUNT A WILD MAMMAL WITH DOGS, CONTRARY TO THE HUNTING ACT, 2004...
THE END

COVERS GALLERY

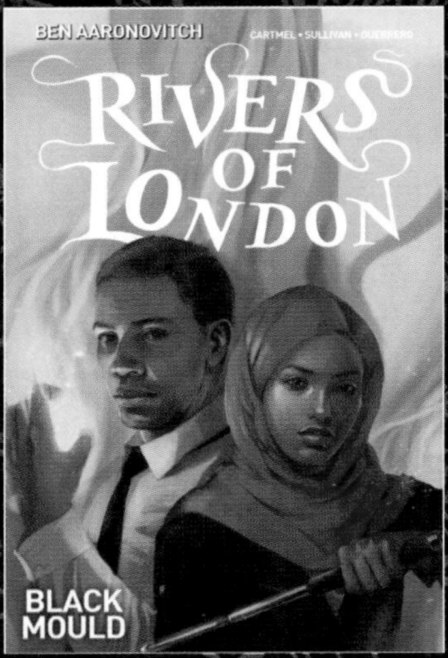
BEN AARONOVITCH
CARTMEL • SULLIVAN • GUERRERO
RIVERS OF LONDON
BLACK MOULD

ISSUE 1 - Cover A •
Claudia Caranfa

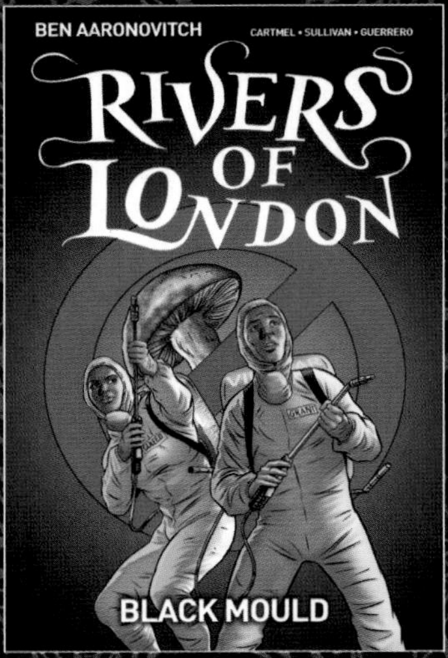
BEN AARONOVITCH
CARTMEL • SULLIVAN • GUERRERO
RIVERS OF LONDON
BLACK MOULD

ISSUE 1 - Cover B •
Lee Sullivan & Luis Guerrero

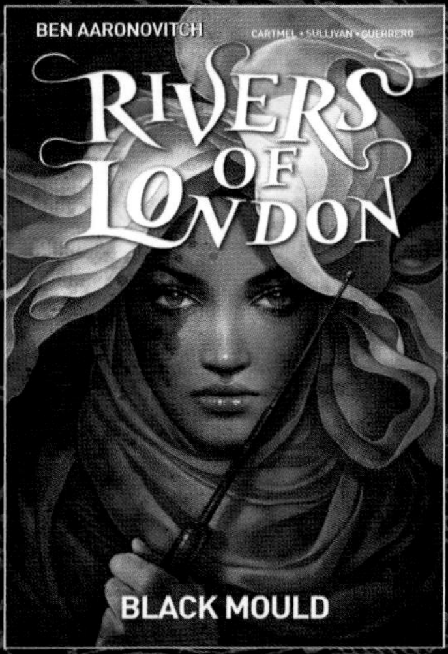
BEN AARONOVITCH
CARTMEL • SULLIVAN • GUERRERO
RIVERS OF LONDON
BLACK MOULD

ISSUE 1 - Cover C •
Anna Dittmann

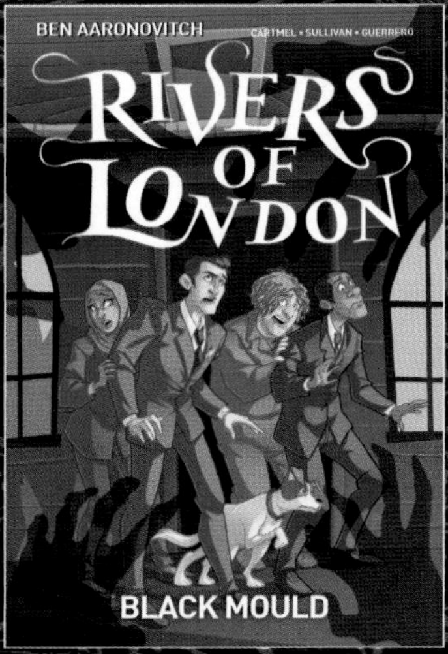
BEN AARONOVITCH
CARTMEL • SULLIVAN • GUERRERO
RIVERS OF LONDON
BLACK MOULD

ISSUE 1 - Cover D •
Arianna Florean

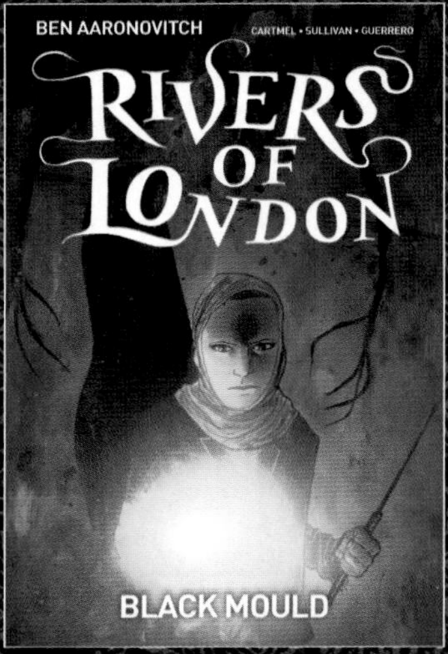
BEN AARONOVITCH
CARTMEL • SULLIVAN • GUERRERO
RIVERS OF LONDON
BLACK MOULD

ISSUE 1 - Cover E •
Ben Templesmith

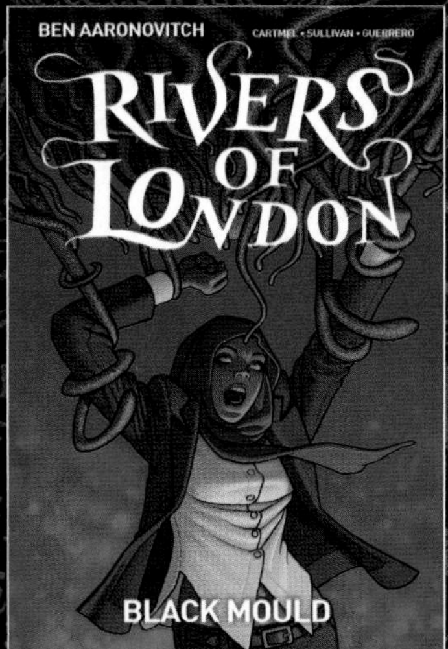
BEN AARONOVITCH
CARTMEL • SULLIVAN • GUERRERO
RIVERS OF LONDON
BLACK MOULD

ISSUE 2 - Cover A •
Paul McCaffrey

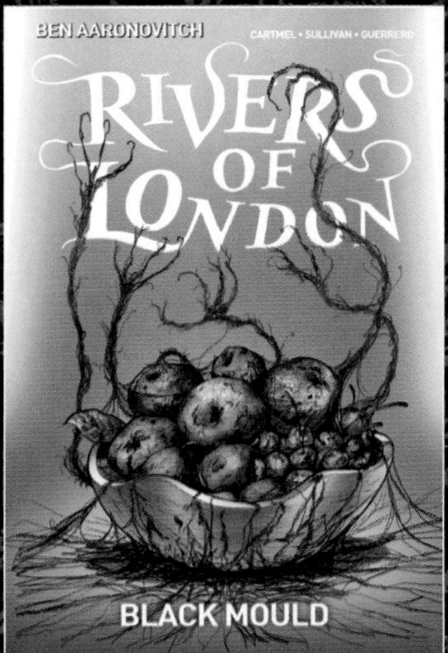
BEN AARONOVITCH
CARTMEL • SULLIVAN • GUERRERO
RIVERS OF LONDON
BLACK MOULD

ISSUE 2 - Cover B •
Lee Sullivan & Luis Guerrero

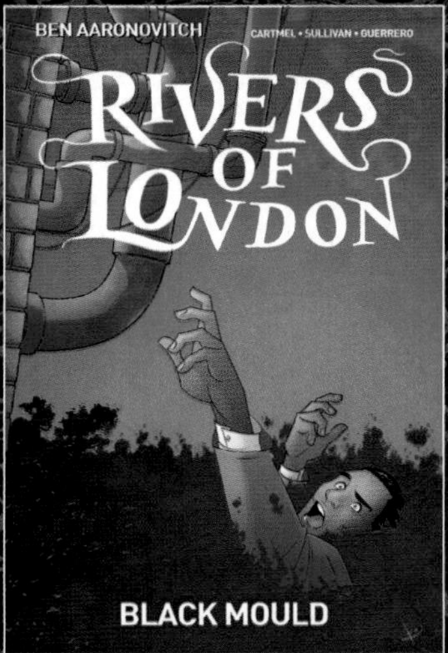
BEN AARONOVITCH
CARTMEL • SULLIVAN • GUERRERO
RIVERS OF LONDON
BLACK MOULD

ISSUE 2 - Cover C •
Dan Boultwood

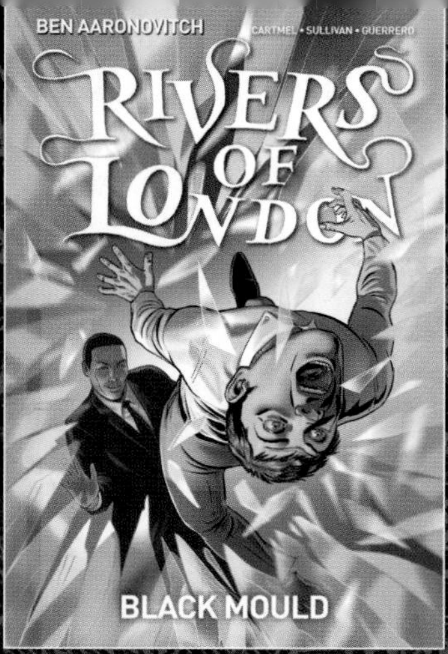
BEN AARONOVITCH
CARTMEL • SULLIVAN • GUERRERO
RIVERS OF LONDON
BLACK MOULD

ISSUE 3 - Cover A •
Lee Sullivan & Luis Guerrero

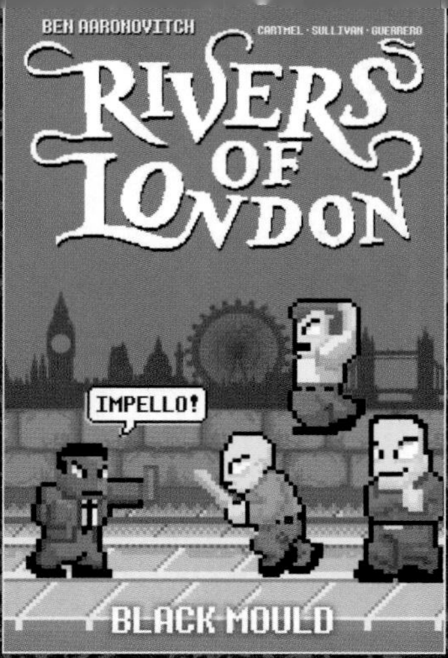
BEN AARONOVITCH
CARTMEL • SULLIVAN • GUERRERO
RIVERS OF LONDON
IMPELLO!
BLACK MOULD

ISSUE 3 - Cover B •
Matthew Waite

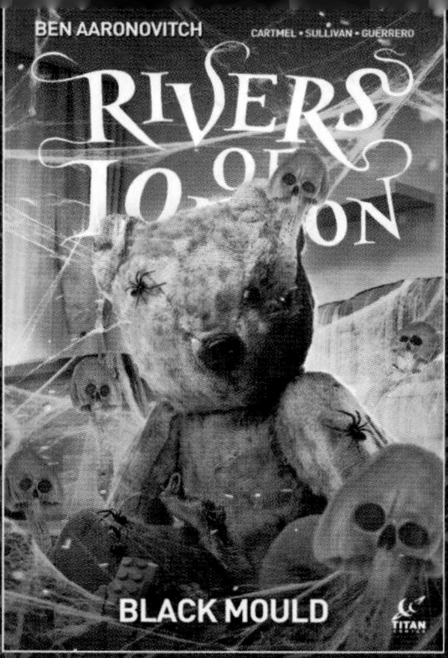
BEN AARONOVITCH
CARTMEL • SULLIVAN • GUERRERO
RIVERS
BLACK MOULD
TITAN

ISSUE 3 - Cover C •
Will Brooks

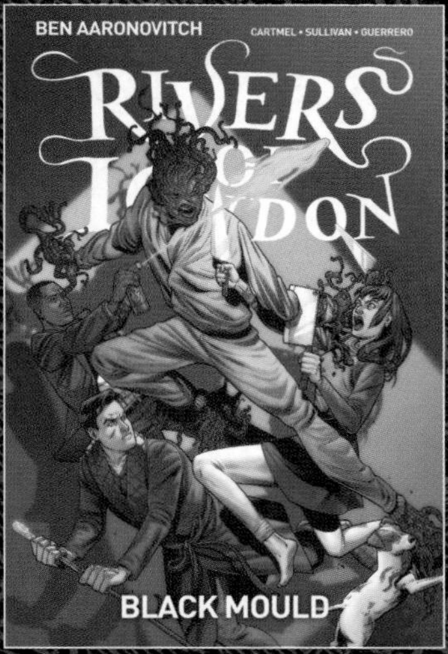
BEN AARONOVITCH
CARTMEL • SULLIVAN • GUERRERO
RIVERS
BLACK MOULD

ISSUE 4 - Cover A •
Rachael Stott & Luis Guerrero

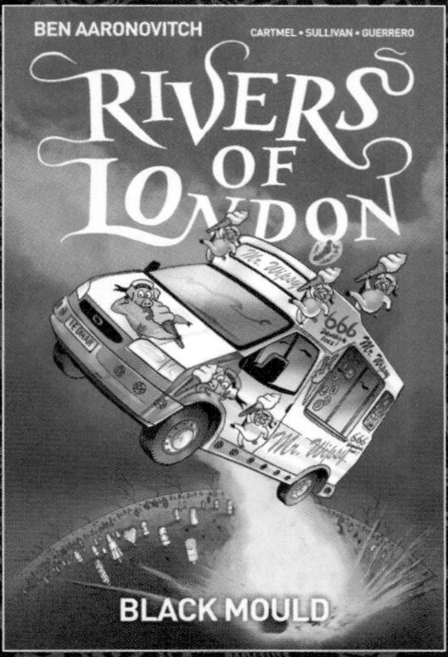
BEN AARONOVITCH
CARTMEL • SULLIVAN • GUERRERO
RIVERS OF LONDON
BLACK MOULD

ISSUE 4 - Cover B •
Lee Sullivan & Luis Guerrero

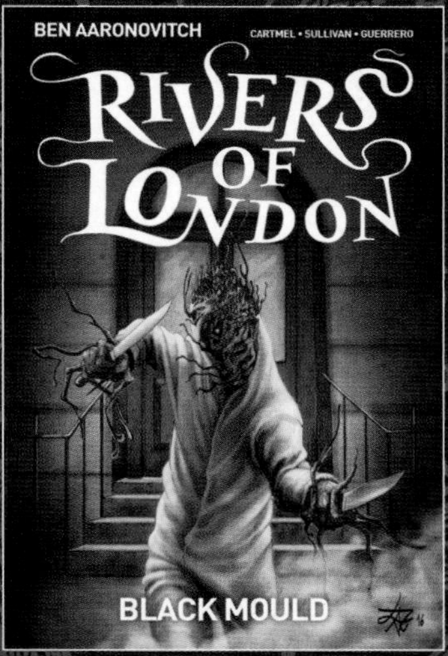
BEN AARONOVITCH
CARTMEL • SULLIVAN • GUERRERO
RIVERS OF LONDON
BLACK MOULD

ISSUE 4 - Cover C •
Lorena Assisi

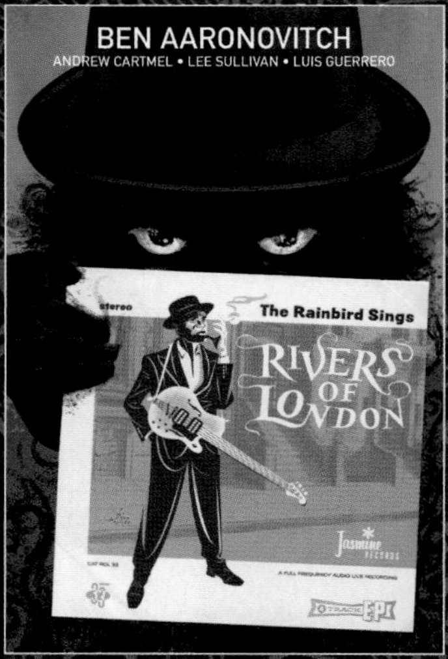
BEN AARONOVITCH
ANDREW CARTMEL • LEE SULLIVAN • LUIS GUERRERO
stereo
The Rainbird Sings
RIVERS OF LONDON
Jasmine

ISSUE 5 - Cover A •
Rian Hughes

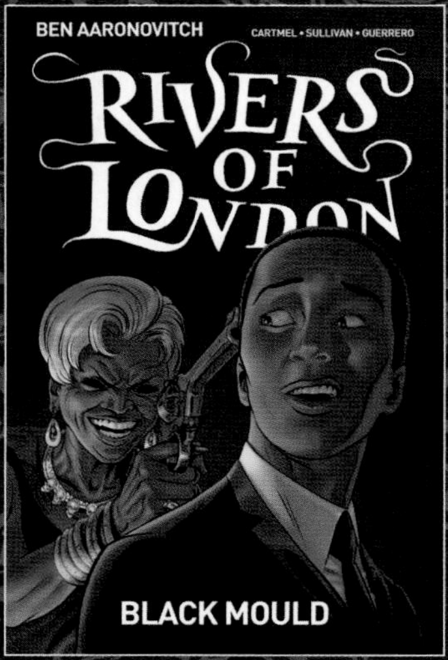
BEN AARONOVITCH
CARTMEL • SULLIVAN • GUERRERO
RIVERS OF LONDON
BLACK MOULD

ISSUE 5 - Cover B •
Lee Sullivan & Luis Guerrero

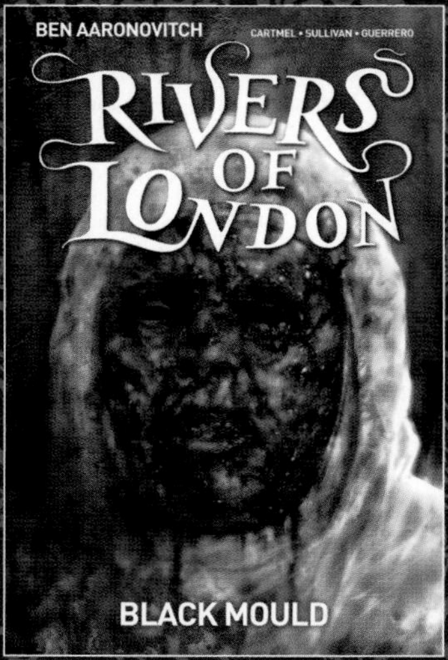
BEN AARONOVITCH
CARTMEL • SULLIVAN • GUERRERO
RIVERS OF LONDON
BLACK MOULD

ISSUE 5 - Cover C •
Nick Percival

RIVERS OF LONDON

READER'S GUIDE

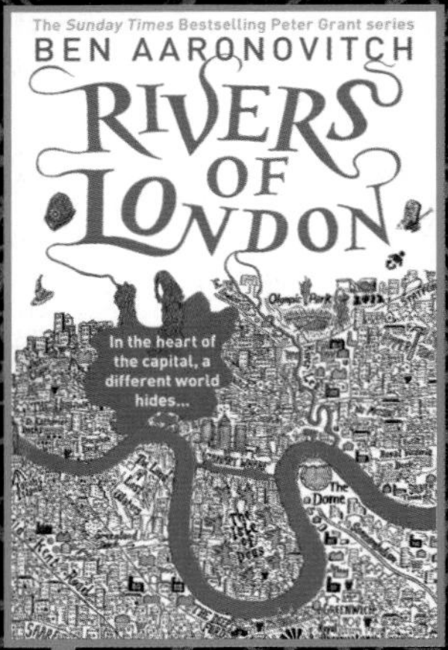

The *Sunday Times* Bestselling Peter Grant series

BEN AARONOVITCH

RIVERS OF LONDON

In the heart of the capital, a different world hides...

RIVERS OF LONDON / MIDNIGHT RIOT

Novel 1

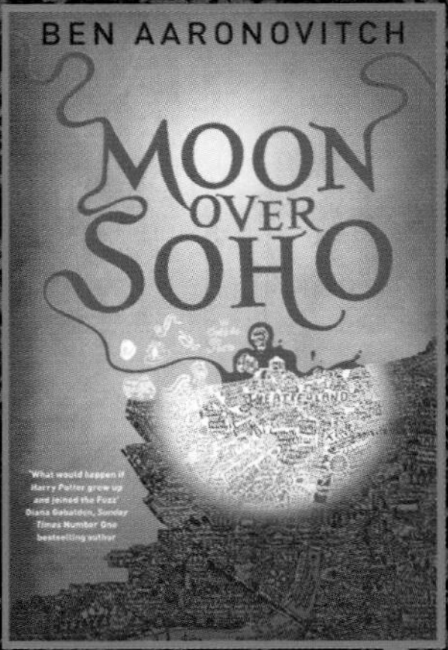

BEN AARONOVITCH

MOON OVER SOHO

'What would happen if Harry Potter grew up and joined the Fuzz' Diana Gabaldon, *Sunday Times* Number One bestselling author

MOON OVER SOHO

Novel 2

BEN AARONOVITCH
The *Sunday Times* bestselling series

WHISPERS UNDER GROUND

If you've been on the Underground you know what horrors await . . .

WHISPERS UNDER GROUND

Novel 3

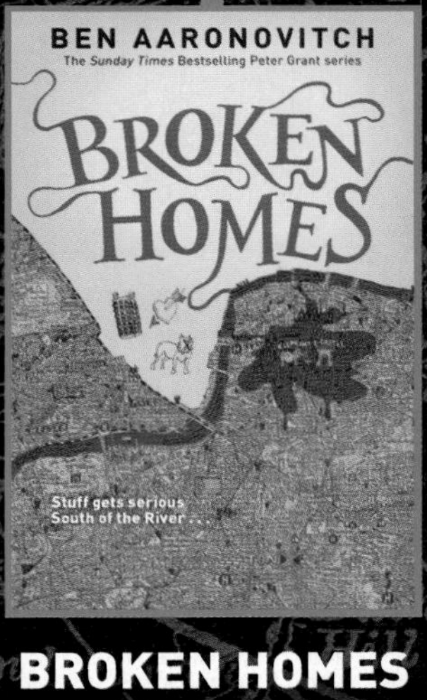

BEN AARONOVITCH
The *Sunday Times* Bestselling Peter Grant series

BROKEN HOMES

Stuff gets serious South of the River . . .

BROKEN HOMES

Novel 4

The *Rivers of London* comics and graphics novels are an essential part of the saga. Though they each stand alone, together they add compelling depth to the wider world of Peter and the Folly!

This helpful guide shows where each book fits in the ever-growing timeline of the *Rivers of London* universe!

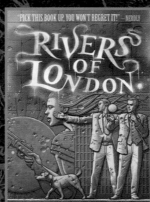

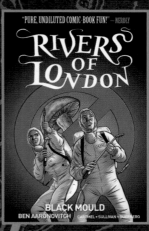

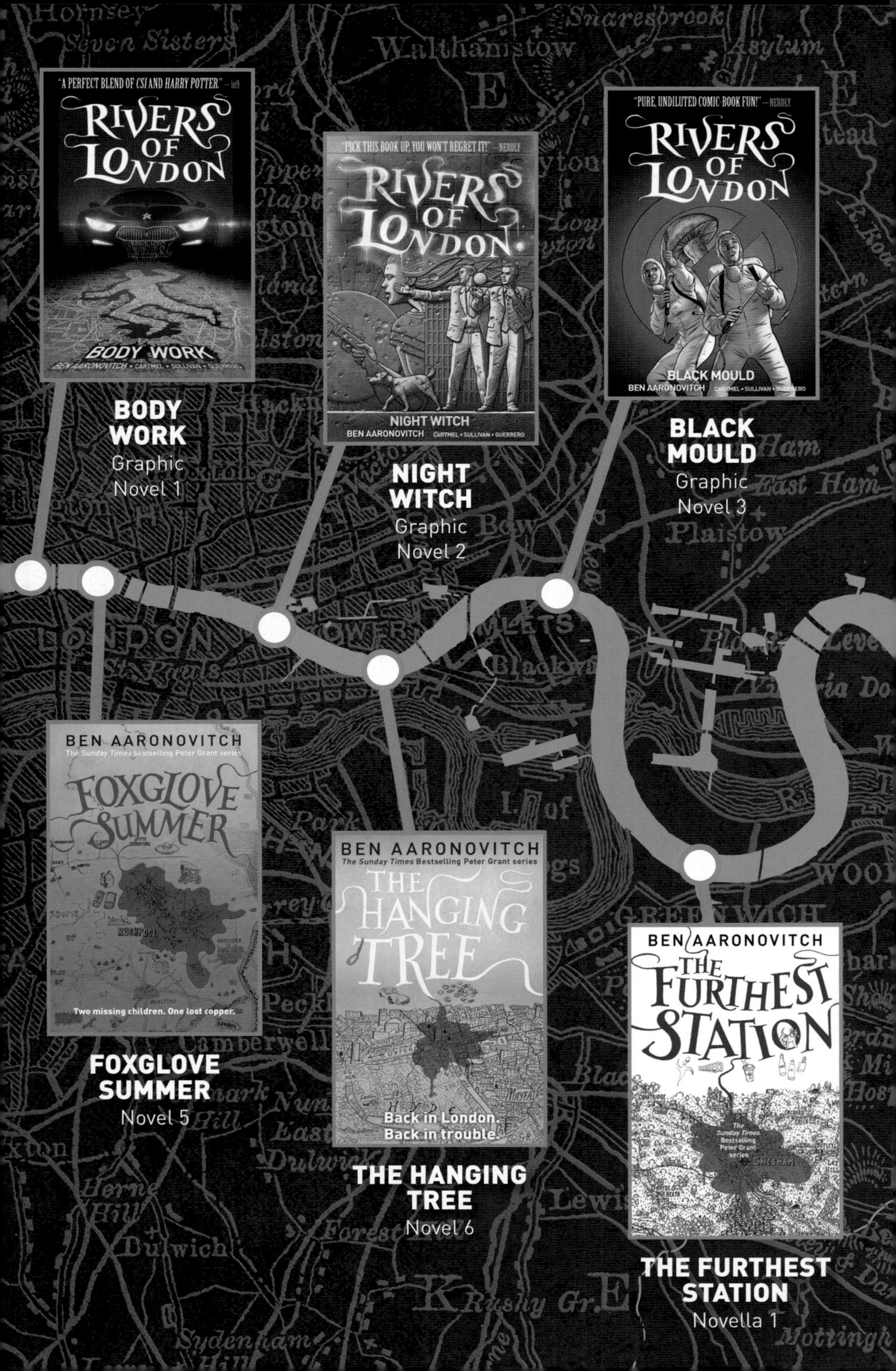

"A PERFECT BLEND OF CSI AND HARRY POTTER." — io9
RIVERS OF LONDON
BODY WORK
BEN AARONOVITCH • CARTMEL • SULLIVAN • GUERRERO
BODY WORK
Graphic Novel 1
"PICK THIS BOOK UP, YOU WON'T REGRET IT!" — NERDLY
RIVERS OF LONDON
NIGHT WITCH
BEN AARONOVITCH CARTMEL • SULLIVAN • GUERRERO
NIGHT WITCH
Graphic Novel 2
"PURE, UNDILUTED COMIC-BOOK FUN!" — NERDLY
RIVERS OF LONDON
BLACK MOULD
BEN AARONOVITCH CARTMEL • SULLIVAN • GUERRERO
BLACK MOULD
Graphic Novel 3
BEN AARONOVITCH
The Sunday Times bestselling Peter Grant series
FOXGLOVE SUMMER
Two missing children. One lost copper.
FOXGLOVE SUMMER
Novel 5
BEN AARONOVITCH
The Sunday Times Bestselling Peter Grant series
THE HANGING TREE
Back in London. Back in trouble.
THE HANGING TREE
Novel 6
BEN AARONOVITCH
THE FURTHEST STATION
The Sunday Times Bestselling Peter Grant series
THE FURTHEST STATION
Novella 1

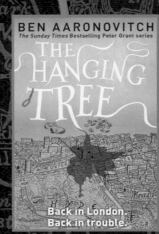

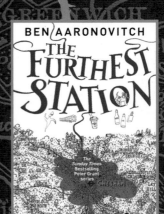

Murder. Mystery. Magic.

Forget everything you think you know about London.

*Get on the case with PC Peter Grant
in the Sunday Times bestselling series.*

*'An incredibly fast-moving magical
joyride for grown-ups'*
THE TIMES

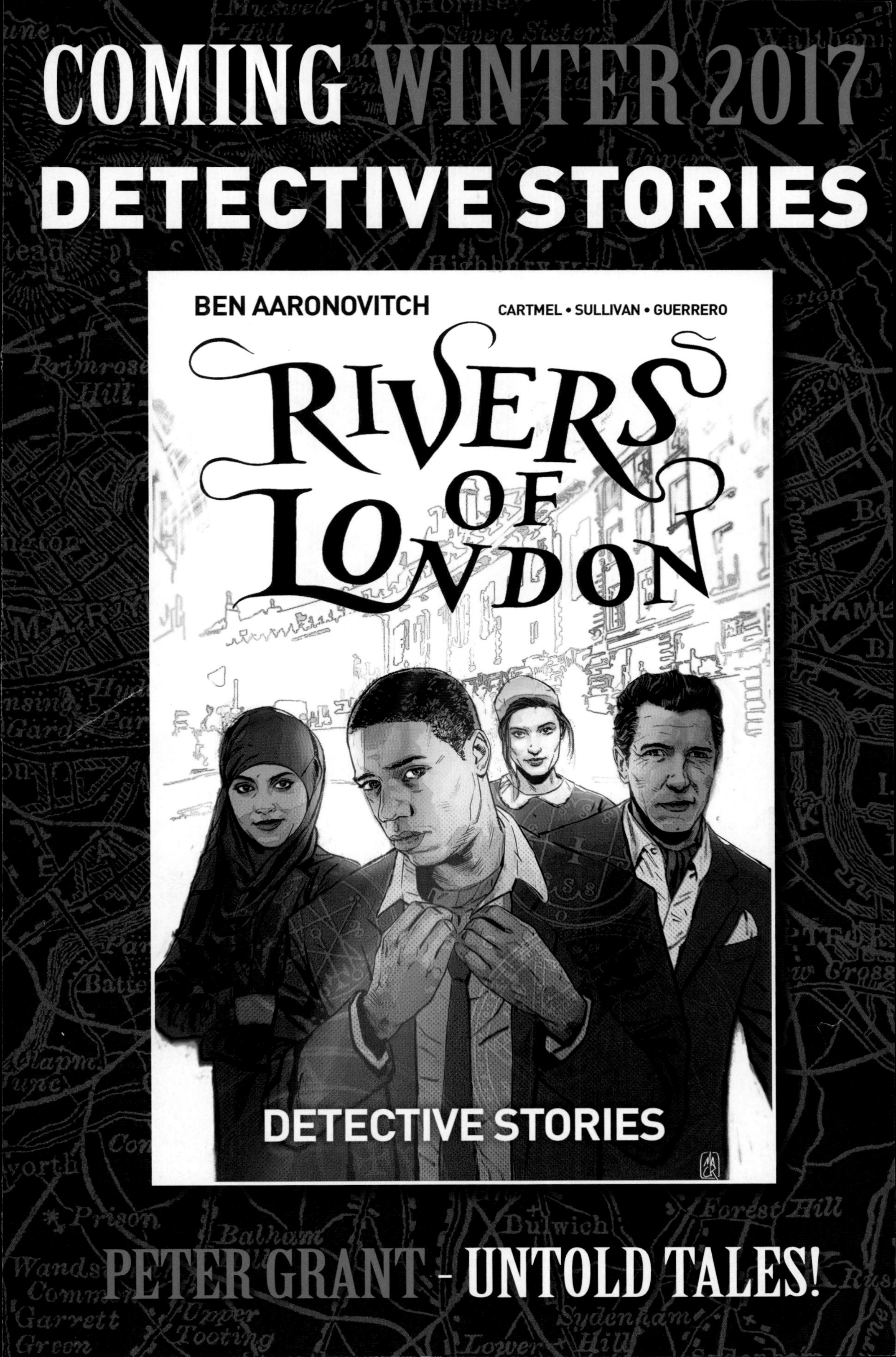
COMING WINTER 2017
DETECTIVE STORIES
BEN AARONOVITCH
CARTMEL • SULLIVAN • GUERRERO
RIVERS OF LONDON
DETECTIVE STORIES
PETER GRANT - UNTOLD TALES!

CREATOR BIOGRAPHIES

ANDREW CARTMEL

began a long and varied career in TV and publishing when he was hired as script editor on *Doctor Who* in 1986. He had a major (and very positive) impact on the final years of the original run of the TV show, after which he worked as script editor on *Casualty*. He is also writing the *Vinyl Detective* series of crime novels for Titan Books; the second, *The Run-Out Groove*, is available now. In his spare time, he likes to do stand-up comedy.

LEE SULLIVAN

began his comics career at Marvel UK, drawing *Transformers* and *Robocop* for the US before moving on to *Judge Dredd* and *Thunderbirds* – but it is with *Doctor Who* that he is most closely associated. He continues to draw the Doctor for a variety of publishers.

He played saxophone in a Roxy Music tribute band for a decade. He has dotted various Roxy Music-related gags through this series!

LUIS GUERRERO

Luis is a relative newcomer to comics. A native of Mexico, his earliest published work was for Big Dog Ink's 2012 series, *Ursa Minor*. Since then, he has been a regular fixture at Titan Comics, coloring interiors and covers for a number of series including *Doctor Who, The Troop,* and *Mycroft Holmes,* as well as *Rivers of London*.

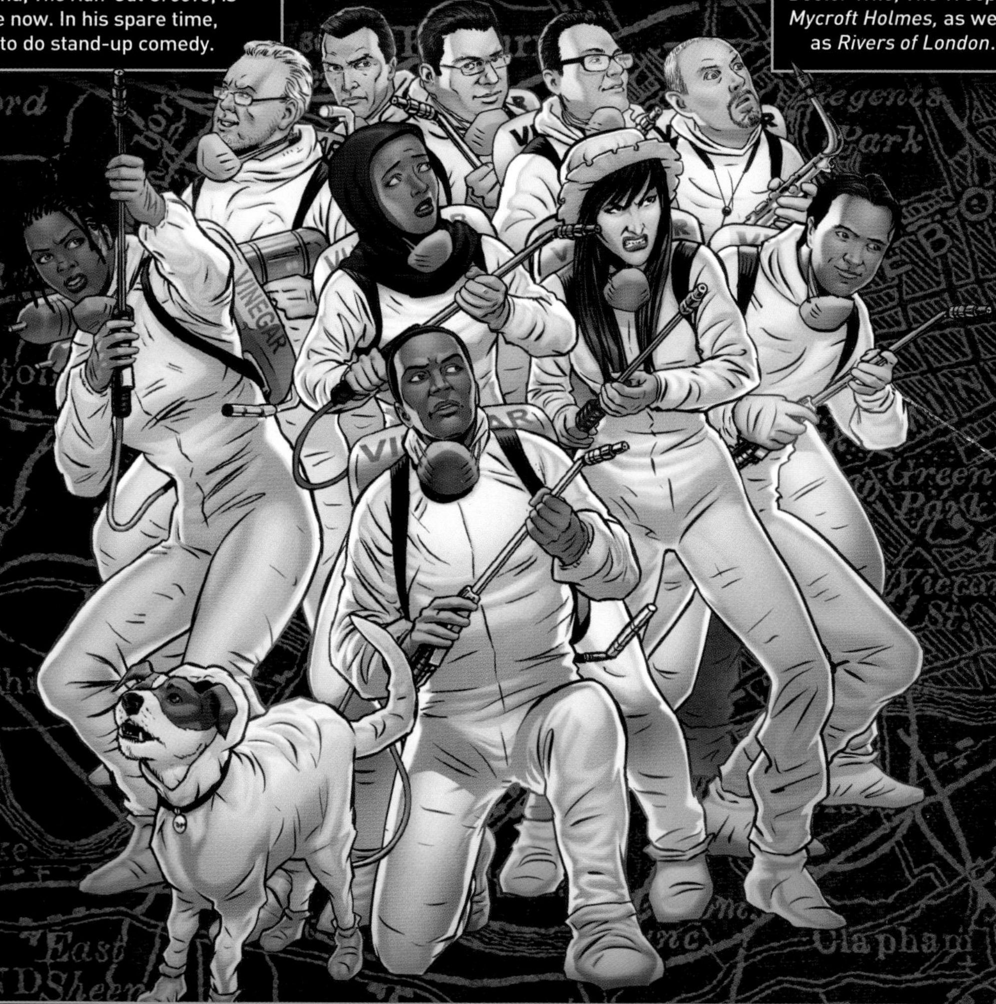
VINEGAR

BEN AARONOVITCH

Ben is perhaps best known for his series of Peter Grant novels, which began with *Rivers of London*. Mixing police procedural with urban fantasy and London history, these novels, the latest of which is *The Hanging Tree*, have now sold over a million copies worldwide. A new Peter Grant novella, *The Furthest Station*, releases in late 2017.

Ben is also known for his TV writing, especially on *Doctor Who*, where he wrote fan-favorites *Remembrance of the Daleks* and *Battlefield*. He also wrote an episode of long-running BBC hospital drama, *Casualty*, and contributed to cult British sci-fi show, *Jupiter Moon*.

Ben was born, raised and lives in London, and says he will leave the city when they prise it out of his cold, dead fingers.